The Diffusion of Electronic Data Interchange

Contributions to Management Science

Ulrich A. W. Tetzlaff
Optimal Design of Flexible Manufacturing Systems
1990. 190 pages. Softcover DM 69,–
ISBN 3-7908-0516-5

Fred von Gunten
Competition in the Swiss Plastics Manufacturing Industry
1991. 408 pages. Softcover DM 120,–
ISBN 3-7908-0541-6

HaraldDyckhoff/Ute Finke
Cutting and Packing in Production and Distribution
1992. 248 pages. Hardcover DM 120,–
ISBN 3-7908-0630-7

Hagen K.C. Pfeiffer

The Diffusion of Electronic Data Interchange

With 53 Figures

Physica-Verlag
A Springer-Verlag Company

Series Editors
Werner A. Müller
Peter Schuster

Author
Dr. Hagen K.C. Pfeiffer
Trills 19
D-4006 Erkrath, FRG

ISBN 3-7908-0631-5 Physica-Verlag Heidelberg
ISBN 0-387-91428-5 Springer-Verlag New York

CIP-Kurztitelaufnahme der Deutschen Bibliothek
Pfeiffer, Hagen K.C.:
The diffusion of electronic data interchange / Hagen K.C.
Pfeiffer. – Heidelberg : Physica-Verl., 1992
(Contributions to management science)
ISBN 3-7908-0631-5 (Physica-Verl.)
ISBN 0-387-91428-5 (Springer, New York)

Druck: Weihert-Druck GmbH, Darmstadt
Bindearbeiten: T. Gansert GmbH, Weinheim-Sulzbach
2100/7130-543210

Preface

This book documents the research I conducted on the subject of Electronic Data Interchange during my time at the Institute of Business Informatics, University of Berne, Switzerland. In this effort I enjoyed a great deal of help from numerous others, including professional colleagues, interview partners, and members of my family. Even though I cannot possibly mention them all, I would like to express my sincere gratitude for their selfless support.

Above all, I am grateful to Prof. Dr. Gerhard Knolmayer who contributed to the book both in its formative stages and throughout its development. He has been an unwavering source of encouragement during the many difficult stages of the investigation and I greatly benefitted from our discussions of the subject matter. Moreover, he was extremely generous with his time in carefully reviewing all the five chapters.

The financial support for this book came from the Hasler Foundation in Berne. I wish to thank the Foundation, and especially its Managing Director, Dr. P.A. Jaeger, for funding the empirical part of the research project. Likewise, I am grateful to the University of Berne for providing me with the necessary computer and other resources. The Institute of Business Informatics should be commended particularly for its very stimulating work environment.

I am indebted to Ms. Petra Koch for assisting me in preparing the questionnaire data for the statistical analyses and her tireless effort in producing a large number of the exhibits through a seemingly endless series of revisions.

Finally, any errors in the book remain uniquely my own.

April 1992 Hagen K. Pfeiffer

Table of Contents

List of Exhibits

List of Tables

1. Introduction

1.1. Research Problem

Electronic aids to support data processing tasks have been used in commercial organizations for almost four decades now[1], but it was not until the end of the 1970s that the utilization of computer based information systems (CBIS) became pervasive in response to technological advances that boosted the performance/price ratio of such systems - particularly with respect to hardware - by several degrees of magnitude[2]. The advent of low-cost, yet increasingly powerful mini- and micro-computers combined with the availability of relatively inexpensive off-the-shelf ("prepackaged") software for common business applications, such as e.g. financial accounting, rendered the acquisition and operation of CBIS economical even for small and medium-sized enterprises (SME). Ubiquity of CBIS, paired with a sophisticated telecommunications infrastructure, provides unprecedented opportunities to enhance the coordination of transaction-related activities between cooperating organizations.

Individual variances notwithstanding, it has been postulated that the utilization of computers in enterprises typically unfolds around certain evolutionary stages[3]. For the majority of organizations, the informatics life cycle commenced with the introduction of electronic data processing (EDP) systems - precursor of CBIS - which were designed to automate a small number of labor-intensive, repetitive processing tasks. While these early systems enhanced organizational efficiency by reducing transaction costs, the subsequent development and proliferation of information systems (IS) to support not only administrative but also managerial decision making tasks[4] had various indirect (strategic) effects beyond cost displacement. Since organizations became increasingly dependent on the well-functioning of their IS, professional management of those re-

---

1) The exact date is 1954; cf. e.g. Johnson (1975) p. 81, Davis/Olson (1985) p. 4.

2) Cf. e.g. Hansen (1986) pp. 46, 312.

3) The earliest and most prominent advocate of a life-cycle theory of information systems (IS) growth is Nolan who developed models consisting of four, five, and six stages. Cf. Gibson/Nolan (1974), Nolan (1979). Refer also to King/Kramer (1983), Benbasat/Dexter/Drury (1984). Stage theories have also been proposed in the context of telecommunications; cf. e.g. Wightman (1987), Donovan (1988), and Keen (1988).

4) Management support systems comprise e.g. so called management information systems (MIS), decision support systems (DSS), expert systems (ES), and executive information systems (EIS). A taxonomy of organizational IS can be found e.g. in Mertens (1988) p. 6 *et seqq*.

sources was more and more perceived as being of critical importance to the continuing competitiveness of organizations[5].

Concomitantly, methodologies for development and implementation of CBIS underwent a paradigm change[6]. Consistent with the aforementioned stage theories of information systems growth, early application systems[7] were largely self-contained in the sense that system developers were primarily concerned with algorithms. Data pertaining to these programs were treated as application-specific, i.e. they were stored in file organizations, closely attached to the program instructions. With a growing installed base of information systems, it soon became apparent, however, that the same data were frequently needed for different applications, giving rise to the database concept which aims at making data independent from a particular usage. By eliminating the need to store data redundantly in several places, storage efficiency improved and, most importantly, the integrity of the organization's data resources could be protected more easily[8].

Thus, databases emerged as the indispensable foundation of an organization's portfolio of application systems since they represent the core of an integrated systems concept. Integration is desirable from the viewpoint of management control because it makes the functioning of the entire organization more transparent to managerial decision makers. The recognition of data rather than algorithms as the common basis for all application systems shifted the focus of attention to the development of tools, such as database management systems (DBMS)[9], and concepts, e.g. the Entity-Relationship Model (ERM)[10], to more effectively manage the typically large data volumes of organizations.

---

5) The complexities associated with the development, implementation, and maintenance of CBIS have often led to the establishment of special IS departments, the head of which is sometimes called Chief Information Officer (CIO), is, or, according to Benjamin/Dickenson/Rockart (1986), ought to be member of the organization's top management. An analysis of the strategic value of Information Technology (IT) for organizations can be found e.g. in Hanker (1990).

6) Paradigm changes as a model for scientific revolutions were introduced by Kuhn (1970).

7) In this text the terms 'application systems' and 'applications' are used interchangeably.

8) The theory of data normalization was specifically developed to protect the integrity and consistency of databases by providing structural design guidelines to prevent the occurence of insert, update and delete anomalies when databases are being modified. Cf. Codd (1972). See further Dutka/Hanson (1989).

9) See e.g. Date (1986), McFadden/Hoffer (1988).

10) Chen (1976). Another example would be the idea of an Enterprise-wide Data Model; cf. e.g. Hars/Scheer (1991).

From a normative standpoint, the design of databases is but a single part of the overall "information engineering"[11] approach that advocates a step-by-step procedure whereby organizational processes are aggregated into clusters of applications with input-output correspondences between them[12]. If total correspondence is exhaustive, systems are said to be 'closed' in the sense that only internal dataflows occur. Occasionally, however, data needed by some applications are generated outside of the particular information system. It has been estimated that about 70% of those external data are generated by other IS[13]. For this reason, it would seem economical to resort to existing means of telecommunication for data transmission purposes instead of having to manually re-enter data which is already stored electronically at a different site. Concepts[14] that enable the automatic exchange of data between remote applications in cases where those systems belong to different organizational entities have frequently been called **Electronic Data Interchange (EDI)**[15]. Thus, EDI may be regarded as the second phase of the systems integration trend in IS management[16]: After integrating previously isolated internal applications to reap the benefits of more efficient transaction processing, lower systems maintenance costs, greater operating transparency, and improved coordination between intra-organizational processes, applications for external business transactions such as ordering and invoicing, that *ex definitione* involve more than one enterprise, are increasingly being targeted for integration by devising mechanisms to enable these independent systems to directly exchange data. As a result, EDI is sometimes subsumed under the more general term "External Integration"[17].

Given the fact that EDI merely facilitates the execution of inter-business transactions, it is intriguing how much attention the concept has recently attracted. Besides the conspicuous symptom of tens of conferences devoted each year to Electronic Data Interchange throughout the world[18], this trend manifests itself in the number of articles published

---

11) An expression probably coined by Martin (1989, 1990a,b). See also Finkelstein (1989).

12) This stepwise procedure to cluster organizational processes according to dataclasses *generated* or *used* has been called Business Systems Planning (BSP). Cf. IBM (1989); see also e.g. Martin (1982), Vetter (1988) pp. 182 - 192, Katz (1990).

13) Cf. e.g. Dearing (1990) p. 4.

14) The term concept is used here in its abstract, scientific sense as "an idea which combines several elements from different sources into a single notion", Chaplin (1975) p. 105.

15) Occasionally, EDI stands for Electronic Document Interchange; cf. e.g. Silber (1987).

16) For a descriptive historic review and analysis of IS management evolution, cf. e.g. Hanker (1990) p. 21 - 27.

17) Petri (1990). Some reflections why the term 'integration' in connection with EDI may not be perfectly appropriate, can be found in section 2.4.1.

18) See e.g. the announcements in the "EDI Calender" which is part of the EDI Yellow Pages; cf. EDI, spread the word! (1989).

on the subject matter. Exhibit 1-1 contains the results of several online literature-database queries and depicts the number of citations found with respect to EDI by year.

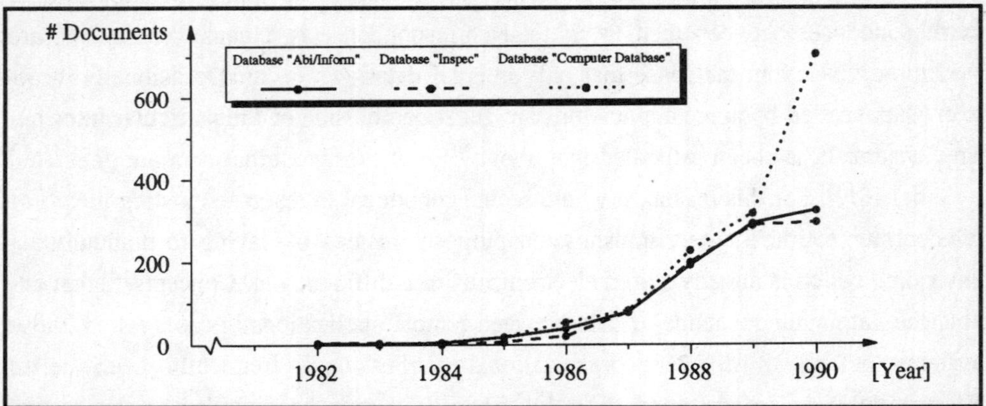

Exhibit 1-1	Number of EDI-related Citations in Selected Literature Databases

While the intersection of those query results may not be empty, the growth patterns seems to indicate that the topic is gaining prominence, at least among practitioners[19)]. Despite the fact that the origins of EDI can be traced back to the 1960s[20)], the concept appears to be a fairly recent phenomenon[21)]. However, if it were only for the administrative savings potential, due to the avoidance of data entry costs and reduced transcription errors, the current popularity of EDI would hardly be understandable.

Claims about the alleged strategic importance of EDI[22)], which is often heralded as a "revolution" that fundamentally alters "the way business is done"[23)], need to be interpreted in the context of current business trends. According to observations by academicians and practitioners, in today's saturated buyer's markets, the basis of competition appears to shift from the traditional dichotomy of cost vs. quality towards a situation where service aspects, such as the ability to quickly and flexibly respond to demand fluctuations and market developments, become as important as price or functional pro-

---

19) Cf. also the delphi study on IS-issues of the 1990s conducted by Niederman/Brancheau/Wetherbe (1990). In this study, EDI was ranked by practitioners as one of the most important developments that IS management needs to embrace. Cf. further Straub/Wetherbe (1989) who interviewed a panel of experts for the purpose of technology forecasting. According to their interviewees, EDI is one of the key information technologies of the 1990s.

20) Mertens (1966).

21) See section 2.5.

22) Cf. e.g. Silber (1987), Schumann/Hohe (1988) p. 518 *et seqq.*, Schwab (1989) p. 27, Sokol (1989), Thomas (1989).

23) Bone (1989) p. 41, Schatz (1988) p. 56. Cf. also N.N. (1989), p. 5.

duct attributes[24]. Thus, time is frequently regarded as a "strategic success factor"[25], as the "next source of competitive advantage"[26], the proper management of which enables companies to distinguish themselves from the competition. New manufacturing concepts such as "just-in-time" (JIT), "zero inventory" (ZI), "lean manufacturing"[27], and "simultaneous engineering"[28] *inter alia* are being pursued in the belief, that they would allow enterprises to prosper in a vertically disintegrated market environment characterized by "time-based competition"[29].

These concepts, however, can only be successfully implemented if both the necessary technological means and a conducive organizational structure are present. With respect to the first prerequisite, advanced manufacturing technologies, like e.g. flexible manufacturing systems (FMS), promise to achieve 'economies of scope' by allowing the production of different items in small batches on relatively general-purpose equipment, thus reducing the cost advantages of traditional mass production ('economies of scale') over customized manufacturing[30]. Similar to other production activities such as product design and material requirements planning (MRP), manufacturing relies heavily on computer assistance. In order to streamline the entire sequence of planning, execution and control activities over the internal value chain of a manufacturing organization, system vendors are striving to develop an integrated systems concept which allows the different computer-aided processes to share data between them, again, obviating the need for tedious manual interfacing . This computer integrated manufacturing (CIM) concept promises to shorten the internal production cycle time[31].

The speed of completing business transactions is partially dependent on the obstacles raised by having to interface between separate business systems. Since not all the data needed for manufacturing control is generated internally but originate in business relationships with customers, suppliers, and other third parties, it would be desirable to im-

24) Cf. Wildemann (1990). Cf. also Porter's generic competitive strategies *cost leadership* and *differentiation* (1980, 1985). See further Szyperski (1980), Warnecke (1988), and Nevins/Whitney (1989) p. 12 *et seqq.*

25) Cf. Simon (1989).

26) Stalk Jr. (1988).

27) Cf. Krafcik (1988), Womack/Jones/Roos (1990).

28) Sometimes also called "Concurrent Engineering" or "Concurrent Design". See e.g. Nevins/Whitney (1989), Bullinger/Wasserloos (1990).

29) Blackburn (1991). Cf. also Szyperski (1980), Stalk Jr./Hout (1990).

30) Cf. e.g. Goldhar/Jelinek (1983), Talaysum/Hassan/Goldhar (1986).

31) Cf e.g. Scheer (1987a).

prove the efficiency of the external interfacing task. By creating a well-defined datalink between independent systems, EDI accelerates the execution of business transactions and is therefore often perceived as an important prerequisite for the introduction of JIT concepts[32]. Thus, EDI purports to indirectly enhance an organization's competitive position even if - as is commonly acknowledged - the overall effect would be difficult if not impossible to measure or disentangle from the aforementioned technical and organizational innovations in other areas. Indeed, even though the virtues of EDI *per se* are frequently extolled in the contemporary management literature, more serious analyses dispute such unidimensional assertions and suggest that competitive effects may only be possible if organizational process changes accompany the introduction of EDI systems[33].

Although EDI tends to shorten inter-business transaction cycles and allows a more comprehensive and detailed control of operations, it is not as widely diffused in practice as should be expected when considering its presumed strategic importance. In fact, while the technologies necessary to implement EDI - largely (the fusion between) information systems and telecommunication networks[34] - have been in place for quite some time, the question arises why, despite all the advantages commonly attributed to it, this innovative concept is presently not in widespread use. According to market research reports, of millions of private and public organizations in industrialized countries, only a few thousand have begun to utilize EDI, and the predicted "explosive growth" in the number of active users always seems to remain just around the corner[35].

While it is generally a worthwhile endeavor to study the diffusion of innovations, because of the assumed positive correlation with public welfare, examining the spread of communication technologies is particularly important. Depending on the chosen definition, EDI may lack some of the features that jointly constitute a technology[36], yet at least special software is needed to provide for the essential input-output transformation[37]. By virtue of this nature, EDI displays a typical characteristic of telecommunication technologies, namely what has been described as "positive network externali-

32) Cf. Annis (1986), Abend (1987), Canright (1987).

33) Cf. Benjamin/De Long/Scott Morton (1990), Knolmayer/Pfeiffer (1990).

34) Cf. Vervest (1987) p. 19 *et seq.*

35) See Joyce (1989). Cf. also section 2.5.2. where diffusion estimates are reviewed.

36) Sahal (1981) p. 15 *et seqq.* provides an overview of three different definitions of the term 'technology', the differences between which are, however, largely irrelevant for the purposes of this text.

37) Cf. e.g. Wittmann (1986) p. 3. Therefore, EDI will throughout this text be called interchangeably a *concept* and a *technology*.

ties"[38]: Similar to technologies such as the telephone, facsimile, and electronic mail, the benefits available to EDI users are to some extent contingent upon the concept's diffusion within the potential user community. As a consequence, a "start-up problem" arises because pioneers would derive little utility from adopting early in the diffusion process[39]. For this reason, it is especially important to conduct research aimed at identifying factors that affect - stimulate or retard - the early adoption of EDI. Furthermore, from the perspective of current users and institutions which are concerned about a high utilization level[40], strategies that may be contemplated to foster the initial diffusion of EDI should be carefully examined, since, according to the theory of network externalities, after some (difficult-to-determine) "critical mass"[41] of EDI users has been reached, diffusion can be anticipated to develop a momentum of its own. Thus, business management as well as public policy makers should be able to benefit from a study which focusses specifically on aspects of EDI adoption and diffusion[42].

Given the generic objective described above, the research documented in this text fulfills a number of normative criteria that management studies should meet[43]:

- The research problem should be based on an identified need in society and should be of practical relevance.

- The anticipated results should be operational in the sense that they can be implemented.

- The results are not trivial, i.e. they contribute to current knowledge[44].

---

38) Cf. with respect to telecommuncations e.g. Rohlfs (1974), Farrell/Saloner (1985), Katz/Shapiro (1985), Allen (1988). See also section 3.1.

39) Rohlfs (1974) p. 18.

40) E.g. suppliers of telecommunication infrastructures and value added telecommuncation services. Refer also to the Trade Electronic Data Interchange Systems (TEDIS) program of the European Communities initiated in October 1987. The main objective of this program is to foster the proliferation and diffusion of non-proprietary EDI systems in Europe; cf. Commission of the European Communities - DG XIII - Telecommunications, Information Industries and Innovation (1987).

41) Cf. Newman (1986). The notion of a critical mass for EDI has also been alluded to in Seither (1988) where it addresses an entirely different issue: The development of standardized EDI software packages.

42) Gurbaxani et al. (1990), p. 87, underscore the practical importance of this problem: "However, there is considerable controversy about how best to proceed with efforts to stimulate diffusion in both production and use of IT. Without a sound understanding of the dynamics of such innovation, there will be little guidance to assist policy makers in both the public and private sectors at the local, national, regional and international levels."

43) Cf. Bomers (1983), Vervest (1987) p. 13.

44) See also Davis/Parker (1979) pp. 44 - 49.

- The timing of the research is commensurate with practical needs, i.e. the results should have an impact on present managerial decision making.

1.2. Prior Research on Electronic Data Interchange

An analysis of the fairly limited amount of published academic research on Electronic Data Interchange reveals that most prior studies were conducted by researchers in the field of administrative science. Besides detailed descriptive analyses of EDI systems found in practice[45)], industrial economists have tried to examine the business advantages associated with the utilization of EDI, mostly in the context of how the application of IT affects an organization's competitive position[46)]. In those studies, the value chain concept[47)] is frequently employed to illustrate how IT in general and EDI in particular might exert influence on Porter's strategic market forces that are supposed to ultimately determine a company's profitability[48)]. While most research aspires to derive meaningful generalizations about the impact of EDI on businesses, some authors implicitly criticize this approach by confining their analyses to particular industries, which suggests that there may exist noticeable inter-industry differences that obstruct attempts to draw generally applicable conclusions[49)].

The intuitive plausibility of arguments for a contingency approach notwithstanding, some macro-level type of research was directed towards analyzing the potential effects of linking the CBIS of different organizations through wide-area telecommunication networks on prevailing transaction governance structures. The notion of "electronic markets and hierarchies"[50)] relates to the question of how electronic linkages between organizations affect vertical integration, by opening opportunities to create "virtual" re-

---

45) Cf. e.g. Mertens (1985). An early, yet highly elaborate examination of possibilities for and implications of external EDP integration can be found in Mertens (1966).

46) Cf. Barret/Konsynski (1982), Parsons (1983) McFarlan (1984), Cash Jr./Konsynski (1985), Mertens/Plattfaut (1986), Benjamin/De Long/Scott Morton (1988), Schumann/Hohe (1988), Scott Morton (1988), Mertens/Schumann/Hohe (1989), Venkatraman/Zaheer (1989), N.N. (1989), Schumann (1990). A research framework for studying the impact of IT on corporate strategy is given in Bakos/Treacy (1986).

47) Cf. Porter (1985) p. 33 *et seqq*. Cf. also Meffert/Benkenstein (1989).

48) See e.g. Porter/Millar (1985), Clemons/McFarlan (1986).

49) An overview of the application of EDI in trade and distribution can be found e.g. in Stern/Kaufmann (1985). Industry-specific EDI applications are also described in ADL (1980), Corey (1985), ADL (1987), Zentes (1988), Sokol (1989) p. 103 *et seqq*., Gibson Jr./Bell (1990), Petri (1990).

50) Malone/Yates/Benjamin (1987). Cf. also Malone/Yates/Benjamin (1989).

lationships[51]. The renewed attention devoted to questions concerning task specialization (i.e. the division of labor among cooperating agents) spawned a new inter-disciplinary field of research referred to as "coordination theory"[52] which investigates the ramifications of information technology assistance for work coordinating tasks of geographically dispersed actors.

In contrast to those *inter*-organizational studies, another branch of research addresses the *intra*-organizational aspects of EDI. Specific attention has been devoted to the business implications, the costs and benefits of EDI in various functional areas such as purchasing[53], logistics[54], manufacturing[55], and cash management[56]. Moreover, the process of implementing EDI systems from a socio-technical viewpoint[57], including hiring and training aspects, and the impact on internal controls have been analyzed[58].

In addition to investigating the business implications of EDI for individual organizations and for the relationships between organizations, EDI has also been studied from a technological viewpoint with particular attention given to telecommunication infrastructure requirements. The explosive growth in data communications, due to the merger between telecommunications and EDP, and the rising demand for specialized telecommunication services led to the emergence of public and private suppliers of Value Added Networks and Services (VANS)[59] and provided a strong impetus to define international standards for open systems interconnection (OSI)[60]. Much work has been devoted to develop a flexible model of a message handling system (MHS) for the de-

---

51) Clemens/Row (1989) p. 345.

52) Cf. Malone (1987, 1988).

53) Cf. La Londe/Emmelhainz (1985), Emmelhainz (1986, 1987), Eidenmüller (1988), Drake/Ciucci/Milbrandt (1990).

54) Cf. e.g. Scheer (1987b), Wildemann (1988), Hill/Hansen (1989), Knolmayer/Pfeiffer (1990).

55) Here specifically with respect to the exchange of CAD data. Cf. e.g. Meijer (1989), Shaw (1990).

56) Cf. Hill/Ferguson (1987a,b).

57) The socio-technical approach postulates that systems implementation is a two-way process. Systems requirements should be determined from both social and technical considerations to achieve a successful IS-project. Cf. e.g. Bostrom/Heinen (1977a,b).

58) Cf. Carter et al. (1987), Monczka/Carter (1988), Hansen/Hill (1989), Norris/Waples (1989), Sadhwani/Kim/Helmerci (1989). See also Burch (1989) and Payne (1989), Sokol (1989) p. 79 *et seqq*., Carlisle (1990), Emmelhainz (1990) p. 132 *et seqq*., Petri (1990) p. 153 *et seqq*.

59) The term "value added" relates to complementing basic message transmission services with specialized processing tasks such as store-and forwarding. An introductory overview regarding providers of VANS is given e.g. in Chang/Hitchcock (1989).

60) The ISO/OSI reference model for open systems interconnection may well be the most famous result of those standardization efforts.

livery of electronic mail messages in a heterogeneous systems environment[61]. Such messaging systems were initially conceived to handle the exchange of "interpersonal" messages between individuals who utilize EDP-hardware for their mutual communication purposes[62]. With the introduction and growing diffusion of EDI applications, the questions arose, whether it would be feasible, in principle, to modify the MHS so as to accommodate the specific requirements of EDI, and if so, which of the design alternatives should be pursued further[63].

With few noticeable exceptions[64] most of the research regarding EDI is based upon either conceptual or empirical analysis, the latter of which is characterized predominantly by "anecdotal", case-study type of evidence[65]. Research strategies vary with respect to the nature of the object under investigation; presuming that case study research is indicative of early examinations about more recent phenomena, such a strategy is clearly appropriate for an innovative concept such as EDI[66]. However, the conclusions drawn often do not adequately take the inherent methodological weaknesses of this approach into account. At best, case studies are useful to provide a deeper understanding of a (still changing) phenomenon. The insights obtained may lead to the formulation of hypotheses which must then be tested in subsequent confirmatory investigations. By no means can case study evidence alone be generalized to a larger population nor establish a causal linkage between a set of variables[67], yet such a cause-effect relationship is unfortunately very often explicitly or implicitly suggested[68].

---

61) CCITT published the set of X.400 recommendations in 1984 that defines the basic components of an MHS. Since then, CCITT and ISO have cooperated in revising the originial model and produced the 1988 version of the X.400 recommendations which have become known as ISO standard ISO 10021. For an introduction to X.400 (88) refer e.g. to Heist (1987), Craigie (1988).

62) Since the primary objective of the MHS was to provide a means for communication between persons, a special interpersonal message service (IPMS) was devised which defines a message structure/end-to-end protocol, very similar to paper-based mail conventions.

63) Cf. the discussion in Genilloud (1988a). See also Genilloud (1988b), INPUT (1988), Dawkins (1989), Häßler (1989), Pope (1989), Herbert (1990).

64) See e.g. Venkatraman/Zaheer (1989) who conducted a quasi-experimental study to determine the strategic benefits of electronic integration; cf. further Hill/Hansen (1989) who used a simulation approach to study the impact of EDI on inventory levels. See also Venkatraman (1990).

65) Benjamin/De Long/Scott Morton (1990) p. 29.

66) Cf. e.g. Yin (1984) p. 13, Bonoma (1985) p. 203.

67) Cf. Stone (1978) pp. 135 - 138, Williams/Rice/Rogers (1988) p. 108.

68) As Vankatraman/Kambil (1990) p. 1 comment: "However, even a casual perusal of the emerging literature would indicate that the underlying linkage between theses systems and changes in market has not been adequately explained, resulting in a rather blind acceptance of the validity and importance of such systems."

1.3. Main Goals of Research

The discussion in the previous section has shown that most EDI research so far focussed on hypothesized external (competitive) or internal (organizational) effects presumed to be associated with its application in business. The investigation conducted in connection with this thesis was driven by some apparent shortcomings of past research efforts as listed below:

(1) While the chosen research methodologies have been quite useful in fathoming the implications of an innovative concept, previous studies failed to subject a more comprehensive empirical data set about EDI to a rigorous statistical analysis, which would be conducive to inferential reasoning. Especially quantitative measures of well-defined variables, obtained on a large, preferably representative set of user organizations, are conspicuously absent in the contemporary research literature on EDI[69].

(2) Whereas the general concept of innovation diffusion has been studied extensively[70], the amount of research devoted to the diffusion of communication technologies such as EDI, which exhibit the previously mentioned property of network externalities that leads to the postulated critical mass effect, is surprisingly small despite the obvious importance of this special characteristic for the evolution of those technologies[71]. As some observers appraise the situation: "Only in recent years have scholars begun to investigate the adoption of the interactive communication media. Consequently, our theory and methods for studying the effects of the critical mass in such diffusion is limited."[72] "The notion of the critical mass calls for important modifications of diffusion theory in the particular case of interactive technolo-

---

69) One may suppose that the innovative nature of EDI shielded this deficiency from widespread criticism so far. At least Emmelhainz (1986) pp. 184 - 186, suggests that quantitative measures on a larger data set would be highly desirable to advance the current state of knowledge about the use and implications of EDI. A similar argument has been made by Williams/Rice/Rogers (1988) p. 77 who regard sample data a mandatory prerequisite for an "ideal study of an interactive innovation". Cf. also Tornatzky/Klein (1982), p. 29 *et seq*., who define seven features that constitute an "ideal" study on innovation attributes: "Surveys, secondary data analysis, and experiments may be methodologically adequate in this sense because they permit both replicability and some degree of cross-study comparability. In contrast, theoretical pieces, and the usual single-site qualitative case study cannot logically provide a basis for generalizing about the innovation process."

70) Refer to section 3.2.1.

71) Some studies do exist which consider telecommunication technologies from the viewpoint of innovation theory. Yet in most cases, the emphasis was placed on the technical evolution of innovations, so called "trajectories", rather than the diffusion of a particular technology. A counterexample can be found in Vervest (1987).

72) Williams/Rice/Rogers (1988), p. 72.

gies."[73] "It is almost as if past diffusion research had been perfectly designed not to focus on the critical mass in the diffusion of an interactive communication innovation."[74]

(3) Finally, to the extent that systems implementation must be accompanied by a redesign of certain administrative organizational procedures in order to fully harness the advantages offered by EDI, it represents a technological as much as an administrative innovation. However, "existing studies focus almost entirely upon the diffusion of technological innovations"[75].

In conclusion, besides a general shortage of broad empirical research on EDI, one important aspect of Electronic Data Interchange, the process of adoption within a community of potential users, has largely been neglected in the literature[76]. Consequently, the primary motivation of the research presented here was to eliminate part of this apparent knowledge gap. In order to accomplish this objective, it is necessary to operationalize the generic goal described above and make it amenable to practical research. Hence, the following specific objectives were defined at the outset of the project:

- Develop a theoretically simple, yet highly discriminating definition which allows to distinguish EDI from (even closely) related concepts.
- Identify and discuss the socio-technical prerequisites of EDI.
- Identify and evaluate major business implications of EDI.
- Determine the utilization of EDI in different geographical areas and industrial sectors.
- Systematically collect and analyze information about experiences made by active EDI users.

---

73) Williams/Rice/Rogers (1988), p. 75.

74) Williams/Rice/Rogers (1988), p. 78.

75) Teece (1980) p. 464.

76) Surveys on EDI utilization appear almost periodically in the literature. Those surveys are frequently executed by market research organizations or management consultancies and regularly cover diffusion aspects and EDI market penetration levels for obvious reasons. However, rarely do those surveys address the core question of what measures should be taken to overcome the perceived and/or real impediments to a rapid growth of EDI, let alone capitalize upon the empirical data gathered to test hypotheses related to the diffusion of EDI by means of inferential statistics. In most cases, the data are merely prepared for descriptive purposes and the reader is at the mercy of his ability to draw conclusions based upon a select subset of data usually presented in highly condensed form. See e.g. Butler Cox (1987), Ferguson/Hill (1989a,b), Mulder (1989) pp. 226 - 228, Wigglesworth (1989).

- Evaluate EDI from an innovation diffusion perspective by identifying or deriving factors that are likely to impact the diffusion process, and integrate determinants found into a causal model that can serve as a research framework for an empirical investigation.

- Gather empirical data to test hypotheses about various, practically relevant aspects of EDI, placing special emphasis on questions concerning the adoption, implementation, and diffusion of EDI.

In conformance to the nature of the specific research objectives, this thesis has been characterized as a management study. A contingency approach to study a contemporary phenomenon of significant practical relevance as opposed to a purely analytical examination strictly calls for an empirical research strategy[77)]. Particularly in a situation where no or little empirical data are publicly available, collecting such data alone was considered to merit the effort of an investigation (irrespective of the typically transient value of cross-sectional analyses) and therefore represents one of the major deliverables of this research undertaking. Since the diffusion of EDI can at least conceptually be separated into an internal part which deals with the adoption of the technology by a single organization (individualistic view) and an external part where organizations strive to persuade their trading partners to go along (relational view), collecting information on both aspects was deemed important.

To summarize, this study seeks to contribute to theory-building /-confirmation by examining factors that influence the diffusion of a joint technological and administrative innovation which additionally exhibits the special feature of network externalities. From the perspective of practitioners, the study should be useful in evaluating intervention alternatives of decision makers in public and private organizations who intend to stimulate the proliferation of EDI systems in practice. A framework for such institutional intervention has recently been proposed[78)], but no empirical data have been published that would allow a comparative analysis of the effectiveness of various intervention mechanisms. Moreover, since EDI standards, software, and infrastructure components are still in a state of rapid change, research at this time offers an opportunity to conduct a "formative evaluation"[79)], i.e. results of this investigation may help to reduce the amount of uncertainty faced by providers of EDI products and services through en-

77) Cf. Staehle (1989) p. 47.

78) Cf. Gurbaxani et al. (1990).

79) Cf. Williams/Rice/Rogers (1988) p. 117.

hancing their ability to determine (latent) market demand with greater precision. At the same time, potential users who are obliged to choose between a confusingly large number of alternative system configurations may benefit from an improved market transparency since timely research feedback facilitates the task of maintaining systems compatibility within trading clusters and reduces the risk of having to alter entrenched organizational procedures. Thus, both theory and practice alike should gain from the collection and careful analysis of a more comprehensive empirical data set on EDI.

1.4. Organization of Research

This thesis is conceptually divided into two main parts: Part one consists of chapters 2 and 3 and contains a descriptive analysis of Electronic Data Interchange. Part two is comprised of chapters 4 and 5 and provides detailed information regarding execution and findings of the empirical research project. The specific layout is as follows:

Chapter 2 examines Electronic Data Interchange from the viewpoint of its theoretical foundations, drawing upon communications and database theory. Using an analogy from linguistics about how meaning can be shared between human communication partners, a working-definition of EDI is derived which represents a radical departure from conventional definitions. This was deemed necessary in order to clarify the distinctive characteristics of EDI. Following, the socio-technical requirements and configuration options of EDI systems are considered, paying careful attention to communication standards. After examining intra- and inter-organizational business implications of EDI, a brief overview of the concept's utilization in practice is provided.

Chapter 3 is devoted to analyzing relevant adoption and diffusion aspects of EDI. At the outset, the concept of network externalities is introduced to underscore the importance of diffusion for the viability of innovative communication technologies. The discussion continues with a review of major elements of innovation diffusion theory to instill a more profound understanding of diffusion processes and their respective determinants. Following, the implications of network externality effects for innovation diffusion are being investigated, the most important of which is the notion of a 'critical mass'. Finally, the applicability of the obtained results with respect to EDI is assessed and the conclusions drawn are integrated into a conceptual EDI diffusion research framework which guides the empirical part of the investigation.

Details of the empirical project are elaborated in chapter 4. The project consists of an exploratory field-study - in the course of which approximately 30 EDI-user organizations and services providers were interviewed - and a mail survey of 128 responding user-organizations in North America and Europe. Most of this section is devoted to a presentation of the investigation's exploratory findings and selected results of the statistical analyses, primarily testing of the 31 specific hypotheses derived from the foregoing conceptual examination.

The final section provides a summary of the research and presents its major conclusions. Subsequently, implications for user organizations, public policy, and telecommuncations services providers are discussed. Some suggestions for future research on the subject matter are given.

2. Electronic Data Interchange

2.1. Introduction

In chapter 1, the notion of positive network externalities was introduced to explain the importance of studying the diffusion of Electronic Data Interchange. Due to the fact that EDI has to be simultaneously regarded as a technological and an administrative innovation, it appears plausible to hypothesize that the diffusion of EDI is to some extent dependent on its technological and administrative characteristics. This assumption is vindicated by a paradigm of innovation diffusion theory which asserts a relationship between innovation and adopter attributes and adoption rates. It would obviously be an oversimplification to assume that all types of innovations diffuse identically, and therefore a consensus has been reached that characteristics of the innovation itself as well as characteristics of the adopting system will have repercussions for the adoption rate[1]. As a consequence, this section of the text is devoted to explore and determine the relevant characteristics of EDI, first from a technical viewpoint and later from the perspective of the adopting organization.

In order to identify diffusion-relevant attributes it seems necessary at the outset to derive a suitable working definition which will allow to distinguish EDI from related concepts, e.g. distributed databases. Similar to technologies such as electronic mail (E-Mail), EDI is but one offspring of the merger between telecommunications and data-processing; a discriminative definition must therefore be based on sufficiently specific, non-technological criteria. Definitions in general, and within the framework of MIS research in particular, can be broadly categorized according to a dichotomous grouping[2]: Definitions of the first kind may be referred to as *systemic* in the sense that a concept is defined in terms of its components or building blocks as well as the specific relationships between them. The recursive nature of this approach implicitly assumes that all branches of the ensuing incarnations will terminate at some point without any need for further explanation. By contrast, the second group of definitions may be called the *functional* approach since it essentially regards the concept to be defined as black boxes

---

1) Cf. e.g. Rogers (1983) pp. 14 - 16 who evaluates innovations according to the following five criteria: Relative advantage, compatibility, complexity, trialability, and observability; see section 3.2.1. Cf. further Brown (1981) p. 152 *et seqq.* who underscores the importance of adopter attributes such as e.g. firm size or degree of competition among adopting firms.

2) Cf. Ein-Dor/Segev (1978) p. 1065 and the literature quoted there.

with no transparent internal structure, and classification is accomplished by means of the concept's functionality.

One may speculate that, especially during the early stages of product and process innovations, the functional viewpoint dominates until the most effective design has been determined. As soon as structural modifications become rare, a state of maturity is reached and subsequent definitions tend to fall into the systemic category. A dissenting view could argue that definitions tend to become increasingly abstract over time as the scope of the concept broadens. The following sample definitions suggest, that neither the first nor the second evolutionary pattern fits the development of EDI definitions very well:

> "X.12's Electronic Document Interchange (EDI) standard, based on the work done by the Transport Data Coordinating Committee for the Office of Facilitation of the U.S. Department of Transportation, can be used to exchange completely standardized documents between different organizations' computers."[3]

> "EDI *always* involves one computer in contact with at least one other, usually transmitting specific documents such as invoices, waybills or puchase orders."[4]

> "Electronic data interchange (EDI) is the computer-to-computer linkage between buyer and seller and the automatic transmission of purchase orders and invoices between the parties involved."[5]

> "EDI is essentially a data processing concept that is neutral to different data communications protocols. It just specifies a way of formatting business data, not unlike a standard business-letter format for person-to-person correspondence, so that computers on either end of a communications line can understand it."[6]

> "EDI is now widely understood to mean the transfer of structured data, by agreed message standards, from computer to computer, by electronic means."[7]

> "The transfer of formatted data between computer applications, running on different machines and using agreed standards, to describe and format the data contained in the messages."[8]

---

3) Jones (1982) p. 123.

4) Maraschiello (1985) p. 48, emphasis in the original.

5) Emmelhainz (1986) p. 2, source cited is Norris (1984).

6) Kemezis (1987) p. 64.

7) Sarich (1988) p. 7.

8) Smithers/Bailey (1988) p. 187.

"Electronic data interchange (EDI) is the INTER-COMPANY COMPUTER-TO-COMPUTER communication of STANDARD BUSINESS TRANSACTIONS in a STANDARD FORMAT that permits the receiver to perform the intended transaction."9)

"EDI ist der bi- oder mulitlaterale Austausch von applikationsorientierten Daten zwischen unabhängigen Informationssystemen per Telekommunikation."10)

The early definitions are consistent with the argument presented in chapter 1 that EDI may be viewed as a natural evolutionary step in the utilization of IT by business organizations. Many applications which had been developed to support the execution of common business transactions, such as order processing, are relying on external data sources, primarily other organizations with whom business relationships are maintained. With a growing systems penetration level, it was found that between 70 and 90% of the transactions data to be processed were prepared by application systems of business partners11). These circumstances, in addition to recent technological advances in data telecommunications over wide-area-networks (WAN), particularly the availability of low-cost modems, gave rise to a search for instruments - henceforth called EDI - to accomplish the transport of these application specific data by electronic means rather than traditional, paper-based methods.

While those definitions emphasize the conspicuous effect of EDI by citing the specific paper documents EDI is intended to replace, more recent definitions abstract from particular types of transactions. Thus, a limited number of essential features can be identified which together constitute EDI, namely:

- At least *two organizations* having a business relationship, i.e. conducting joint business transactions.

- Data processing tasks at both (all) organizations pertaining to a transaction are supported by *independent application systems.*

- The integrity of the data exchange between application systems of transaction partners is guaranteed by *ex ante* agreements concerning *data coding* and *formatting rules*, eliminating or at least reducing the need for human intervention.

---

9) Sokol (1989) p. 12, emphasis in the original.

10) Knolmayer/Pfeiffer (1990) p. 32.

11) Cf. e.g. Schindler (1987) p. 21, Dearing (1990) p. 5, Justenhoven (1990) p. 114.

- Data exchange between the application systems is accomplished via *telecommunication links*.

It may be worthwhile to note what is *not* required for EDI: Organizations which jointly execute a business transaction do not have to be ownership-independent. To state it differently, EDI can take place between two wholly-owned subsidiaries of the same enterprise. Crucial, however, is whether the application systems involved are independent, i.e. no intentional prior alignment may exist between them.

Yet even those more abstract definitions are unnecessarily narrow for they fail to fully appreciate the fact that, because application systems usually retrieve data from databases, EDI ultimately entails a data exchange between independent databases. While this interpretation of EDI is yet to be fully reflected in the literature[12)], some authors have begun to express similar views[13)]. If one were to accept the notion that EDI systems can conceptually be divided into the basic components databases and telecommunications, two separate tasks would have to be accomplished: One, it would be necessary to extract data from the database of one transaction partner according to the requirements of the predetermined transaction and store those data into the corresponding database of the other, while preserving semantic. Two, the extracted data must be transmitted over a communication link. Since databases and communication infrastructure exist independently of EDI, the EDI concept reduces to a data formatting and messaging mechanism[14)]. In order to derive a formal EDI model, the following sections provide reviews of database and communication theory as far as they are relevant for this purpose[15)].

---

12) See e.g. Emmelhainz (1990) p. 4 who insists that "Electronic Data Interchange is the interorganizational exchange of business documentation in structured, machine-processable form."

13) Cf. e.g. Smithers/Bailey (1988) p. 193: "Data which is required to build the standard EDI messages should be extracted from the existing databases... Data received into the machine is de-formatted before being passed to the existing applications and used to update the system data bases." Cf. also Forge (1989) p. 16: "Eventually EDI will link databases of different companies in a fairly direct manner, ...". Cf. also Petri (1990) p. 208 and the conceptual EDI model shown in Knolmayer/Pfeiffer (1990) p. 32.

14) Cf. also ADL (1980) p. 13: "For electronic data interchange to take place...it is useful to split the problem into two major and largely independent parts: message standards and communications standards."

15) It should be noted that industrial economists have proposed completely different, non-technical, non-procedural definitions of EDI. Classification/distinction from related systems may e.g. be accomplished by means of measurement on two nominal-scale dimensions: Market governance structure (electronic hierarchy vs. electronic market) and system functionality (transaction processing vs. task support); cf. Benjamin/De Long/Scott Morton (1990) p. 31. Alternatively, the degree of cooperation between transaction partners with respect to systems and organizational processes could be used; see e.g. Schumann (1990) pp. 309 - 311.

2.2. Foundations of EDI

2.2.1. Communication Theory

2.2.1.1. A Communication Model

Communication (derived from the latin word "communis" which means together) by definition implies a relationship between objects. More narrowly interpreted, the purpose of communication is to transfer information between at least two agents (interchangably referred to as sender/receiver, source/destination), in order to affect the actions of the receiver. The circular nature of this definition underscores the close interrelatedness between communication and information[16]. In fact, information theory has been introduced as the "Mathematical Theory of Communication"[17]. The activities subject to a linear communication process are usually illustrated by the schematic model of a communication system depicted in Exhibit 2-1. The Shannon/Weaver model shows that any communications process relies on four basic elements: (1) A source, (2) a message, (3) a medium, and (4) a destination.

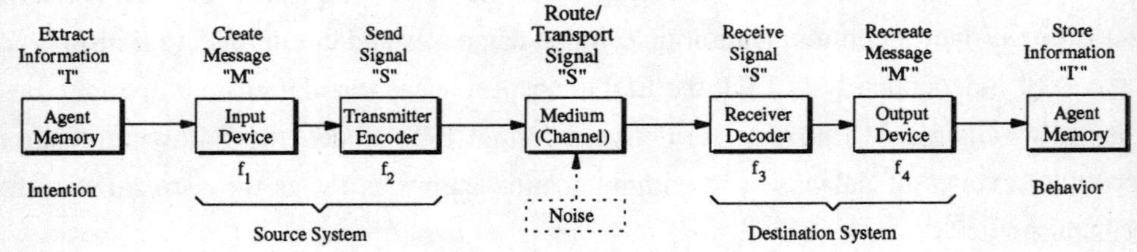

Exhibit 2-1	Schematic Block Diagram of a Communication System[18]

All elements of the system must have a certain minimum functionality in order for the communications process to transpire. The first component, the *sending agent*, must be able to preserve data about itself or the environment in a memory space. Secondly, the source must be able to intentionally select a specific subset of the stored data which has

16) If information is defined as e.g. in Davis/Oson (1985) p. 205: "Information is data that has been processed into a form that is meaningful to the recipient and is of real or perceived value in current or prospective actions or decisions", and if data relates to any representation of facts or concepts, communication implies information and *vice versa*.

17) Shannon (1948), Shannon/Weaver (1949), cf. also Wiener (1949).

18) After Shannon/Weaver (1949) p. 34, Cf. also Stallings (1988) p. 2.

implications for the future actions of the recipient, and turn this information into a *message*[19] by means of some encoding device. The message is subsequently transmitted over a *medium* (channel) to the destination system. Thus, the communication medium serves as a bridge for the message to overcome the physical distance between source and destination system. The destination system must be able to receive and decode the message and submit the information to the *receiving agent.* This agent must then change his current or planned future actions.

Communications processes (e.g. between human actors) can therefore be described as a series of functional mappings or coding operations on information. At the outset of the process, some information I is selected from the memory of the sending agent where it is stored according to the idiosyncratic rules of some internal representation form of the agent. Then, the information is encoded into a message M by means of a (rule based) translation mechanism (functional mapping f_1[20]). Subsequently, the transmitter of the source system takes the message, converts it into a form (e.g. signals) S that is suitable for the transmission medium (functional mapping f_2) and submits it to the medium for transport. The receiver of the destination system converts the transmission back into a message M' (functional mapping f_3) and finally, the decoder transforms the message into information I' for the receiving agent where it is stored according to the particular rules of the agent's internal representation form (functional mapping f_4).

In order for the communication process to achieve the desired results, the functional mappings are required to meet certain correspondence constraints. Obviously, functions f_1 and f_4 must be compatible to each other in the sense that sender and receiver may have dissimilar internal representation forms for information but have reached agreement *ex ante* (e.g. by a negotiation process) of how information is to be coded into a message between them, i.e. they have agreed on a common symbolic or other form of representation[21]. Secondly, functions f_2 and f_3, channel encoding and decoding, must be aligned such that f_3 may be the inverse of f_2 ($f_3 = f_2^{-1}$)[22]. And finally, the informa-

19) According to Wiener (1949) p. 16, a "message is a discrete or continuous sequence of measurable events distributed in time - precisely what is called a time-series by the statisticians." For the purposes of this text it suffices to view a message as a collection (or sequence) of symbols drawn from a set of symbols that carries meaning for the communicating agents.

20) This could in fact be called mapping f_2 since the information stored in the sending agent's memory must have been received either via another communications process or via sensual perception which requires at least another transformation function.

21) The complex negotiation/reconciliation process has been labeled the "problem of reference". Cf. e.g. Lindsay/Norman (1977) p. 479.

22) If more than one medium would be used during the communciations process a sequence of encoding/decoding pairs of functions (f_2'/f_3', f_2''/f_3'', etc.) would be required.

tion was selected and transmitted by the sending agent in order to influence the behavior of the recipient. Successful communication therefore requires that the sender has a correct causal model regarding the determinants of the recipient's behavior.

Thus, it is possible to divide the communication problem into three distinct hierarchical levels, each of which must be solved separately[23]:

- Technical level. How accurately are the symbols being transmitted over the communications medium and replicated by the receiving system? (Correspondence between f_2 and f_3)

- Semantic level. How accurately do the symbols convey the intended meaning? (Correspondence between f_1 and f_4)

- Effectiveness level[24]. To what extent does the message induce the receiving agent to behave in the desired way? (Correspondence between behavioral model and action)

Since this distinction will be important in describing and analyzing the various requirements of EDI as well as to differentiate EDI from related concepts, the technical level of the communication problem will be referred to as the Technical Communication Problem (TCP), the semantic level will be labeled the Semantic Communication Problem (SCP), and the effectiveness level will be called the Pragmatic Communication Problem (PCP).

Given these definitions, it is quite clear that the development of early communication systems such as the telephone was dominated by the search for finding effective solutions for the TCP. At that time it was argued that "the fundamental problem of communications is that of reproducing at one point either exactly or approximately a message selected at another point. Frequently the messages have meaning; that is they refer to or are correlated according to some system with certain physical or conceptual entities. These semantic aspects of communication are irrelevant to the engineering problem."[25] The original contribution of Shannon was therefore to present a mathematical model of

---

23) Cf. Shannon/Weaver (1949) pp. 4 and 24 - 28, Wiener (1950) pp. 88 - 91. See also Davis/Olson (1985) p. 202, Vervest (1987) p. 57.

24) This problem has also been called the *pragmatic* problem of communication. Cf. e.g. Mag (1980) col. 1033, Roger/Kincaid (1981) p. 33.

25) Shannon/Weaver (1949), p. 31.

signal transmission rather than of human communication[26]. However, since means for solving the SCP and PCP of human communication were already established, thanks to natural language and predictability of behavior, finding an effective solution for the TCP was all that was required. In fact, as long as a communication process involves human agents on both sides, irrespective of whether it is computer-mediated like e.g. in E-Mail or not, solving the TCP is sufficient to guarantee effective communication between both agents. On the other hand, as soon as information systems replace humans as communication agents, which is obviously the case for EDI considering the aforementioned definitions, SCP and PCP re-emerge as important issues in addition to finding a suitable message transport mechanism[27]. As was pointed out above, EDI was primarily designed to support the execution of inter-organizational business transactions such as sending and processing orders. The "behavior" of the IS participating in the communication process is predetermined by coded program instructions on either side which reflect the established norms for such business transactions. Therefore, it is possible to disregard the pragmatic communication problem and instead focus attention on the SCP[28].

To understand more precisely the requirements for solving the semantic problem in IS-communication, it seems advantageous to briefly review the analogous problem with respect to communication processes between human agents.

2.2.1.2. Semantic Aspects of Communication between Human Agents

When human agents are involved in a communication process, they resort to natural language in order to solve the SCP, i.e. in order to attach meaning to the signals transmitted over whatever communication medium. This implies that only the physical representation of a message - i.e. the sequence of symbols drawn from an *a priori* defined symbol set - can be transmitted, never can meaning[29]. Learning to use a natural lan-

---

26) Cf. Robers/Kincaid (1989) p. 31: "The theory did not consider the semantic or pragmatic levels of communication". Human communication requires a message that carries meaning for the communication partners.

27) In fact, due to the historical development of communications technology, solving the SCP and PCP take precedence because a message transmission infrastructure to support communication between human agents has already been established and can at least theoretically be utilized for communication processes between IS, which is the whole purpose of the discussion about how to use X.400 systems for EDI communication (refer to section 2.3.3.3.).

28) The established business norms govern the execution of transactions entirely unrelated to the physical characteristics of the communication system.

29) A fundamental aspect of communication: Meaning is derived by the cognitive process of interpretation. Cf. e.g. Herrlitz (1973) p. 35.

guage is the mechanism by means of which semantic can be associated with a collection of symbols, a task which must be accomplished by each communication partner alone. Therefore, effective communication requires a binary relationship between communicating agents: First, symbols (or signal transforms of symbols) must be physically transmitted between them. Second, a shared interpretation code[30] is required which relates symbols to their meaning. Given the conventional assumption that all agents have over time acquired a personal code set, the intersection of the code sets of communication partners must cover all symbols used during the communication process (see Exhibit 2-2); otherwise communication fails[31].

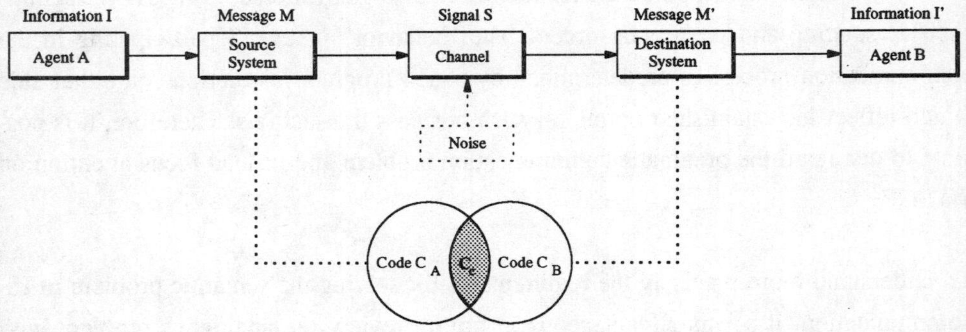

Exhibit 2-2	Human Communication Model[32]

In mathematical notation:

Let there be two communication agents A and B as well as a message M which is sent from A to B. Furthermore, let

M_A := the set of all messages available to A,

30) A code by definition is any function that maps a set of symbols into another set of symbols. Cf. e.g. Deutsches Institut für Normung e.V. DIN 44300: "Code: 1. Eine Vorschrift für die eindeutige Zuordnung (Codierung) der Zeichen eines Zeichenvorrats zu denjenigen eines anderen Zeichenvorrats (Bildmenge). 2. Der bei der Codierung als Bildmenge auftretende Zeichenvorrat."

31) Cf. Kreckel (1981) p. 4: "Each individual's conceptual organization of reality is unique. It reflects his experiences with and his knowledge of the social and physical environment." How this personal code set for human communication is acquired is of no direct concern here. It can basically be described as a cognitive learning process which creates a correspondence structure between perceptual characteristics and "labels". Cf. Atkinson/Kilby/Roca (1988) pp. 346 - 349. See also Clark (1973).

32) Adapted from Herrlitz (1973) p. 41, Figure 6. It should be noted that this model is frequently extended by distinguishing further between a "denotative" and connotative" meaning of messages. This distinction is particularly important in the context of human communication but can be excluded from further consideration because only analogous aspects of EDI and human communication are relevant here.

M_B	:=	the set of all messages available to B,
S_A	:=	the set of semantic A associates with M_A,
S_B	:=	the set of semantic B associates with M_B,
C_A	:=	the code used by A to relate M_A to S_A,
C_B	:=	the code used by B to relate M_B to S_B.

It follows that C_A and C_B are functions f_A and f_B[33)] such that:

$$C_A = f_A: M_A \rightarrow S_A$$

$$C_B = f_B: M_B \rightarrow S_B$$

Communication occurs if

$$M \subseteq (M_A \cap M_B) \quad \text{and} \qquad (2.1)$$

$$C_A(M) = C_B(M). \qquad (2.2)$$

Hence, a collective (common) code $C_c = C_A \cap C_B \neq \{\}$ (the shaded area in Exhibit 2-2) must exist on which the communication process can be based[34)]. It should be noted that conditions (2.1) and (2.2) both must be met simultaneously for a communication process to succeed. In fact, analogous to optimality criteria in calculus, (2.1) could be called the *necessary* and (2.2) the *sufficient* condition of a communication process.

Such codes or languages normally consist of a three level architecture to capture semantic: The lowest level is comprised of the basic symbol set (e.g. characters of some alphabet) available to communicating agents to compose messages. In general, no meaning is conveyed by those atomic symbols since, by virtue of their small number, they cannot possibly denote environmental entities such as objects or concepts[35)] in sufficient variety. Therefore, serial collections - strings - of symbols (words) drawn from the symbol set represent the basic units to reference those objects or concepts as well as

33) The notation used has been introduced for simplicity reasons. It would actually be more precise to define two types of functions (mappings) to relate message and meaning: One for coding $C = f: S \rightarrow M$ and another one for decoding $D = f: M \rightarrow S$. However, since C is assumed to establish a one-to-one correspondence between M and S, the inverse function of C ($C^{-1} = D$) can be disregarded and, depending on whether coding or decoding is meant, C(S) and C(M) may be used.

34) Again, nothing will be said here about how such a common code is developed between human communication agents. An introduction into the development of 'shared knowledge' or 'shared maps' can be found e.g. in Kreckel (1981) p. 24 *et seqq.*, Lewis/Pucelik (1982).

35) Here, "concept" refers to "products of classified knowledge an individual holds about objects, events and states". Cf. Kreckel (1981) p. 24 and the references cited there.

relationships between them[36]. However, with respect to relationships between entities, words are incapable of expressing the direction of the relationship which is why words must be qualified somehow. Hence, words are grouped into higher level structures, sentences (serial collections of words), in which the relative position of the words - the syntax[37] of the sentence - indicates their precise meaning[38].

To summarize, in order to solve the SCP of agents who wish to communicate with each other, it would be necessary for them to agree on a collective code for the symbolic representation of environmental objects, concepts, etc. Such a code normally consists of a three-level hierarchical architecture composed of symbols, words, and sentences. Not surprisingly, if those agents turn out to be IS, as is the case with EDI, *full agreement* concerning and *compliance* with standards on all three levels represent only two of several mandatory prerequisites of any EDI implementation[39]. Non-availability or multiplicity of standards on any level would seriously erode the potential for a rapid diffusion of EDI systems in practice due to the increased likelihood of miscommunication which occurs when the 'sufficient' communication condition (2.2) is not fulfilled.

2.2.2. Database Theory

2.2.2.1. Database Architecture

The second major component of EDI systems besides a communication module are databases. The architecture of database systems is commonly described by a three-level organization which is illustrated in Exhibit 2-3. This model was first proposed by the

36) Any more than rudimentary treatment of linguistics theory is certainly beyond the scope of this text. Nonetheless, it may be in order to remark that attempts to determine a satisfactory, language-invariant definition of a "word" other than the smallest-common-denominator manifest: "words occur between spaces" proved to be difficult, which is why linguists instead prefer to resort to morphemes as "the smallest meaningful unit in any language at all"; cf. Atkinson/Kilby/Roca (1988) p. 134.

37) Paradoxically, there is even definitional confusion/disagreement between linguists and communication scientists on key terms, exemplified e.g. by the apparent homonymic character of the term *syntax* which, for linguists refers to the internal structure of sentences, i.e. the organization of words within sentences, while at least some communication scientists would use *syntax* as a referent for sending signals/symbols over a communication channel. Cf. e.g. Atkinson/Kilby/Roca (1988) p. 155, Akamajian/Demers/Harnish (1979) p. 138, Mag (1980) col. 1033.

38) For example, consider the words "Person A", "Person B", and "Supervises". Each unambiguously references either an object or a relationship between objects. Yet only the structure of the sentence is able to clearly indicate who supervises whom.

39) To emphasize the difference between a mere data interchange, that is the transmission of a sequence of symbols or bit-strings with no meaning attached according to some technical protocol, and a communications process which involves the transfer of information, EDI should more accurately be called "electronic information interchange" (EII). However, since pronunciation is less convenient and due to the normative power of established facts, the conventional term can be expected to prevail. Cf. also Mark/Roussopoulos (1987).

ANSI/X3/SPARC Study Group on Database Management Systems in 1978[40]. Essentially, it distinguishes between an *internal* and an *external* view of a database, where the former is relevant for systems professionals who are interested in particular design and implementation features of the database system, and the latter refers to the perspective of end-users who access the database for the purpose of executing (business) transactions. To bridge the gap between both views, the study group proposed to create a conceptual schema which "in machine readable form" describes the information contained in the database. This schema should be known to the *database management system* (DBMS) which is an integrated software package that controls access to and manipulation of the contents of the database system on all three levels. Moreover, the conceptual schema requires that internal and external views be always consistent with it.

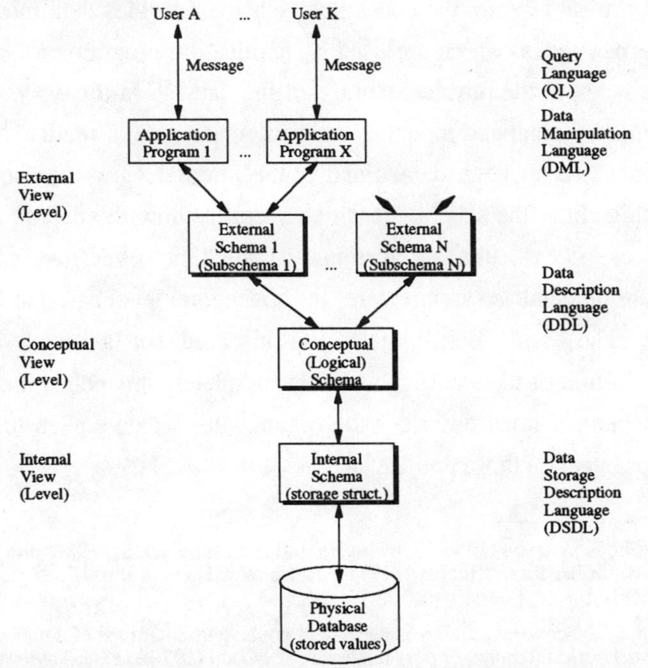

Exhibit 2-3	Three-Level Architecture of a Database System

Given the assumption that the database serves an entire organization, a typical user would only be interested in a certain portion of the database, the external view of that particular user. A description of a view has been called a schema, and therefore external

40) Tsichritzis/Klug (1978), p. 179. Cf. e.g. Date (1986) p. 30, Encarnação/Lockemann (1987) p. 25, Schwarze (1987) p. 55, McFadden/Hoffer (1988) p. 54 *et seqq.*, Yannakoudakis (1988) p. 24, Hars/Scheer (1991) p. 38.

views are defined by subschemas that are subsets of the conceptual (logical) schema of the overall database.

Several, not necessarily mutually exclusive methodologies for database design are found in practice. Besides the more frequently used top-down approach, which seeks to determine a suitable design through a process of continuous refinement, the "view integration" method, according to which user views are elicited (e.g. through interviews) and later combined into the conceptual (logical) schema, has received considerable attention[41]. The conceptual schema is a comprehensive description of the entire information content of the database in a logical sense, which means that those objects and relationships between objects that are relevant to the organization are being described in a machine-processable data description language (DDL) in terms of datastructures and referents[42]. At the same time, the conceptual schema provides data independence and shields the external views, which are used by application programs to access the database, from details about the physical storage of the data[43]. In this way, the conceptual schema represents a formalized model of the particular "slice of reality"[44] about which the organization needs to keep data. Finally, the internal view represents the lowest level of the architecture, the schema of which specifies how the data is actually stored on storage devices, access paths, etc. It should be noted, however, that (especially in the German literature on database architecture) the conceptual level has also been called the "logical" level. The term "conceptual" was reserved for an even more abstract ("semantic") definition of the database which is completely independent of any database model. This conceptual level describes the organization's data e.g. in terms of entities and relationships between those entities[45].

---

41) Cf. Navathe/Elmasri/Larson (1986). See also Batini/Lenzerini/Navathe (1986) and the literature cited there. See further Raver/Hubbard (1977), Yannakoudakis (1988) p. 162 *et seqq.*, Spaccapietra/Parent (1990).

42) The definition of the conceptual view is dependent on the particular type of database employed, be it hierarchic, network, relational or post-relational; see Codd (1970), Frank/Taylor (1976), Tsichritzis/Lochovsky (1976).

43) This is, however, a fairly idealistic view of a conceptual schema. In reality, the notion of data independence may actually be achieved by existing DBMS products, yet few, if any of those systems provide application independence or e.g. sophisticated mechanisms to enforce semantic integrity constraints on the data.

44) Klein/Hirschheim (1987) p. 8 who present a framework for various data modelling paradigms. It is also referred to as "Universe of Discourse (UoD)"; see Nijssen (1974). The notion that the conceptual model is nothing else but a representation of reality in symbolic form raises a number of interesting questions, e.g. whether it is both feasible and advisable to develop an *enterprise-wide datamodel*, which are, however, beyond the scope of this text.

45) Cf. e.g., Schlageter/Stucky (1983) p. 42 *et seqq.*, Stucky/Krieger (1990), p. 845 *et seq.* See also Batini/Lenzerini/Navathe (1986) p. 324 *et seq.* Navathe/Elmasri/Larson (1986) p. 51. Cf. Chen (1976), Hull/King (1987), Peckham/Maryanski (1988) for semantic data models as well as Biller/Neuhold (1978) and Kent (1978) for the relationship between semantics and data stored in databases. Cf.

The motivation for such a three-level (four-, respectively) database system architecture emerged from the desire to separate the end-user requirements for access to the organization's data as much as possible from the technical considerations associated with gathering, storing, and administrating this data. If one were to accept such a layered architecture of database systems, it is easy to see how a typical end-user accessing the system invokes a series of communication processes. First, by means of some *query language* (QL), *data manipulation language* (DML), or *application program*, the user selects a message from the set of all messages available (or derivable) through the external view. This message is then forwarded via mapping function to the conceptual/logical schema of the database. If the message meets certain integrity constraints, it is mapped to the internal schema where the requested operation is physically executed. The system eventually returns one or several messages (e.g. information or status messages) to the user. Thus, accessing a database can be viewed as a communication process.

2.2.2.2. Data Dictionary

The institution responsible for managing the database system is the *database administrator* (DBA) which is rather a role than a person. The DBA assumes such tasks as the planning, design, implementation, and maintenance of the database. In addition, policies and guidelines for using the database are largely defined by the DBA who is generally "charged with managing the firm's data resource"[46]. Due to the size and complexity of organizational databases on the one hand, and the limited ability of human beings to cope with complexity on the other[47], effective execution of the DBA function requires support tools to assist the responsible personnel. Such a tool is the *data dictionary* (DD), sometimes also called *data dictionary/directory system* (DD/DS)[48]. As a result of the DD's importance in managing a database system, many, yet not all DBMS vendors also offer DDs[49].

---

further Codd (1979), Tsichritzis/Lochovsky (1982), Karszt (1984), Furtado/Neuhold (1986) Part B, Bowers (1989), Everest (1989).

46) Canning (1972). Even though the DBA fulfills a fairly wide range of technical and operational tasks, it must not be confused with the separate task of *data administration* which is concerned with decisions regarding the information content of the database.

47) Concept of bounded rationality; cf. March/Simon (1958). See further McFadden/Hoffer (1988) p. 338 *et seqq.* and the rather cynical remarks in Spaccapietra/Parent (1990) p. 2.

48) E.g. Leong-Hong/Plagman (1982), McFadden/Hoffer (1988) p. 382 *et seqq.*

49) Cf. Wertz (1986) p. 56, Yannakoudakis (1988) p. 98. Such a product does not necessarily imply integration with a particular DBMS, it may be a completely DBMS-independent DD.

As its name implies, the data dictionary is nothing else but a database. Yet while a regular database describes the relevant environment of an organization, the DD describes the contents of a database, i.e. the description of the environment. Hence the notion that the DD stores meta-data. According to proponents of DD systems, the data dictionary can have an almost unlimited capacity to assist the DBA in various stages of the lifecycle of a database system[50)]. At least, however, by storing descriptive information about data structures and elements, it provides a comprehensive definition of the database on all three levels as well as the necessary mechanisms to permit inter-level mapping[51)]. It is convenient to classify the great variety of meta-data types that can be stored in a DD according to a two-dimensional scheme. On the first dimension, DD entries are dichotomously categorized regarding whether they describe data contained in the database or usage of that data (e.g. via programs). On the second dimension entries are also separated into two groups, the first group relates to logical concepts (e.g. entities or events as described in the conceptual schema) or to physical representations of those concepts (e.g. records or programs as described in the internal schema). Thus, a four-cell matrix is created and all DD entries unequivocally either fall into one of those cells or describe the relationship between the elements of adjacent cells, i.e. mapping and access rules[52)].

Using the DD as a tool to effectively manage a database requires that all structural or procedural modifications of the database are immediately reflected in the corresponding entries of the DD. While the concept of the data dictionary has recently been extended to also encompass application systems development aspects[53)], the DD features two main properties which are relevant from a communications perspective: One, the DD defines the symbolic representation of the environmental concepts captured in the database. Two, by providing a "narrative" description of the data stored in the database, it essentially bridges the semantic gap between the data stored in the database and the entities and relationships in the users' perception of the relevant organizational en-

---

50) Cf. e.g. Leong-Hong/Plagman (1982) p. 25 *et seqq.*, McFadden/Hoffer (1988) pp. 353 - 356. Cf. further Everest (1986) p. 602: "A data dictionary supplements a database definition; it is like a 'super' database definition."

51) Cf. Tsichritzis/Klug (1978) p. 185.

52) Cf. BCS (1977) p. 5.

53) In this extended role, the DD has been called a "repository" or "encyclopedia" that supports the entire information engineering process and contains design information about data and application architectures. Cf. e.g Strunz (1988).

vironment[54]. Thus, by virtue of storing meta-data, a DD contains the code which enables users to communicate with the database.

2.2.3. EDI Communication Model

Having introduced the general requirements of communication processes as well as the basic structure of databases, it is a fairly straightforward endeavor to derive an EDI communication model which helps to comprehend the amalgam of problems reported in the literature about EDI implemention in practice, such as the need to change internal application systems or the proliferation of EDI standards, which are perceived as being major inhibitors to the diffusion of EDI[55]. The EDI model depicted in Exhibit 2-4 essentially is a composition of two ANSI/SPARC databases and a communications system in between for message handling.

For EDI to function properly, all three levels of the communication problem defined earlier must be solved. With respect to the *effectiveness level,* business transaction cycles such as order and order acknowledgement have either been specifically agreed upon *ex ante* between the business partners or they have evolved into a standard business practice so as to be part of the established norms of commercial conduct. Since the effectiveness of a business transaction does not depend on the means of communication, fulfillment of this requirement, which is not peculiar to EDI, can usually be taken for granted. However, the effectiveness of legal recourse, due to the failure of one party to abide by those established norms of commercial conduct, may under certain circumstances be hampered with EDI as a consequence of the difficulty of electronic communication records to be admitted as legal evidence in court proceedings[56]. Regarding the *technical level,* a messaging system must be available which not only provides for the physical transport of the message but also routes the message safely through a network. Similar to the effectiveness question, the message handling problem is not unique to EDI, it applies equally to other forms of electronic communication records such as e.g. E-Mail. Thus, the *semantic level,* the association of a concept and

---

54) This does not necessarily imply narrative descriptions in natural language. Explication can also be accomplished e.g. by means of a semantic network of expressions. The ability of the DD to capture semantic associated with database entries allows the DBA to exert control over the integrity of the database by avoiding or helping to discover and resolve naming conflicts such as homonyms and synonyms, etc.; see e.g. Myrach/Jordan (1990).

55) Cf. N.N. (1990)

56) For the problem of electronic contracting, cf. section 2.3.4.2.

its symbolic referent, remains as the defining element of the EDI communications process.

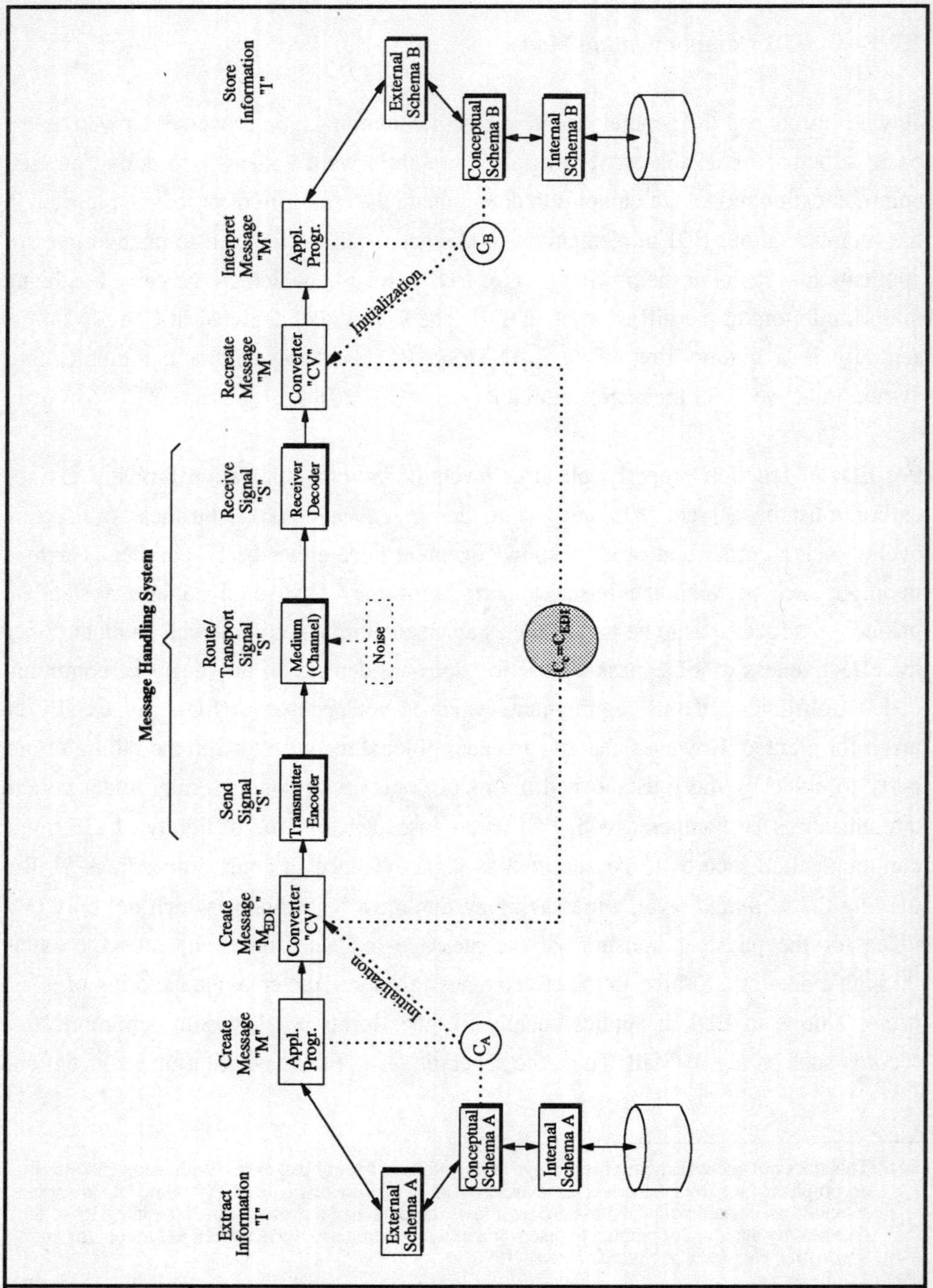

Exhibit 2-4	Schematic EDI Model

It is now possible to give two definitions of what constitutes Electronic Data Interchange. The *broad* definition subscribes to the view that EDI can only be differentiated from other forms of message exchange when the semantics issue is fully separated from hardware and network considerations, which are at any rate necessary prerequisites for conducting EDI. Such an interpretation could be formulated as follows:

> **Electronic Data Interchange (EDI) can be defined as any mechanism that provides a solution to the semantic communication problem of a data exchange between autonomous databases or application systems.**

To state it differently, EDI is a *language* that allows autonomous databases or application systems to communicate, i.e. a semantic preserving exchange of data. The second, more *narrow* definition pays tribute to the current usage of EDI in practice:

> **Electronic Data Interchange (EDI) can be defined as a set of message standards to enable the exchange of commercial transaction data between autonomous application systems without human intervention.**

This view effectively confines the scope of EDI to electronic renditions (equivalents) of conventional paper-based business documents used in the context of commercial transactions. While it must be regarded less appealing from a theoretical perspective, all sections of this thesis dealing with empirical aspects presuppose the latter definition of EDI.

To concentrate attention initially on the broad definition of EDI, and disregarding both the TCP and the pragmatic communication problem, the analogy between EDI and human communication is evident. Traditionally, organizational databases were designed considering internal requirements only and gradually evolved over some time period of continuing development. As a result, the conceptual schemas of autonomous databases, i.e. databases which are design-independent, not only differ but may in most cases be pairwise disjoint. This implies that without external intervention, no message can be exchanged at all between them, the common situation for databases even within the same enterprise.

Capitalizing upon the notation introduced earlier, suppose a business transaction is to be executed between two partners A and B, each of which uses a database as depicted in Exhibit 2-4. For this purpose, a transaction message M_T is sent from database A to database B. Independent of the communications mechanism employed, the transaction can only be completed if the semantic S_T associated with that message is a subset of the semantic captured in both databases[57]:

$$S_T \subseteq (S_A \cap S_B) \quad (2.3)$$

In most situations (2.3) can be taken for granted. Indeed, an established business relationship between both partners implies that this condition is fulfilled. Secondly, similar to (2.1):

$$M_T \subseteq (M_A \cap M_B) \quad (2.4)$$

If M_T violates this condition, the message cannot be processed by one of the two systems (due e.g. to a different character set). Analogous to a communication process between human agents, the most stringent requirement can be stated as follows:

$$C_A(M_T) = C_B(M_T) \quad (2.5)$$

Assuming that the databases are autonomous and design-independent, condition (2.5) will normally be violated - i.e. $C_A(M_T) \neq C_B(M_T)$ - and thus prevent the automatic exchange of data. To overcome the problems caused by the incompatible, non-integrated nature of databases[58] two basic approaches are conceivable.

According to the first method, the conceptual database schemas, as defined in the respective data dictionaries, are being modified to accommodate requirements imposed by the need to communicate with external databases. Thus, the databases partially lose their autonomy since certain design aspects are no longer freely disposable. This approach represents the essence of a proposal made by Petri (1990) in which case it would be justified to use the expression "external integration". Three different options exist:

- $C_A(M_T) = C_{B'}(M_T)$ — C_B is adjusted according to C_A
- $C_{A'}(M_T) = C_B(M_T)$ — C_A is adjusted according to C_B
- $C_{A'}(M_T) = C_{B'}(M_T) = C_c(M_T)$ (2.6)

The final option implies that both C_A and C_B are adjusted according to a collective (exogenous) code C_c.

57) Not even paper-based transactions would be possible under those circumstances.

58) See e.g. Smith et al. (1981) p. 487.

The second approach recognizes that integration can only be achieved *ex post* and seeks to both preserve the *status quo* of a database design, that was refined (as argued before) in the course of an extended evolutionary process, and the flexibility of the individual database designer to proceed with the development at the cost of increased complexity and redundancy[59]. In this approach, compatibility between databases is achieved by setting up an additional mapping layer that transforms messages from one idiosyncratic representation into another or into a standard form and *vice versa,* which obviates the need to modify the conceptual schemas. However, the device - henceforth called "converter" - that performs the conversion between idiosyncratic and/or standard codes must be initialized at the outset which means that a coding table must be prepared. The functionality of a converter (CV) can generally be described as follows:

$$CV = \{f: C_i(M_T) \rightarrow C_j(M_T)\,,\; f^{-1}: C_j(M_T) \rightarrow C_i(M_T)\} \tag{2.7}$$

This solution is the most prevalent form of EDI today. Two basic alternatives exist:

$$CV_{AB} = \{f: C_A(M_T) \rightarrow C_B(M_T)\,,\; f^{-1}: C_B(M_T) \rightarrow C_A(M_T)\} \tag{2.8}$$

The first alternative requires to initialize a *single* converter that directly interfaces between C_A and C_B. Choices remain concerning the installation point of the converter which could be set up on either end of the message handling system. The second alternative, which is the one being depicted in Exhibit 2-4, requires the installation of *two* converters which transform messages from autonomous coding systems C_A and C_B into a *standard collective code* C_c.

$$CV_{Ac} = \{f: C_A(M_T) \rightarrow C_c(M_T)\,,\; f^{-1}: C_c(M_T) \rightarrow C_A(M_T)\} \tag{2.9a}$$

$$CV_{Bc} = \{g: C_B(M_T) \rightarrow C_c(M_T)\,,\; g^{-1}: C_c(M_T) \rightarrow C_B(M_T)\} \tag{2.9b}$$

While this alternative apparently necessitates twice as many converters as the previous systems architecture, it represents nonetheless the more efficient solution. Within a multi-lateral trading community where each member has business relationships with several other members, the number of converters required to directly interface between systems increases quadratically with the number of community members n[60]:

---

59) Hammel (1975) p. 67 stresses that structural modifications of databases for communication purposes remains a long-term goal at best. Up until then, compatibility between systems can only be achieved by means of establishing functional interfaces.

60) Rather than exponentially, as is stated e.g. by Sarich (1988) p. 12.

$$\text{No. Converters} = n! / [(n-2)!\,2!] = n(n-1)/2 \tag{2.10}$$

This is the extreme case of a *closed user community*. By contrast, with a standard collective code, each member only needs to maintain a single converter to map between its idiosyncratic code and the standard. Thus, the user community is open in the sense that all community members can freely exchange messages among each other without having to switch code standards. Therefore, the number of converters that must be initialized and maintained increases merely *pari passu* with the number of community members[61]:

$$\text{No. Converters} = n \tag{2.11}$$

The EDI model described above facilitates the classification of various implementation problems frequently complained about by practicioners as serious impediments to EDI's growth. Common examples include the incompatibility of communication hardware (signal processing), the proliferation of closed EDI user groups[62], the ambiguousness of international standards such as EDIFACT[63] as well as the imminent emergence of standard subsets, and the need to adjust internal application systems/databases[64].

On the upper most level, problems can be separated as to whether they are germane to the message handling system[65], whether it is a matter of database content, or whether differences or shortcomings of database design are to be blamed. For instance, in cases of technical equipment incompatibility, or membership in different and unconnected telecommunications networks, the inability to conduct EDI stems from the messaging system. Again, such problems are not peculiar to EDI; conducting E-mail would not be feasible either. By contrast, the initial proliferation of bilateral agreements between major trading partners concerning codes for data exchange, which led to closed EDI user communities, is a result of the historic evolution of EDI which was initially characterized by low penetration levels and the non-availability of public EDI standards. Lacking a collective code C_c, organizations had no choice but to resort to bilateral message exchange agreements. The growing size of the EDI user community, however, imposes intolerable maintenance and administrative burdens on the use of private codes.

---

61) If converters allow only unidirectional mapping, *2n* such devices must be maintained.

62) Cf. Emmett (1991).

63) Electronic Data Interchange For Administration, Commerce and Trade.

64) Cf. Butler Cox (1987) p. 3, Canright (1988b) p. 84, Norris (1990) p. 22.

65) As was pointed out earlier, solving the TCP does not belong to the province of EDI. Finding a solution, however, represents an indispensible prerequisite.

The later development of a collective code penalizes EDI pioneers with switching costs since they are obliged to at least modify their converter mapping tables to accommodate the new code.

The seemingly innocuous change of migrating towards a public standard can, however, have much farther reaching consequences for EDI users. Public standards *ipso facto* need to cover a wide range of typical business situations. Since requirements for individual organizations and trading relationships do in fact differ, a public standard must be a *superset* of micro-level requirements. If this collective code contains some mandatory semantic, which was not a necessary element of the previously employed private code between transaction partners, migration would in the best case imply that the application programs, which extract the information relative to a transactions message from the database, must be modified to retrieve and process heretofore unused data *in addition* to changing the converter tables ($M_T \notin (M_A \cap M_B)$, see (2.4) above). In the worst case, the semantic S_T of the message, as defined by the collective code, is not captured in the databases of EDI users ($S_T \notin (S_A \cap S_B)$), which implies that not only converter tables and application programs must be changed, but also the structure and contents of the databases involved in the communications process are subject to design modifications[66].

2.2.4. Concepts Related to EDI

The schematic EDI-model derived in the previous section provides a *systemic* definition of EDI which aids in differentiating it from related concepts whose properties/requirements partly overlap. Those concepts which include electronic mail, online database communication, and distributed databases, can be distinguished from each other according to a two-level classification scheme depicted in Exhibit 2-5[67].

---

66) This may be illustrated by means of an example. Suppose two, only domestically operating organizations are exchanging EDI transactions, e.g. orders and invoices, according to a private coding scheme and decide to migrate towards a public standard which was designed to also handle international transactions of the same kind. Therefore, 'currency' may be a mandatory data element of the respective transaction message of the collective code. Since neither of the organizations' databases contains a currency data element, their structure has to be modified in order to generate messages that comply with the requirements of the public code. The reverse situation may also occur: An application system needs more data to execute a transaction than is contained in the EDI message. In cases like this special programs have to be developed that add the missing components. Cf. e.g. Groß (1990).

67) A similar idea to classify EDI has been put forth in Kemmler (1989) p. 160.

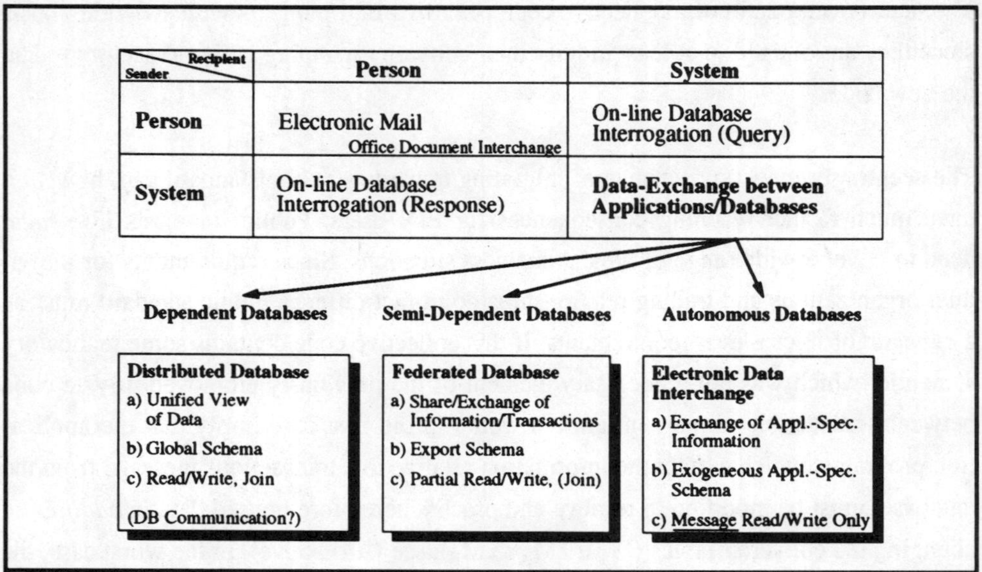

Exhibit 2-5 EDI in Comparison with Related Concepts

While recognizing that all those forms of communication may be computer-mediated, the upper-level perspective categorizes concepts by determining the 'nature' of the ultimate message sender and recipient. The domain of the attribute 'nature' consists of only two values: 'person' and 'system'. If sender and receiver both fall into the category 'system', which implies that the data exchange/communications process occurs between application systems or databases, a second, lower-level criterion is applied which measures whether the databases involved are autonomous, in the sense that their conceptual schemas are design-independent, or whether the schemas were aligned or integrated.

2.2.4.1. Electronic Mail

From a communication theory perspective, E-mail is merely a *technical* problem because neither the SCP nor the PCP need to be solved due to the fact that messages are exchanged between persons who themselves assume responsibility for the semantic and pragmatic aspects of the communications process. Thus, only a technical infrastructure for handling electronic messages, i.e. routing and transporting messages from sender to addressee, must be made available, providing all communication partners are endowed with suitable terminal equipment to create messages, submit them to the MHS, as well as receive (process) and display messages. It is therefore not surprising that, apart from the here mainly irrelevant business implications[68], E-Mail is often discussed in the framework of the complex technical problems encountered for interfacing between the great variety of incompatible communications gear found in practice[69].

Thus, similar to E-Mail, EDI presupposes some transport system for the delivery of (well-structured) electronic messages; yet whereas with EDI, messages are passed between IS, where further processing takes place, E-Mail was developed to interconnect between human agents, where message content is of no concern since any message processing is considered to be exogenous. Therefore, E-mail can actually be equated with a message handling system of a certain functionality. This particular MHS may, however, serve as a *platform* for exchanging EDI messages[70].

2.2.4.2. Online Database Communication

Any end-user accessing a database in on-line or batch mode invokes a bidirectional communications process between a human agent and a system, irrespective of the physical distance between them. A prime example of a remote database access would be sending a query to a commercial on-line database system which retrieves the requested information, encapsulates that information into a message which is subsequently sent back to the end-user[71]. Similar to E-Mail, an electronic communications infrastructure is necessary to transport messages. This time, however, the query has to comply with certain format standards in order for the system to correctly (i.e. consistent with the purpose of the transaction as defined by the information needs of the end-user) process the message[72]. As a result, interrogating on-line databases implies that the SCP must be solved *unilaterally* in addition to the technical communications problem, a task

---

68) Examples include the management of introducing E-mail systems into organizations or the utility of E-mail in supporting the execution of business processes;. cf. e.g. Picot (1987), Caswell (1989), Dean (1989).

69) Much of the literature on this topic is devoted to a description of multi-layer models for systems interconnection, the most famous of which is probably the ISO/OSI model for open systems interconnection; see International Standards Organization (1981). Cf. also Heist (1987), Moshos (1989) p. 173 *et seqq.*, Plattner et al. (1990).

70) Cf. Bairstow (1987), Dalton (1989), Sacher (1989).

71) An overview of electronic information services is given in Mulder (1989).

72) Since the query response recipient is a human agent, the message returned can essentially be free-format.

which is normally accomplished by exploiting the inherent flexibility of the human agent to adapt to the rigid requirements of the system[73)].

2.2.4.3. Distributed Databases

The last cell of the matrix shown in Exhibit 2-5 refers to a communications process between two systems or databases. It has already been pointed out that this cell can be further divided into sub-categories by the degree of schema-independence between the respective databases.

In principle, the total system required to conduct EDI deceptively resembles a distributed database environment which is commonly described as a collection of computer nodes that are interconnected by means of a telecommunications network; the question therefore arises, which differences can be identified. To begin with, the primary purpose of distributed database systems is to permit the execution of transactions against several databases via a *single logical access point*[74)]. A global conceptual schema presents users of the distributed database with a unified view of the entire system. The functionality of this system is likely to be a direct result of either the database design history or the philosophy of the integration approach.

The database designer may decide during the design process to physically partition a logically unified database into several smaller databases which are installed in geographically dispersed, interconnected computer nodes[75)]. Since only a single conceptual schema exists, the system provides *location transparency* to end-users or application programs, which means that processing requests do not have to contain information about the actual location of the program required and/or the data. Instead, the system

---

73) An exception to that rule would e.g. be a natural language interface to a DBMS, a technology which is yet to become widely available. See e.g. Yannakoudakis (1988) p. 109 *et seqq.* and the references cited there.

74) Cf. Sloman/Kramer (1987) p. 109.

75) Alternatively, the database could be replicated, which implies that copies of the database are physically stored at arbitrary nodes.

itself will keep track of it and shield the user from this additional complexity[76]. Moving data from one local database to another - if such a need occurs at all under those circumstances - is fully user-transparent and thus remains just a technical issue without any need for data translation since the semantic of the data is retained automatically by the global dictionary. In cases where a distributed database system is created *ex post* from a set of previously isolated local databases, that were independently developed and installed with idiosyncratic schemas[77], several types of distributed systems architectures with different functionalities may be distinguished[78], depending on whether the local schemas are *consolidated*[79] or *represented separately* in the global schema of the distributed system[80].

While the integration of several local databases into a distributed system offers end-users the entire range of database processing capabilities, such as e.g. *joins*, consolidation reduces the structural autonomy of the component databases. Moreover, the derivation of a global schema may be difficult to attain due to *semantic relativism* and may not even be required from a business perspective. In order to reconcile the conflicting goals of preserving as much autonomy of individual databases as possible while still permitting them to share information and transactions, a "federated architecture" has been proposed which mitigates the problems associated with developing a global schema and the necessary mapping functions. This architecture is based on a *semantic datamodel* and dispenses with the need of a centralized authority to control execution of

76) Such an integrated distributed system has certain advantages over a conventional centralized database. Besides providing the opportunity to exert ownership control of the data on a local level without restrictions to access data stored at other sites, a distributed system may simply be too large to be implemented at a single location. Furthermore, reliability is increased because a breakdown of a local node does not necessarily cause the entire system to fail. A distributed system economizes on communication costs, and finally, operating efficiency may improve due to lower response times when data and programs are moved closer to the points of regular usage so that most access is local. Cf. e.g. Date (1983) p. 294 *et seq*., Lyngbaek/McLeod (1983) p. 364, Sloman/Kramer (1987) pp. 103 - 105, Özsu/Valduriez (1991) pp. 8 - 10. To be sure, a distributed system has also some disadvantages. Apart from the additional administrative overhead required to cope with the higher complexity, transactions that involve several nodes are usually slower, which increases the risk of contention and deadlock. Indeed, synchronization and concurrency control tend to cause major problems in a distributed database environment. See Ceri/Pelagatti (1984) p. 180 *et seqq*., Özsu/Valduriez (1991) pp. 12 - 16, p. 276 *et seqq*. See further Leong-Hong/Plagman (1982) p. 234 *et seqq*., Stamper (1986) p. 432.

77) Cf. Davenport (1981).

78) Cf. Ram/Chastain (1989) p. 79 *et seqq*. Besides the question of how local schemas are represented in the global schema, distributed systems can be further characterized as *homogeneous* or *heterogenous* depending on whether local databases use the same or different types of DBMS. Multi-layered architectures have been proposed to handle the problems introduced by a heterogeneous database environment. See e.g. Cardenas/Pirahesh (1980), Miles et al. (1981). For schema translation refer e.g. to Sen/Ching (1986).

79) A methodology to accomplish consolidation is e.g. provided in Codd (1990a,b). A comparative analysis of schema integration methodologies can be found in Batini/Lenzerini/Navathe (1986).

80) "Multidatabase" architecture; see Ram/Chastain (1989).

transactions across the federation. Instead, interoperability is achieved by special "export schemas" which define "the information that the component is willing to share with other components"[81].

Even though individual databases retain a fair amount of autonomy, this architecture has been called "semi-dependent" in Exhibit 2-5 because some constraints must still be imposed. For instance, the evolution of the federation is controlled by a "federal dictionary" which is a separate, mandatory component of any federation. Secondly, the problem of semantic relativism must be resolved explicitly, e.g. by direct negotiation between the various database administrators involved[82]. As opposed to a distributed database, a federation does not remove redundancies among its constituents. In fact, while in a composite, one-transaction-at-a-time database information exchange is mostly external, a federation is characterized by multiple local transactions which create the need for federation-internal communication processes, inexorably inducing redundancy.

The difference between EDI and the federated architecture is primarily evident in the ability of the component databases in a federation to directly access (read) the export schemas of their counterparts and extract remote data[83] or carry out remote transactions. By contrast, EDI as defined above provides *no* access to external databases at all, which represents the fundamental difference between the EDI concept and all other forms of database integration. Since it is assumed that in most cases the database administrators of different organizations with a business relationship have no intention to make their organizational databases mutually accessible, the initiative for an information exchange always rests with the *sender* of a message rather than with the *recipient*. Hence, EDI-users grant no read-access to each others' databases, and because they cannot directly engage in negotiations to resolve semantic conflicts with an unknown

---

81) Heimbigner/McLeod (1985) p. 260; see also Lyngbaek/McLeod (1984), Alonso/Barbará (1989). This approach has also been called "multidatabase" Litwin/Abdellatif (1986), the same term that carries a different connotation in Ram/Chastain (1989). It is intriguing to notice, that even individuals who are professionally concerned with devising methods about how to resolve naming conflicts, such as homonyms and synonyms, in the process of merging previously isolated databases apparently fall prey to the disease of creating such ambiguities.

82) In the "multidatabase" approach, administrators are required to develop "dependency schemas" for this purpose. See Litwin/Abdellatif (1986) p. 11.

83) This could be regarded as a *latent message* that can be retrieved by the communications partner. The characterization of a federated database architecture as a semi-dependent system is not without problem. This is partly due to the innovative nature of this concept in database theory which is exemplified by the still evolving terminology and the lack of commercial systems. A comprehensive review and analysis of the relevant literature on federated database systems can be found in Sheth/Larson (1990).

set of potential business partners, a reasonably small number of user representatives must assume the responsibility for defining exogenous application-specific schemas which is only feasible on a very limited scale, namely for supporting a few highly standardized types of business applications[84)].

2.2.4.4. Office Document Interchange

While it is generally correct to distinguish EDI and E-Mail by pointing to the different message processing requirements, the assumption that messages exchanged between individuals carry no further structural information clearly represents an oversimplification. Especially within office environments, messages with some common logical and representational architecture - so called documents - are sent back and forth between office workers. Due to the incompatibilities of the office equipment used to produce those documents, it becomes necessary to devise a hard- and software independent standard for defining document structures. The Office Document Architecture (ODA) model, ISO standard 8613, has been developed to enable the exchange of documents between independent systems such that the content of the document, which may be comprised of text and graphics, is presented and can be consistently processed in accordance with the nature of the document as defined by its original author[85)].

To achieve those two objectives, the ODA model separates the information pertaining to a document into the three categories *logical*, *layout*, and *content*[86)]. The logical information describes the logical structure of a document in terms of its components and the relationships between components, independent of content and representation, while the layout information defines how the contents of a document are to be presented by a

---

84) A process which leads to open standards. It appears worthwhile to mention that another conceptually different method for information interchange has been proposed in the context of so called "self-describing databases". The basic idea of this approach is that in order to achieve an information interchange, the data transmitted during a communications session must be accompanied by metadata which will help the recipient interpret the symbolstring. The subsequent chain of intension-extension links terminates in the recursive definition of a meta-schema which contains the set of available rules to define schemas. Besides featuring an active, integrated data dictionary, a self-describing database system provides users who wish to access the database with a set of data management tools to develop an overview of the database content and to organize the information interchange process. Similar to the federated database architecture, the fundamental difference between this concept and EDI is the fact that a self-describing database system is accessed by users who extract information according to their own formating requirements; see Mark/Roussopoulos (1987). Again, the sender is in a reactive mode which is contrary to EDI where the initiative for a communications process always rests with the sender; cf. e.g. Sokol (1989) p. 90.

85) ODA was originally developed by the European Computer Manufacturers' Association (ECMA) and became ECMA standard 101. It was later adopted by ISO and CCITT (CCITT recommendations T.410). Refer to Campbell-Grant (1988) for further details.

86) Cf. e.g. Robinson (1990).

display device (e.g. terminal or printer). To exchange documents described by this architecture between independent office systems, they have to be encoded (by the sender) and decoded (by the recipient) according to the rules defined by the ODA interchange format (ODIF). Thus, EDI and ODIF have certain similarities in the sense that both define a data interchange format. However, in contrast to EDI, the ultimate purpose of ODA/ODIF is to support *interpersonal* communication which implies that SCP and PCP must still be resolved by individuals; to state it differently, any processing of the systems involved in the interchange is not affected by a document's content. This solely belongs to the province of the communication partners[87].

2.3. Requirements of EDI

The descriptive analysis concerning the nature of EDI presented in the previous section shows that for EDI to happen, a fairly large number of requirements must be fulfilled. Again, those requirements may be classified according to the three categories (TCP, SCP, PCP) identified within the framework of the general communication model. However, a finer-grained level of analysis seems desirable from the viewpoint of practitioners who are concerned about implementation issues of EDI rather than about a purely theoretical examination. For this reason, it may be preferable to decompose a typical EDI implementation into its main components and discuss those components separately. In light of the schematic EDI model depicted in Exhibit 2-4, five prerequisites for conducting EDI can be identified: (1) Message standards, which can be further disintegrated into *character*, *data element*, and *syntax* standards, (2) information systems for generating and processing messages, including EDI converters, (3) technical data communication standards to enable message exchange between (potentially) dissimilar hardware equipment, (4) a message handling infrastructure for transporting messages between sender and recipient, and (5) operational control agreements for organizing the communication flow between business partners.

87) Further information regarding ODA/ODIF can be found e.g. in Maciejewski (1989). A comparison between EDI standards and ODA/ODIF is provided e.g. in Rösch (1989).

2.3.1. Message Standards

2.3.1.1. Character Standards

Characters represent the lowest level in the hierarchy of communication standards required to construct interpersonal messages. Since EDI refers to a data exchange between systems rather than individuals, using a character set pertaining to human communication modes for the purposes of EDI is not a mandatory requirement. However, since databases normally provide character-based interfaces for end-users and since the internal data storage relies on chunks of bit-strings representing characters, it seems convenient to build EDI messages by capitalizing upon given standards. The feasibility of this approach presupposes that the character set used for creating messages is a subset of the character set which can be processed by the systems of all communication partners, irrespective of their actual bitwise representation in the various information systems[88]. Given the diversity of international alphabets, finding a suitable common denominator has been the responsibility of supra-national standards organizations such as the International Standards Organization (ISO) or the Comité Consultatif International Telégraphique et Telephonique (CCITT). Perhaps the most widely used code in messaging systems is the International Alphabet No. 5 (IA5)[89] which is a 7-bit code that allows to define a set of 128 printable and control characters. IA5 can be adapted to accommodate special national requirements such as *diacritics*. The advantage of this flexibility is somewhat mitigated by the fact that different national versions - the most important of which is arguably the American Standard Code for Information Interchange[90] (ASCII) - are incompatible with each other[91]. These limitations do not apply to 8-bit codes such as IBM's EBCDIC[92] or to the international teletex alphabet specified in CCITT recommendation T.61 which are able to handle a wider set of characters. While data coding aspects determine the number and type of symbols that can be used

---

88) The task of converting between different data representation forms could e.g. be handled by the presentation layer of the ISO/OSI reference model. Similar to the semantic problems encountered with exchanging EDI-messages, mapping between data representation forms requires a third, standard representation. Such a standard was defined in ISO standards 8824 and 8825 and has been called Abstract Syntax Notation One (ASN.1). For further information see e.g. Gora (1990), Plattner et al. (1990) p. 41 *et seqq.*, Taylor/Howard (s.a.).

89) CCITT Recommendation T.50, ISO 646. The precursor of IA5 is the 5-bit Baudot code which was originally conceived by Murray in the last century. Despite its age, a standardized version of the Baudot code (ITA2) is still being used for Telex applications. Cf. e.g. Loomis (1983) pp. 150 - 152, FitzGerald (1988) pp. 61 - 63.

90) Also known as the American National Standards Code for Information Interchange, American National Standards Institute ANSI X3.4-77.

91) See e.g. Plattner et al. (1990) pp. 84 - 87.

92) Extended Binary Coded Decimal Interchange Code.

to create messages and control data transmission processes, EDI messages may only consist of printable characters with no regard for the peculiarities of the chosen message transport facility[93)].

2.3.1.2. Data Element Standards

The next level of message standards relates to *data elements* which are the smallest unit of an EDI message that carries meaning. Since EDI was primarily devised to facilitate (international) trade, the data elements that are commonly recorded and maintained in public data element dictionaries cover transactions of this kind[94)]. For instance, the United Nations Trade Data Elements Directory (UN/TDED)[95)] provides (1) a listing of hundreds of trade related data elements containing 4-digit tags that can serve as the key to uniquely identify elements, (2) formatting guidelines, (3) a description which defines the meaning to be conveyed, as well as (5) the message segments (explained below) to which an element belongs in a given syntax. Because such a directory cannot possibly be exhaustive in light of the large variety of business requirements, user groups have the liberty to define additional, *private* data elements that can be integrated with standard elements into proprietary messages[96)].

2.3.1.3. Syntax Standards

Given a library of data elements, messages for various purposes can be assembled by drawing the appropriate elements from the directory and bringing them into a sequential order. The rules for constructing messages from data elements comprise the *syntax* of the EDI standard employed. As a consequence of the historical evolution of EDI, which originated within certain industries and countries, classifying syntax standards according to their application areas seems convenient. The two-dimensional grid shown in Exhibit 2-6 differentiates between four categories of standards depending on whether

93) According to the recommendations of ISO 9375 which specifies the EDIFACT syntax rules, the ISO 646 standard should be used unless trading partners have specifically agreed to employ an 8-bit code such as ISO 6937.

94) However, proposals have been made to extend this basic vocabulary with technical elements which may be relevant for certain business applications. See e.g. Mertens (1985) p. 82.

95) Conforms to ISO 7372. An alternative dictionary, X 12.3, primarily used in North America belongs to the ANSI X.12 family of EDI standards developed by the Accredited Standards Committee (ASC) established in 1979. A listing of those standards is e.g. provided by Norris (1988) p. 727.

96) Cf. e.g. Sarich (1988) p. 20.

they were designed for domestic or international use and whether they specifically apply to certain industries only.

	National	International
Industry-Specific	**VDA**	**SWIFT** **ODETTE** **(EDIFACT-Subsets)**
Non-Industry-Specific	**TRADACOMS** **ANSI X12** **(EDIFACT-Subsets?)**	**EDIFACT**

Exhibit 2-6	Categories of EDI-Standards[97)]

The two arguably most important EDI syntax standards currently in use consist of the family of ANSI X12 standards in North America and of the international EDI standard EDIFACT which is becoming increasingly popular in continental Europe as well as for international applications. Both standards are similar in their use of variable-length data elements.

2.3.1.3.1. ANSI X12

The ANSI/ASC X12 standard for electronic business data interchange (EBDI) was developed in order to promote trade related electronic communication across industries in the U.S.[98)] Standardized electronic messages or documents are referred to as "Transaction Sets" in X12 vernacular[99)]; transaction sets are not directly constructed from data elements but from so called "Data Segments". Similar to records in file organizations, data elements are assembled into data segments which represent an intermediate layer of data structure. Data segments are also standardized and kept in a separate directory which not only specifies the exact structure of each data segment but also stipulates in which transaction sets a particular segment is used. A sample data segment is shown in Exhibit 2-7:

---

97) Cf. e.g. Hofer (1990) p. D-3-13.

98) Cf. ANSI ASC-X12 (1987) p. 2. See further Jones (1982).

99) The reasoning behind creating the artificial term "transaction set" instead of e.g. "electronic document" is discussed in Bass (1989) p. 114.

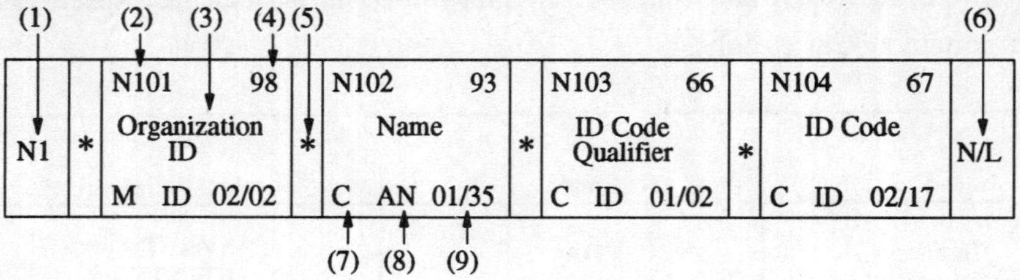

(1) Data Segment Identifier
(2) Data Element Reference Designator
(3) Data Element Title
(4) Data Dictionary Reference Number
(5) Data Element Separator
(6) Data Segment Terminator
(7) Data Element Requirement Designator
(8) Data Element Type
(9) Data Element Length

Exhibit 2-7 ANSI X12 Sample Data Segment[100)]

The actual transmission contains only the necessary reference characters, such as the 'Data Segment Identifier', the 'Data Element Separators' (required due to variable data element length), and the 'Data Segment Terminator', in addition to the values of the data elements. Data elements can either be a *mandatory*, *conditional* or *optional* part of a data segment as indicated by the 'Data Element Requirement Designator'. The ommission of non-mandatory data elements is easily detected by two adjacent element separators.

The set of data segments accounts for a self-contained part of the X12 standards and is defined in the ANSI X12.22 Data Segment Directory. Transaction sets that have been developed in accordance with the X12 syntax identify the required data segments and provide sequencing rules to enable the construction of complete EDI messages. The whole complexity of an EDI language becomes apparent when the multi-layered structure of interdependent standards is considered. The preceding discussion illustrates, that within ANSI X12 no less than three levels of message standards (data element, data segment, and transaction set) must be maintained and carefully controlled for preservation of inter-level integrity when modifications become necessary. Due to the ongoing standard development process, "releases" are published as frequently as every six months by the X12 committee[101)].

---

100) Adapted from Milbrandt (1987) p. 45.

101) Cf. e.g. Emmelhainz (1990) p. 79.

Having introduced the hierarchical structure of an ANSI X12 transaction set, it is now possible to visualize an arbitrary EDI session between trading partners. Assuming that several transaction sets are to be transmitted within a single session, messages are separated by type and organized into one or several 'Functional Groups', each of which can likewise contain one or several transaction sets of the same type. Exhibit 2-8 provides a schematic overview of an "Interchange" that highlights the use of *control segments* to structure the transmission[102].

While it is possible - and for efficiency reasons even advisable - to batch transaction sets into functional groups, and multiple functional groups into a single *interchange envelope*, a communication session will in practice involve only a single addressee, unless the services of a VANS are being employed who could assume responsibility for receiving and distributing messages for different recipients within the same session[103].

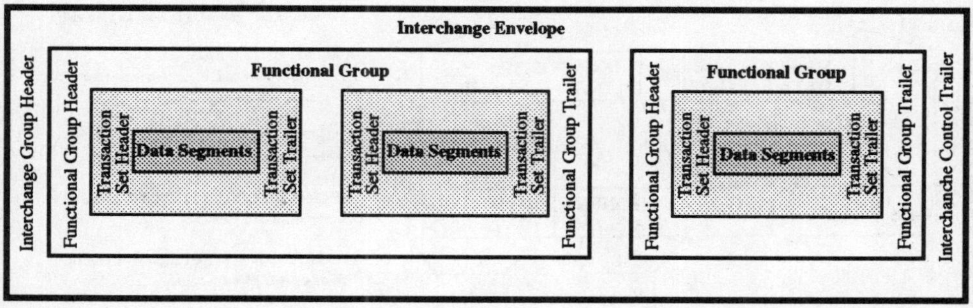

Exhibit 2-8	ANSI X12 Interchange Model

2.3.1.3.2. EDIFACT

EDIFACT is the second important syntax standard for EDI which has gained a large followership, particularly among the EC and EFTA countries with the notable exception of the U.K. for historical reasons. The United Nations (UN) EDIFACT Standards are structurally rather similar to ANSI X12. Besides the syntax rules, as defined in ISO 9735, there are directories of data elements (TDED), data segments (EDSD) and mes-

102) Cf. ANSI ASC-X12 (1987) p. 6. See also Meier (1989) p. 59.

103) Refer to section 2.3.3.

sages (EDMD), respectively[104]. Exhibit 2-9 illustrates the hierarchical architecture of an EDIFACT Interchange.

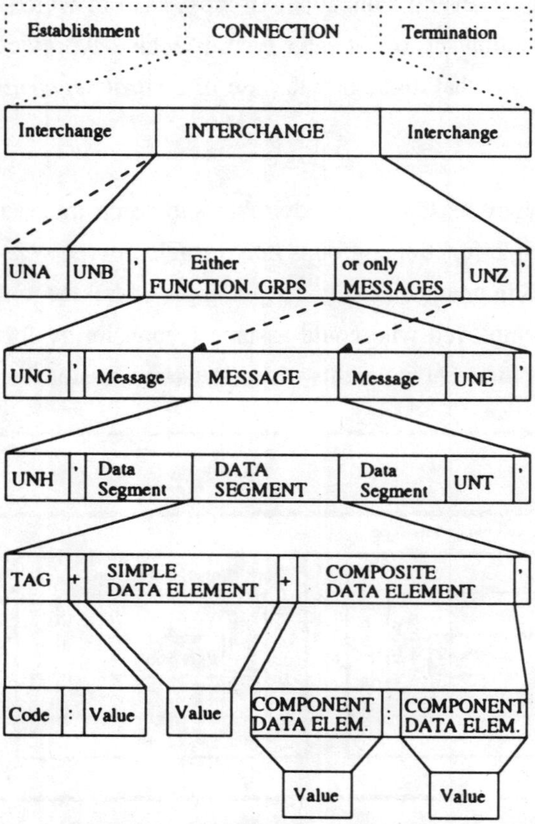

A CONNECTION contains one or more interchanges. The technical protocols for establishment, maintenance and termination etc. are not part of this standard.

An INTERCHANGE contains:
- UNA, Service String Advise, if used
- UNB, Interchange Header
- Either only Functional Groups, if used or only Messages
- UNZ, Interchange Trailer

A FUNCTIONAL GROUP contains:
- UNG, Functional Group Header
- Messages of the same type
- UNE, Functional Group Trailer

A MESSAGE contains:
- UNH, Message Header
- Data Segments
- UNT, Message Trailer

A SEGMENT contains:
- A segment Tag
- Simple data elements or
- Composite data elements or both as applicable

A SEGMENT TAG contains:
- A segment code and, if explicit indication, repeating and nesting value(s).

A SIMPLE DATA ELEMENT contains:
- A single data element value

A COMPOSITE DATA ELEMENT contains:
- Component data elements

A COMPONENT DATA ELEMENT contains:
- A single data element value

Exhibit 2-9	EDIFACT Interchange Model[105]

While at the time of this writing there are in excess of 150 different transaction sets within the framework of ANSI X12, only a small but rapidly growing number of EDIFACT message have achieved formal recommendation status by the UN/ECE as of

104) The terminology used in the literature is not always consistent. Compare e.g. Sarich (1988) p. 20 and Plattner et al. (1990) p. 191. While there is a significant amount of similarity between EDIFACT and ANSI X12, the EDIFACT syntax is in fact slightly more complex due to the introduction of Composite Data Elements and implicit as well as explicit nesting techniques for data segments. See ISO 9735 (1987) p. 9 *et seq*. A detailed discussion of the EDIFACT syntax rules can also be found e.g. in Mehnen (1989), Petri (1990) p. 178 *et seqq*. See further Weid (1989).

105) ISO 9735 (1987) p. 4.

yet[106]. The EDIFACT syntax is a successor to the Guidelines for Trade Data Interchange standards (GTDI). Due to a growing international commitment, the movement towards EDIFACT is likely to gain additional momentum, at least within Continental Europe, where e.g. national customs organizations are obliged to utilize EDIFACT standards "for data exchanges between customs administrations of the ECE, and between those customs administrations and the trading community"[107].

2.3.1.3.3. Other Syntax Standards

Besides ANSI X12 and EDIFACT a number of alternative EDI standards proved their viability over time because they were developed prior to the emergence of more generic standards, and were particularly well-suited to address the business needs of more or less self-sufficient trading communities. Prominent examples of sectoral standards include SWIFT[108] for banking transactions, the VDA-guidelines for data exchange in the German automotive industry[109], or the ODETTE[110] standards employed internationally within the European automotive industry[111]. The most successful national standard apart from ANSI X12 (which is also adhered to in Canada) may be TRADACOMS[112] which is used in the U.K. across a wide spectrum of industries[113]. TRADACOMS resembles EDIFACT in that it is based on the UN/GTDI. But since messages have been intentionally created for national use, the prescribed message architecture is more specific, which underscores the disadvantages associated with the development of a completely generic standard. In order to comprehensively accommodate diverse requirements/habits across industries and countries, a generic syntax must provide users with a certain amount of flexibility to code messages. As a consequence, unless a con-

---

106) EDIFACT messages are subject to a formal development and approval process which qualifies messages according to their life cycle stage. It is common to distinguish between (a) electronic documents that are under development by a working party, (b) documents that have been proposed to a "Group of Experts" for endorsement, (c) messages that have been released for test purposes, and (d) those which have been formally approved by the UN/ECE. The EDIFACT standards development process and the various coordination groups involved are described e.g. in Thomas (1987), ECE (1988) p. 12 *et seq.*, Willenz/Walker/Danikiewicz (1989), Hofer (1990), Roden (1990) p. D-2-12.

107) Sarich (1988) p. 21.

108) Society for Worldwide Interbank Financial Telecommunication.

109) VDA is the acronym for "Verband der Automobilindustrie" which is quite similar to the American "Automotive Industry Action Group" (AIAG).

110) Organization for Data Exchange by Teletransmission in Europe.

111) Information about industry-specific standards in the U.S. can be found e.g. in Kemezis (1987).

112) Trade Data Communication Standards.

113) See e.g. McGuffog (1988) p. 70, Tate (1989).

verter was utilized whose functionality allowed one to cope with synonymous coding, trading partners would have to agree in advance about the specific *subset* of the standard to be used. Considering that within EDIFACT addresses can be coded in three different ways and due dates on invoices in seven, the development of industry-specific EDIFACT subsets is widely anticipated[114].

In addition to the specificity of message design rules, EDI syntaxes may also differ in other respects, which does not necessarily render them entirely incompatible. The VDA guidelines, for instance, define a system which is composed of records with fixed-length data elements, as opposed to ANSI X12, EDIFACT or ODETTE which use data elements of variable length. Thus, the semantic of a data-element can be derived only from its relative position within the record structure. Despite those structural variances, using a converter to translate back and forth between e.g. EDIFACT and VDA messages is nonetheless possible[115]. Compatibility between standards is more difficult to accomplish in cases where the data element dictionaries or segment structures utilized are incongruent. This is a particular problem for translating between EDIFACT and ODETTE messages. While ODETTE is also based on ISO 7372, it does not use generic data segments and so called "qualifiers", as EDIFACT and ANSI X12 do, to uniquely identify data elements; instead, ODETTE defines a set of single purpose data segments[116]. For example, the same *address data segment* yet with a different qualifier may be used in a commercial document to refer to buyer and seller of a trade transaction; alternatively, different buyer and seller address data segments may exist.

As was already pointed out, existing EDI standards, which were originally devised to facilitate the interchange of commercial data, could without too much complication be extended to support *technical* data as well. The chemical industry, for example, is already debating a proposal to include a message for quality control purposes into the EDIFACT syntax[117]. To enhance the functional scope of EDI standards, data element and segment dictionaries would have to be supplemented and even the syntax rules may

114) Cf. Schubenel (1989), Hermes (1990) p. 30 *et seq.* See further Mehnen (1989).

115) From a data transmission perspective, such a translation would be efficient since all fill-blanks within the VDA records could be removed during the initial translation and re-added after transmission. Tests have shown that transmission volume could be reduced by 30 to 40%; see e.g. AWV (*s.a.*) p. 18. Another example of a comparison between a generic standard and a dedicated message syntax in the realm of Electronic Funds Transfer (EFT) shows that if batching of messages is feasible, generic standards do not necessarily imply higher transmission costs; see e.g. McEvoy (1990).

116) A brief comparison of the ODETTE, EDIFACT and ANSI X12 syntaxes can be found in Gerus (1988). Refer to Bierschenk (1990) for a comparison between VDA, ODETTE and EDIFACT.

117) Cf. Brändli (1991) p. 15. See also e.g. Sokol (1989) p. 130 who describes efforts to develop quality messages within the framework of the ANSI X12 standards.

be subject to minor modifications. However, the basic message structure and processing requirements would remain unaffected. This picture changes considerably as soon as Computer Aided Design (CAD) or product structure data are to be exchanged between application systems. Such a situation frequently arises when orders are placed or requests for quotes (RFQs) are received that contain drawing specifications or bit-map images of the transaction object, as is the case e.g. in the automotive and aerospace industries or in the military procurement sector, where the capability to receive and process external CAD data may become a mandatory requirement for companies to retain their supplier status[118)].

The reason for the difficulties involved relates to the necessity of a close alignment between interchange format and database schema design[119)]. CAD databases are inherently more complex than conventional databases since they have to store not only textual images of user-world entities and relationships between those entities, but also information about the graphical representation of those stored objects on a display device. Drawing entities usually consist of combinations of certain geometric primitives such as lines, rectangles and spheres, as well as ancillary data which further describe the structure created from those primitives[120)]. Such data structures cannot be accommodated by current EDI syntaxes. The great variety of CAD systems with proprietary object storage and representation mechanisms found in practice, combined with the need to share objects among those systems, led to the development of specialized CAD data interchange formats, the most widely used of which is probably the Initial Graphics Exchange Specification (IGES) which was introduced as early as 1980 and has continuously been updated ever since[121)]. IGES defines about 100 different primitive data

---

118) Cf. e.g. Benini (1986) p. 40, Dahl/Eversheim/Schütze (1986) p. 22, Blacker (1988) p. 21, Fenton (1988) p. 34, Wilmot (1988) p. 18, Meier (1989) p. 62, Orr (1989) p. 112, Shaw (1990) p. 33, Hartenbach/Faller (1991) p. 88.

119) See e.g. Encarnação/Lockemann (1987) p. 181: "... the format must support the exchange of the whole miniworld defined by the database schema without any loss of syntax or semantic. To fulfill this requirement, close agreement between format design and database schema design is desirable."

120) Functional requirements for CAD-DBMS can be found in e.g. Encarnação/Schlechtendahl (1983) p. 25.

121) The need to exchange drawings between different CAD systems not only arises from cooperation dependencies between several departments of the same organization or with external parties, but also in cases where a migration to the next generation of CAD systems transpires and previous drawings have to be processed with new systems. Proper archival of CAD drawings is the main objective pursued with the SET standard (Standard d'Echange et de Transfert) which is particularly prominent in the European aerospace industry. A comprehensive overview of CAD data interchange formats and their respective development stages besides SET and IGES (version 3.0 of which has become ANSI standard Y 14.26M) is provided by Brändli (1991). Nowacki (1990) and Hartenbach/Faller (1991) discuss some deficiencies associated with current standards which triggered the development of STEP, the Standard for the Exchange of Product Model Data, which is supposed to replace over time all existing interchange formats. Refer also to Meijer (1989), Scholz (1989).

elements ("entities") and relies on files that contain only ASCII characters. Thus, a simple solution to the problem of handling CAD data with EDI messages can be given: Provided that the transaction partners are able to agree *ex ante* upon a specific interchange format for product definition data, the EDI syntax could be expanded by a single data element which indicates the number of characters of *non-standard EDI data following immediately*. A conventional, table driven converter program could then separate both parts of such a graphics-appended EDI message - e.g. a request for quote (RFQ) - for further processing. Apparently, at least one product has emerged on the market which provides this capability[122)].

Even if such an approach represents a quick and theoretically operational remedy to an urgent business requirement, it is certainly not a long-term solution. Given the unlikely assumption that the proliferation of proprietary product definition data formats can be reversed, interchanging drawings within EDI messages over WANs may still be impractical due to the low data transfer rates achieved. While typical EDI messages contain at most a few hundred characters that can be transmitted over a conventional 9'600 baud communication link within just a few seconds, even small drawings can require Megabytes of storage space and lead to transmission cycles of several minutes for single messages. Therefore, the growth of EDI graphics exchanges will be impaired until the advent of digital data networks such as ISDN, or fibre optics, that offer considerably higher transmission capacity than existing packet-switched systems.

2.3.2. Systems

2.3.2.1. Hardware

Implementing EDI systems generally does not dictate a particular hardware-configuration. The type of configuration preferred will be as much contingent upon an organization's historical use of information systems to support the execution of business transactions as upon the costs and functionality of commercial EDI products. According to the schematic EDI model depicted in Exhibit 2-4, exchanging transactions data electronically can be conceptualized as a three-step process. From the viewpoint of the sender, the first step requires that a purpose-specific application system retrieves the necessary data from a database and stores that data into a transaction file with a predefined data format. In step two, this transaction file is translated into a standard EDI syntax by

---

122) Cf. Emmelhainz (1990) p. 219.

means of a converter. Finally, the EDI transaction file is transmitted via telecommunication link to the addressee of the message[123]. Assuming that organizations can use mainframe or mini-computers, or micro-computers (i.e. a PC), or any combination thereof to accomplish those three tasks, $2^3 = 8$ different hardware-configurations are conceivable, depending on which type of hardware is used to perform those tasks. Because a choice exists for two of those designs that involve a combination of a mainframe and micro-computer, whether both are directly linked to each other (Front-end solution) or not (Stand-alone solution), a total of ten configurations can be distinguished which are listed in Table 2-1[124].

Config.	Config.-Reference	Application	Conversion	Communications
1)	**Full Mainframe**	**Mainframe**	**Mainframe**	**Mainframe**
2)	Communications-PC	Mainframe	Mainframe	Micro
3)	Conversion-PC	Mainframe	Micro	Mainframe
4a)	Front-end Mainframe	Micro	Mainframe	Mainframe
4b)	Stand-alone Mainframe	Micro	Mainframe	Mainframe
5)	Communications Mainframe	Micro	Micro	Mainframe
6)	Conversion-Mainframe	Micro	Mainframe	Micro
7a)	**Front-end PC**	**Mainframe**	**Micro**	**Micro**
7b)	Stand-alone PC	Mainframe	Micro	Micro
8)	**Full PC**	**Micro**	**Micro**	**Micro**

Table 2-1 Alternative EDI Hardware Configurations[125]

Disregarding stand-alone solutions, the most common types of EDI systems consist of pure mainframe/micro-computer architectures as well as a setup in which a micro-computer serves as a front-end EDI conversion and MHS interface to relieve the mainframe from most EDI processing tasks. However, other system designs are equally feasible. If e.g. an organization is pursuing a client-server concept for its hardware architecture, the data to be formatted and transmitted via a communications-PC will not be stored in a mainframe computer but will be received via LAN from other micros. Likewise, as

123) Cf. also e.g. Emmelhainz (1990) p. 98, who uses the term "formatting" to describe the EDI translation task while "conversion" is reserved to indicate the retrieval of transactions data from the database. The validity of the three-step view is underscored e.g. by Leinfuss (1990) p. 63.

124) Stand-alone configurations are only conceivable in cases where the application system generates a paper document first which is then manually entered into the other computer system for conversion and communications. Such a setup may actually occur quite often in practice since it neatly insulates the pre-EDI application system from the EDI conversion and communications part. While the ease of this implementation approach holds the advantage of allowing organizations to rather quickly participate in EDI trading communities (the internal setup is invisible to communication partners), this operating mode cannot be subsumed under EDI in the sense of the definition derived earlier. This view is consistent with perspectives of other observers who have coined the expression "door-to-door EDI"; see e.g. Hill/Ferguson (1989) p. 6, Emmelhainz (1990) p. 99.

125) The most frequently chosen implementations are printed in boldface type.

micro-based EDI syntax conversion software packages are generally much less expensive than mainframe products[126)], a PC may be used for conversion tasks alone, especially when a mainframe port has previously been reserved for external communication purposes. Exhibit 2-10 shows such a setup that was implemented by a user in the electronic components industry[127)].

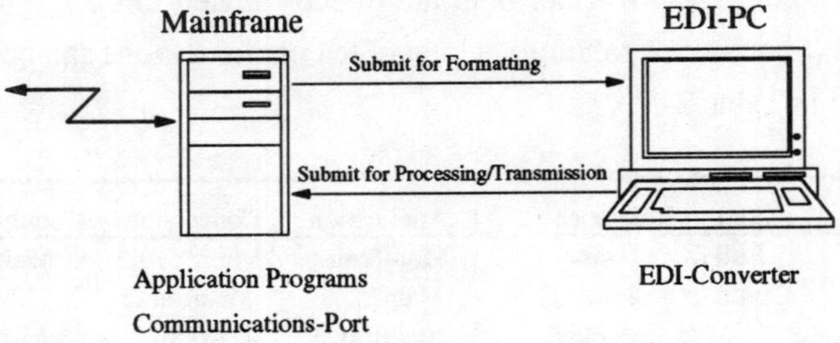

Exhibit 2-10	Front-end PC for EDI Syntax Conversion

Thus far it was always assumed that any EDI message exchange is a series of strictly sequential batch transactions. If e.g. a front-end PC is used in connection with a mainframe computer to convert between in-house and EDI format, as well as to handle the data communications task, transaction data are first extracted from the database residing on the host processor. Secondly, the file is downloaded onto the PC which has been temporarily disconnected from the external communications link. Thirdly, the datafile is converted into the EDI message; and finally, the PC is re-connected to the communications network in order to transmit the message to the recipient, and subsequently switched into a waiting mode for receiving messages during which it cannot be used for other operations[128)]. However, in time-critical/on-line applications or situations where the front-end PC must be able to perform several tasks simultaneously a multi-tasking system is required, e.g. receiving transactions from several internal sources (e.g. several LAN-connected PCs) and preparing them for transmission while receiving and acknowledging external EDI messages, maintaining of a transaction-log for back-up and recovery as well as auditing purposes, etc. It is therefore not surprising that several vendors have introduced dedicated *EDI workstations* with multi-tasking capability (e.g.

126) See e.g. Sokol (1989) p. 85.

127) See also Falke (1989) p. 272.

128) The scenario would be slightly different when a provider of Value added Network Services were employed as intermediary between two communication partners. The PC simply retrieves the messages from the organization's VANS-mailbox and could subsequently be used for other activities until further EDI message handling is required.

UNIX operating system) that have been equipped with EDI conversion software, a variety of interfaces for external and internal communications, and with voluminous secondary storage devices to archive a large number of transactions[129]. A more detailed description of such a system is given in section 2.5.3.

2.3.2.2. Software

The specific software needed to execute a data interchange between application systems/databases can be considered the core of any EDI implementation. While user organizations may decide to develop their own EDI software, at the time of this writing more than 100 commercial software packages have appeared on the market to perform some or all of the three basic interchange functions identified earlier: *Data extraction* (storage), *format conversion*, and *communications*[130]. Irrespective of the procurement approach, the functionality to be provided either by software alone or by a combination of software and manual operations can be visiualized as shown in Exhibit 2-11.

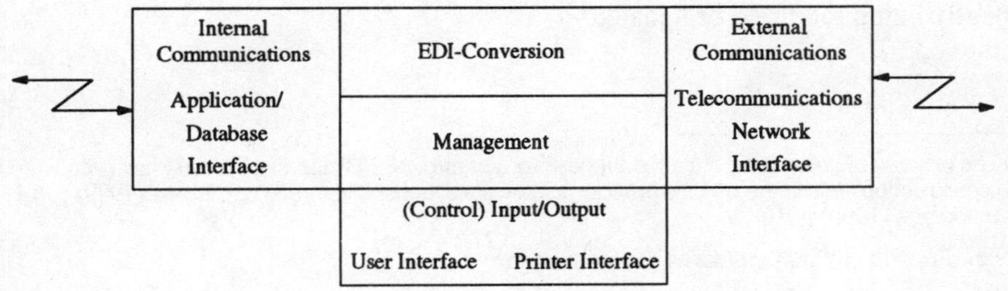

Exhibit 2-11	Functional Modules of EDI Software[131]

129) The need for multi-tasking also arises when an X.400 message handling system without intermediate message store capability is used. The expression "EDI workstation" lacks standardization. It can have different meanings in different contexts, as will become evident in the discussion of EDI software where it refers to a piece of software with certain functionality rather than an entire system composed of software and hardware as it is meant here.

130) See e.g. Seither (1988) p. 18, who mentions that there are approximately 50 vendors of EDI translation software in the U.S. market, and Bakkenist Management Consultants who have tested and compared 70 such products mainly from Europe in a study that was conducted on behalf of the Commission of the European Communities. The following discussion of EDI software relies heavily on the findings of that study; see Bakkenist (1990). The question whether to use standard EDI software or custom-tailored solutions is discussed in Emmelhainz (1990) p. 94 *et seq.*, Groß (1990), Schmoll (1990).

131) Adapted from Bakkenist (1990) p. 9.

Five different main functions can be distinguished:

(1) Conversion

Conversion is the most important function of any EDI software as it provides for the mapping between some inhouse data format and the EDI message format. Some authors distinguish between different generations of conversion modules, depending on (a) whether EDI messages are constructed[132)] from intermediate flat-files[133)] that contain the required data, (b) whether those modules directly access one or several databases to extract that data, or (c) whether such converters[134)] are integrated into application programs[135)]. Most commercial EDI converters are still based on flat-files generated by organizational application programs. Syntactic and semantic conversion[136)] between inhouse and standard format is normally a table-driven process where an editor must be used to initialize conversion tables (i.e. define format correspondences) before message construction or translation can commence. Since those tables may be regarded as *converter databases*, mapping by table rather than by programming instructions facilitates the maintenance task which is particularly important in situations where either format is frequently being modified or updated[137)].

---

132) The process of converting from the inhouse format into the EDI message format has been called "construction" while the reverse process is known as "translation". See e.g. Burns (1989) p. 145, Bakkenist (1990) p. 10.

133) I.e. files without implicit (derived) data structure.

134) "Convertors" according to Bakkenist (1990).

135) Cf. e.g. Weid (1989) p. 415.

136) See Bakkenist (1990) p. 11.

137) Cf. e.g. Kemezis (1987) p. 66. The virtues of a table-based conversion approach are also emphasized by Emmelhainz (1990) p. 93. Standard maintenance in EDI software is a particularly interesting side aspect of Electronic Data Interchange. Various possibilities exist to assign the responsibility for keeping EDI formatting tables current. For instance, it could simply be left up to the users to modify or extend their conversion tables since they own the software installed on their premises. However, this approach does neither appreciate the economies of scale that can be derived from a more centralized maintenance method nor does it adequately address the synchronization requirements within EDI trading communities. Instead, message maintenance could be made the responsibility of the software vendor who would be charged with continuously releasing updated versions of the converter software. This solution appears at first glance to be efficient (providing the syncronization problem could be resolved), yet it neglects the fair amount of initialization required before a converter can be put to use. It is hardly conceivable to expect users to re-initialize their converters every six months when standard updates are being released (however, most current products support multiple standard versions). Thus, it would be desirable to provide some kind of release migration mechanism to copy the inhouse table descriptions and migrate correspondence definitions. Finally, message table maintenance could be made the province of central EDI authorities each of which assumes responsibility for a particular user group. This approach specifically addresses synchronization, providing suitable methods for efficient distribution of updates can be devised. For a brief commentary refer to Bakkenist (1990) p. 36.

Another difficulty that increases the complexity of the mapping task relates to the inherent flexibility of some EDI standards to define messages. Thus, different data elements may be required for different communication partners, which implies that tables must reflect different EDI user profiles, i.e. specific subsets of the standard applying to particular users. Furthermore, syntaxes such as EDIFACT and ANSI X12 rely on the qualifier technique to identify data elements which is rarely found in conventional databases. Thus, conversion modules should have the capability to automatically create or delete qualifiers according to the direction of the conversion process[138).]

(2) Internal communications

If a converter is based on intermediate flat-files, the internal communications function essentially provides an interface between internal databases/application programs and the EDI conversion process. In cases where the data pertaining to a single EDI message are processed by several application programs, the internal communications function must also have *grouping* and *splitting* capabilities to merge data from various sources into messages and to decompose messages in the reverse process.

(3) External communications

The external communications component defines an interface between the conversion process and the telecommunication networks (e.g. VAN) utilized for exchanging messages with business partners. It establishes (by means of one or several standard communication protocols such as e.g. X.400, X.25, remote job entry), controls, and terminates communication sessions with trading partners and, in case of direct linkages, maintains access numbers of trading partners for automatic dialing[139)]. In addition, it can possibly provide sophisticated security functions including password protection, (smart-card) data encryption and message authentication techniques[140)].

---

138) Various other requirements for EDI converters, such as e.g. *error reporting*, are discussed e.g. in Falke (1989) p. 275.

139) See also Emmelhainz (1990) p. 91.

140) For EDI security concepts refer e.g. to Rihaczek (1989).

(4) Management

The management module provides basic housekeeping and maintenance functions such as transaction logging, audit trails, error- and status-report generation, etc. Moreover, user and application profiles should be maintained by a systems administrator.

(5) Input/Output

A versatile user interface is frequently included for the purpose of exerting direct control over the other four functions and producing hardcopies of the reports generated with the management function. Furthermore, at the beginning stage of using EDI, organizations typically resort to manual data entry in order to create EDI messages instead of passing messages directly between network and databases/application programs via flat-file. Again, this may not be EDI according to the definitions given above. It nonetheless represents an important element in most commercial EDI software packages.

Depending on which of the five functional components displayed in Exhibit 2-11 are supported, three different categories of EDI software can be distinguished[141]:

- *EDI Converters* are considered the most basic type of EDI tool available as they only provide mechanisms to perform construction or translation operations and a limited amount of incidental services, such as generating error files.

- *EDI Gateways* provide full converter capability plus internal as well as external communication functions. Gateways can operate independent of human supervision, i.e. in unattended mode, and must therefore support a large number of the message exchange management functions defined earlier[142]. Frequently, the automatic handling of so called "functional acknowledgements"[143] is desirable.

---

141) The following classification is based on Bakkenist (1990) p. 13 *et seqq.*; it contrasts sharply with the converter taxonomy introduced earlier by Weid (1989).

142) In this respect, see also Burns (1989) p. 146.

143) A functional acknowledgement is a specific type of dependent EDI message, acknowledging the successful reception and interpretation (implying correct syntax) of incoming messages to the sender. Functional acknowledgements are e.g. defined in ANSI X12.

- *EDI Workstations* are defined as EDI Gateways with manual data entry functionality. Thus, EDI Workstations must provide a special user interface (e.g. data entry screens) to permit users to manually enter data for message construction. Those systems may occasionally lack the option to interface with existing application systems. Moreover, they may be limited to process only a subset of the entire spectrum of existing messages in which case they are sometimes called *specific workstations* as opposed to *generic* ones that are not subject to such restrictions.

2.3.3. Message Delivery

2.3.3.1. Conventional Methods

When database extracts have been turned into messages that comply with the formatting rules defined by the EDI message standards, in order for the transaction to transpire, those messages must somehow be delivered to the addressee. Delivering messages has two prerequisites: A transport mechanism to move a message over a physical distance and a routing mechanism to control the message transport between the endpoints of the communications process, i.e. sending and receiving location. With EDI, several alternative means of message delivery are available, notably those that are based on networks with value-added telecommunication services. EDI messages could also be stored in files on standard physical storage devices, such as tapes or floppy disks, which could then be distributed by a postal service to the message recipients, who would mount the devices onto a reader for message retrieval or submission to the respective application system for further processing.

While such a physical delivery method does not capitalize on the speed advantage offered by transmitting messages via telecommunication lines, it eliminates the need for the receiving organization to manually re-enter the data into the internal DP systems. Being based on proven technologies for data storage and on a mature distribution system, this method is very reliable and especially appropriate in cases where a comparatively large volume of data must be exchanged periodically between communication partners such that clerical data handling accounts for the bulk of the transmission delays incurred. As a consequence, physical delivery of EDI messages stored on data carriers amenable to automatic processing is still widely used in practice[144]), and can be expected to remain a viable alternative to using telecommunication networks for some applications, at least as long as WAN transmission rates are several degrees of magnitude slower than writing to and reading from secondary storage devices[145]).

Exchanging messages through the conventional mail system between trading partners is unnecessarily slow since it foregoes the advantages of telecommunications to transmit data almost instantly between processing systems over - for all practical purposes - arbitrary distances. The benefits EDI has to offer in terms of reducing the delays of commercial transactions can only be fully exploited when the transaction-specific information which has been coded according to the rules of the EDI language is relayed to the recipient by telecommunications. Therefore, while acknowledging the viability of physical data carrier EDI for a limited number of commercial applications, the term EDI conventionally implies utilization of a telecommunications network.

Exhibit 2-12 shows that there are two basic alternative ways to exchange messages between different locations over a network regardless of message format or content: Either both partners engage in a *joint* communications session - which means that both parties must *simultaneously* access (open) an existing physical line connection between them - or the network itself or a third party *decouples* sending and receiving system by providing an intermediate message store capability to temporarily hold the message until the recipient is ready to receive it. In the latter case, sender and addressee of the message do not directly and simultaneously establish a communication session, even though the existence of a (physical) connection is mandatory.

---

144) See e.g. Morris (1989) p. 61. Another example of such an application is the way in which foreign trade statistics are calculated in France: Customs agents that, by virtue of a large declaration volume, are entitled to follow a simplified customs declaration procedure, have to periodically compile statistics concerning the foreign trade transactions they execute on behalf of their clients. They are obliged to send these data by tape or floppy disk in a prescribed format to the Direction Nationale des Statistiques due Commerce Extérieur (DNSCE) in Toulouse where the data are being aggregated and made available for statistical or economic analysis.

145) Achievable line speeds for data transmission over WANs vary significantly depending on the communication protocols being used. For communication via modem using switched telephone circuits, transmission rates of 2400 bits (2400 baud = 300 characters/s) per second or even lower are common. By contrast, device-internal transfer rates for secondary storage devices such as (floppy) disks and magnetic tapes reach up to several megabytes per second, which is approximately 3 to 4 degrees of magnitudes higher than the telecommunications network. However, this relationship will change considerably with the widespread adoption of fibre optic communication lines, because with this technology, transmission rates of several gigabauds are not inconceivable. Yet even current transmission rates may suffice for most EDI applications due to the generally small size of the messages transmitted and compare favorably with the performance of a data entry clerk who - disregarding economic considerations - is under normal conditions able to manually enter but a few characters per second. See e.g. Hansen (1986) p. 203, FitzGerald (1988) p. 19, Stahlknecht (1989) pp. 71 *et seqq.*, 131.

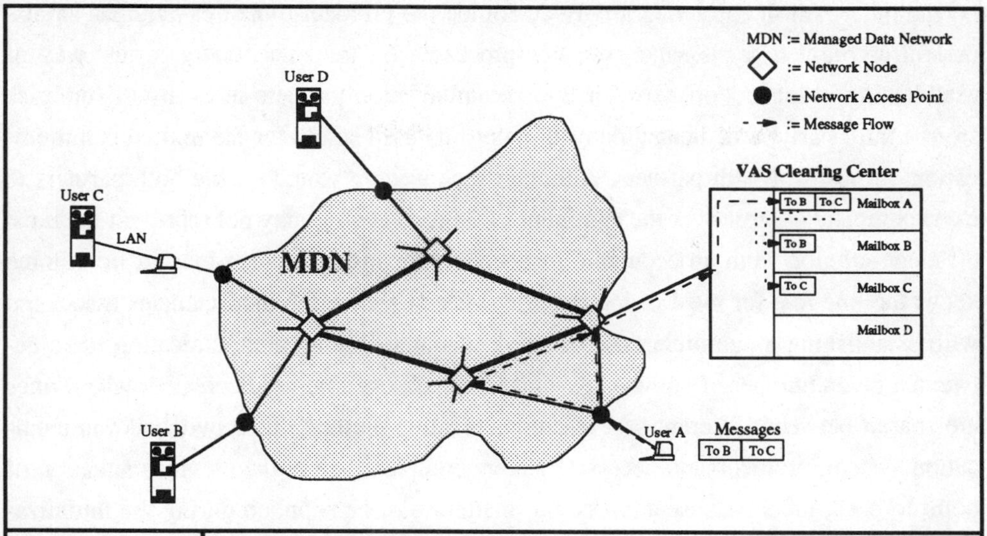

Exhibit 2-12	Sample EDI Network Architecture

Whether or not a direct linkage is established, network characteristics impose certain technical constraints upon the hardware systems involved, as well as define the exact procedures (protocols) both systems must follow in order to successfully initialize, maintain, and terminate a communication session. In consequence, it appears useful to first take a look at communication protocols before discussing private and public solutions to the intermediate message store problem.

A protocol "may be defined as a set of rules governing the exchange of data between two entities."[146] Assuming that telecommunications is applied, any data exchange must ultimately be represented by a series of voltage patterns[147] that are propagated over a communication link (e.g. a wire). In order for the receiving end to correctly (i.e. congruent with the intentions of the sender) transform those signals into data, conventions are needed that precisely stipulate how these voltage patterns are to be interpreted. A protocol is a specific set of conventions which have been agreed to in advance and must be strictly obeyed by all communication partners.

The complexity of a telecommunications protocol is directly related to the functional characteristics of the communications equipment used on the one hand, as well as the structural complexities of the communications link and the messages to be exchanged

146) Stallings (1988) p. 376.

147) Voltage-time profiles.

on the other. All three factors jointly determine the protocol functions required to successfully complete a message exchange process[148]. The conceptually easiest way of establishing a connection between two communication partners is to install (or lease from a third party) a dedicated point-to-point line used solely for the mutual communication purposes of both partners. Although such a setup would enable both partners to exert complete control over the communications protocol, it may not represent the most efficient solution from an economic perspective, for instance when low traffic volume keeps the line idle for most of the time. In order to reduce the inefficiencies associated with establishing a comprehensive network of point-to-point communication links between a given number of entities, a switched network is commonly created, where lines are shared between different sets of communication partners. In a switched communication system, protocols are necessarily more complex than in the previous situation of point-to-point links because address information must be supplied during the initialization stage of a communication session by the sending station to call the desired party. Moreover, the network must be able to recognize if the requested connection is already being used and react accordingly[149]. Even more difficult to handle are circumstances where would-be communication partners do not even belong to the same network. Then, protocols are needed to activate gateways between networks to establish a linkage.

Given the great variety of message types that can be sent over a communications link, it seems intuitively plausible that the task of taking an arbitrary message, turning it into electrical signals that are transmitted over a network to the final destination, and recreating the message is too formidable to be achieved in a single step. For this reason it is customary to cope with the inherent complexity of a communication system by defining a layered (or hierarchical) architecture of system components, each of which supplying only a managable fraction of the required functionality. Exhibit 2-13 shows the typical structure of a layered systems design.

---

148) It is possible to distinguish between certain categories of protocol functions, not all of which need to be a mandatory element of a particular protocol. There may e.g. be functions that disassemble messages into data blocks of predetermined size which are transmitted individually and which must be reassembled at the destination; other functions add communication control data to the message such as sender-receiver identification; still other functions are necessary to ascertain synchronization of sending and receiving devices, to provide connection-, flow-, and error-control, multiplexing, specialized transmission services (e.g. prioritization of messages), etc. An overview of common protocol functions can e.g. be found in Stallings (1988) p. 380 *et seqq.*

149) E.g. return a busy signal, or provide multiplexing services; see e.g. Stamper (1986) p. 149 *et seqq.*

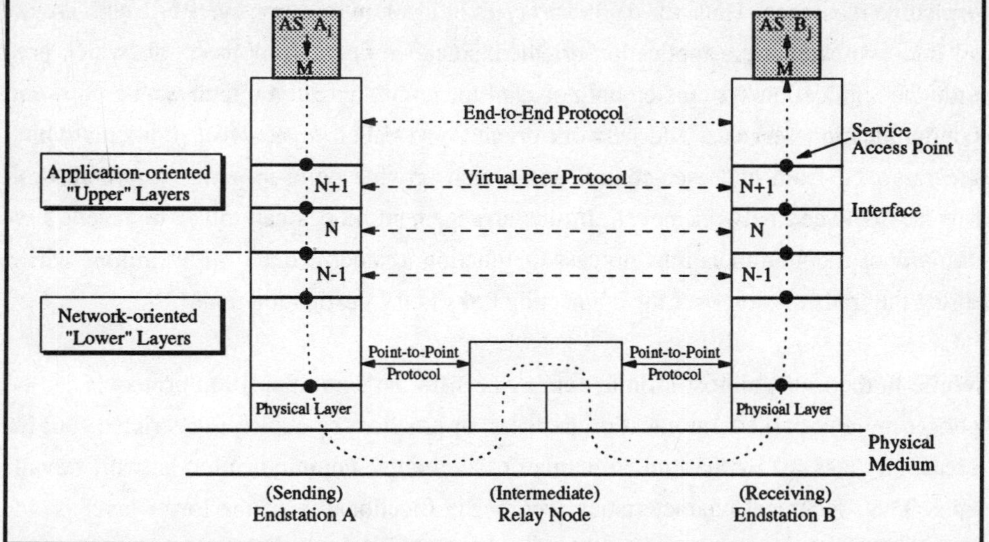

Exhibit 2-13	Communication Systems Architecture[150)]

The purpose of the communication system depicted above is to let two application systems (AS), A_i and B_j, residing at the endstations A and B, cooperate by allowing them to exchange a Message M[151)]. The overall task of applying a particular set of rules to send and receive that message is decomposed into a layered structure of rule subsets (layer protocols). Each layer (N) is supposed to supply a well-defined number of services to the layer immediately above it (N+1) and requests services from the layer immediately below it (N-1) via so called Service Access Points which define interfaces between adjacent layers. As same-level (peer) layers on both ends of the communication circuit provide similar protocol service functions yet are not directly engaged in the data exchange, peer layers are said to be connected by *virtual* links as opposed to the *physical* connection of the transmission medium beneath layer 1[152)]. Unless both endstations are directly linked to each other by a dedicated communication line, the services of a given telecommunications infrastructure, which normally consists of a system of interconnected communication nodes, a network, must be utilized. Technical properties of the infrastructure as well as particular objectives of the network services provider will determine a standardized set of protocol functions that can be used by customers to

150) Cf. FitzGerald (1988) p. 257, Stallings (1988) p. 394 *et seqq*., Moshos (1989) pp. 175, 179. Cf. further Venitz (1990) pp. 191 - 193. Compare also the Figure 2.4 in Vervest (1986) p. 69 which elaborates upon the upmost layers.

151) An EDI message, for example.

152) Cf. FitzGerald (1988) p. 256 *et seqq*.

exchange messages. Thus, the different layers of a communication system can be grouped into two categories, application-oriented, so called *upper-level* protocols which provide the application systems on both ends of the communication circuit with end-to-end communication services, and network-oriented, so called *lower-level* protocols which are removed from end-user control and which provide point-to-point communication services between network nodes. In this arrangement, nodes can either represent *end-stations* of a communciations process or function as intermediate *relay stations* which direct the transmission over the connecting links to the destination node[153)].

While in theory an almost infinite number of different communication protocols can be chosen by any two communication partners, in practice the choice is restricted (but increasingly less so) by the limited number of alternative communication networks available. Their technical characteristics specify the functionality of the lower-layer protocols of the respective communications architecture and the interface to the application-oriented upper layers[154)]. In addition to considering an organization's other internal and external communication requirements and the perceived necessity to integrate those with EDI activities[155)], the decision which network and which communication protocol to select for the purpose of EDI will be determined by such factors as the expansion of the network in terms of reaching the targeted EDI trading partners, the anticipated traffic volume since it qualifies or disqualifies networks due to the achievable transmission rates, the network interface capabilites/requirements of the trading partners, transmis-

153) The currently most widely accepted communication systems architecture featuring a layered design are IBM's Systems Network Architecture (SNA), and the ISO reference model for OSI which is discussed in detail in almost any textbook on data communications. Such a layered architecture has the advantage of providing a reference point for protocol design. The drawback is that the architecture precisely dictates the functionality of layer protocols without regard to contingencies. Therefore, hierarchical architectures have been proposed that alleviate those problems. A comparison of competing communication systems architectures may be found in Stallings (1988) p. 405.

154) An overview of common carrier services and a description of the respective technical performance can e.g. be found in FitzGerald (1988) p. 465 *et seqq*. Besides direct links and private (leased) networks discussed in more detail in the following section, primarily three different types of (public) telecommunication networks may currently be considered for sending and receiving EDI messages: The Public Switched Telephone Network (PSTN), the CCITT network access standard X.25 (Remark: Intra-network protocol is X.75) Packet Switched Data Network (PSDN), and the CCITT network access standard X.21 Circuit Switched Data Network (CSDN), of which only the PSTN and the PSDN are widely available on an international basis. Another option which is expected to gain importance within the foreseeable future is the Integrated Services Digital Network (ISDN). Even though the considerable costs of supplanting ordinary analog switches with digital replacements has retarded the diffusion of ISDN, some EDI software vendors, according to recent product announcements, seem to anticipate considerable growth of ISDN soon. See e.g. Brown (1989), Morris (1989) p. 62, Herbert (1990). See also Buckley (1987), Lefkon (1989), Reichwald/Straßburger (1989).

155) Cf. the discussion in Lee (1988) who emphasizes the need to first select an overall communications structure before deciding upon the particular approach with respect to EDI. Lee distinguishes between *integrated-internal, integrated-external, partitioned-internal,* and *partitioned external* network structures depending on whether internal or external communication processes are based on integrated networks or whether point-to-point links are being used.

sion security which relates to the error detection and correction mechanisms provided[156], and by the tariff structure which determines the transmission costs incurred[157]. The ongoing development and standardization of higher-level communication protocols (in the OSI framework) and the growing availability of systems that conform to these standards is currently providing organizations with new, more flexible choices of how to execute their EDI communication tasks. For this reason, one may speculate that especially for (less time-critical) batch applications, lower-level protocols, which are ordinarily employed in point-to-point connections between trading partners, will eventually give way to the more generic protocols of the application-oriented layers of the communication systems architecture[158]. X.400, which is a protocol germane to the OSI model's top-most layer, describes conventions for how to request a wide range of E-mail services from a telecommunications network. It has recently attracted much attention as an innovative communications mechanism that is almost ideally suited for certain types of EDI applications and therefore, a subsequent section focusses on how EDI may capitalize on the communication services provided by X.400[159].

---

156) Security concerns can be the crucial factor in the network selection decision. The SWIFT network of the banking industry, for example, was designed to reduce the average undetected transmission error rate to less than one erroneous character per billion. See e.g. Hammel (1974) p. 158 *et seqq.*

157) Cf. e.g. Palmer (1988), Gebker (1989) p. 283. Compare further the analysis provided by Hammel (1974) which suffers somewhat from an outdated technical perspective but the conceptual framework is still valid. See further Favre (1989) p. 87, who reports that network selection decisions by business are based on "tariffs, capacity rates, access facilities and ancillary services".

158) Especially with respect to Europe, point-to-point links may well be considered the rule rather than the exception. Data exchange may be achieved e.g. via dial-up with simple synchronous or asynchronous modems over the PSTN; refer to CCITT standards V.2x; see e.g. FitzGerald (1988) p. 293. The character-oriented IBM binary synchronous protocols 2780 and 3780 - commonly known as Remote Job Entry (RJE) - have been called "defacto" standards for EDI in Europe; Gebker (1989) p. 283. Modern, bit-oriented protocols include IBM's Synchronous Data Link Control (SDLC), as well as the ISO standard 3309 High-Level Data Link Control (HDLC) that is also part of the X.25 data communication protocol for PSDN which, due to the large number of network access points and the availability of compatible equipment, can be considered major alternatives of the aforementioned protocols. Cf. e.g. Stamper (1986), p. 189 *et seqq.* Another service mentioned occasionally as suitable for EDI is videotex; see Wildemann (1988), Handwerk (1989), Langen/Tegelhof (1989), Stark (1990) p. 68. See further Palmer (1988) pp. 167 - 169, Schatz (1988) p. 62, Stark (1990).

159) Other OSI model level 7 candidate protocols for EDI message exchange include above all file transfer protocols such as the File Transfer, Access and Management (FTAM) or its sibblings the Organization for Data Exchange by Teletransmission in Europe ODETTE File Transfer Protocol (OFTP) and VDA-FTP 4912/1 that are particular popular in the European automotive industry. As the term FTP suggests, not only raw data are transmitted but also file structure information (i.e. the file's composition in terms of records and data elements) as well as access and presentation attributes. See Stallings (1988) p. 560 *et seqq.*, Rösch (1989) p. 218, Stark (1990) pp. 68 - 71. See also Dawkins (1988) p. 72. While EDI messages can be easily stored in file format, there is reason to question whether the ancillary information provided by FTAM is in fact necessary for EDI, and whether the conceptually more simple E-mail protocol X.400 does not suffice. A comparative technical evaluation of the public network/protocol alternatives available for EDI communication can be found e.g. in Scott (1988) or Handwerg (1989).

2.3.3.2. Using Value Added Network and Services

The preceding analysis of the communciation options among which potential EDI users have the liberty to choose shows that the actual implementation of an EDI network connecting a trading community is a non-trivial endeavor. In order to enable application systems to exchange data, communication partners with potentially very different hardware equipment and operating procedures have to agree upon the following:

- The EDI standard to be used
- The specific subset of the EDI standard
- The telecommunications network to be used for data transmission
- The communications protocol
- The time schedule for the data exchange

Finding solutions for any two communication partners may not pose insurmountable problems, however, as soon as the number of EDI users in the trading community grows, the difficulties of determining mutually agreeable standards, protocols, and schedules may render the task of establishing stable many-to-many EDI relationships at least very time consuming, if not outright infeasible due to the dynamics involved.

One way to address these problems is to restructure the complex *many-to-many* relationships into multiple *one-to-many* relationships by creating the function of an *intermediary* which isolates the communication partners from each other. Thus, a considerable portion of the task to resolve incompatibility problems is turned over to a third party shielding individual EDI users from changes on the side of their communication partners. In the context of EDI, those intermediaries have *inter alia* been referred to as "EDI Suppliers"[160)], "third parties"[161)], RCS[162)], and VADS[163)]. Among this somewhat confusing array of terms with very similar, yet not identical semantic, VANS -

---

160) Coathup/Jackson (1989).

161) Primarily an American expression. Also "third party network". See e.g. Canright (1987) p. 46, Schatz (1988) p. 57, Sokol (1989) p. 62, Emmelhainz (1990) p. 107.

162) Remote Computer Service vendor; see Akerman (1985) p. 8.

163) Value Added and Data Service. This term is frequently used in the U.K. where the Department of Trade and Industry grants VADS licences to applicants since 1982; see Bright (1989) p. 3. See further Bidgood (1988) p. 19, Dawkins (1988) p. 57, Sanders (1988) p. 119, Morris (1989) p. 61, Tate (1989) p. 131.

Value Added Network (and) Services - seems to be the internationally most widely accepted acronym to describe organizations whose primary task is to provide a range of derivative telecommunication services to their clients, of which EDI is but one example[164)]. Due to the diversity of terms and interpretations, clarifying the meaning of VANS, as employed in the context of this study, seems appropriate. From a supplier perspective, a distinction can be made between a *network*, which provides communication facilities for data transmission and routing, and *data processing services* which are attached to the network and *add value* to the basic transmission process. The former will be referred to as a Managed Data Network Service (MDNS) and the latter is called a Value Added Service (VAS)[165)]. It is important to note that while a provider of MDNS would also be a logical supplier of value added services[166)], offering VAS does

---

164) Other services that are said to fall into this category are e.g. E-Mail, On-line Transaction Processing, Electronic Information Services (also referred to as On-line Databases). See e.g. Bright (1989) or Mulder (1989). It may be as much a symptom of the rapid development in the field of telecommunications as it is a result of the very different historical evolution of that industry in North America and Europe that both the wording and the semantic associated with the abbreviation VANS have differed over time and location. Historically, the term Value Added Network (VAN) originated in the U.S. where private organizations established commercial telecommunication networks by renting lines from common (telephone) carriers and adding computer control to the basic data transmission function. In most cases (e.g. ARPANET, TYMNET, TELENET), the expression VAN was akin to providing packet-switching facilities; see e.g. Loomis (1983) pp. 115 - 128, Stamper (1986) p. 253, Stallings (1988) p. 206. By contrast, in many European countries, the public telephone operating (PTO) companies are also offering packet-switching services for data communications which are therefore generally regarded as *base services* rather than *value added*. Until the advent of deregulation it was also legally difficult if not impossible for commercial organizations to create private networks and compete with the PTOs for customers. While the latter obstacle has (partially) been removed, VANS from a European perspective should refer to communication services which go beyond packet-switching. A concurrent view can be found e.g. in Mulder (1989) p. 221. But even if one were to subscribe to this view, there still remains considerable leeway in defining VANS as becomes evident when the widely divergent opinions of international EDI services providers are considered as reported e.g. in Sibler (1990) pp. 42 - 44. See further Chang/Hitchcock (1989).

165) This interpretation is quite consistent with the view expressed in e.g. Smithers/Willis (1989). The expression MDN may therefore be regarded as being synonymous with VAN in the American context; both terms are henceforth used interchangeably.

166) Hence the composite term 'Value Added Network Service' referring to a provider of value added services in addition to a data network; thus, reference is to an organization. For differentiation purposes such an organization has also been called a "Super-VAN"; Loomis (1983) p. 126. A large number of purpose-specific computer networks exist in practice. See Quarterman/Hoskins (1986) for a rather comprehensive listing.

not necessarily require ownership of a network[167]. From a customer perspective, the distinction may not be all that crucial and therefore, the term VANS[168] generally relates to a *combination* of MDNS and VAS.

The market for commercial MDNS evolved primarily in the U.S. As a result of the diffusion of DP equipment, larger organizations with multiple branches were facing a soaring need for long-distance data communication. Due to the disadvantages of modem-based communications over regular telephone lines in terms of transmission rates and error frequency, setting-up private, company-wide telecommunication networks is an effective as well as efficient solution for large organizations to meet their data communication requirements. For lack of the necessary financial resources, or for the difficulty of acquiring and maintaining specialized expertise, SMEs with more sporadic data communication needs are normally unable to make efficient use of a dedicated communications network. Such a situation is a fertile ground for intermediaries to fill the supply gap by pooling the individual demands of many users. The fundamental *raison d'être* of a private VAN (or MDN) is the efficiency gain that can be derived from sharing a resource with fixed supply (and for that matter fixed cost), namely, a network of telecommunication lines with a more or less given capacity to transport messages between users. As long as the sum of the channel capacity demands does not exceed the capacity provided by the system, no user will notice a deterioration of communication services by the admission of a new user into the community; yet because the fixed network costs are distributed over a larger number of participants, each existing user will benefit[169].

167) In fact, it is not only quite conceivable but actually occurring that commercial organizations use existing public and private networks such as e.g. the PSDN to make their specialized services available to customers. Such a cooperative structure seems particularly appropriate where VAS providers lack the financial resources to create their own networks which have the required minimum geographical expansion. Given the fact that only the very large public and private organizations have established data networks, significant barriers to entry into the MDN market may be suspected due to economies of scale. Moreover, in some cases, potential suppliers may be barred by law to enter the market. See e.g. the report on a Swiss VAS presented by Anner (1990). Consider also the German word for VANS: "Mehrwertdienst" which literally translated rather means VAS; see e.g. von Weizsäcker (1987) p. iii, Schneider (1988) p. 769. A cooperation between a public MDN, which not only owns an extensive communications network but also has almost unlimited financial resources, and a private VAS, whose intricate grasp of market needs and technical sophistication allows to develop and supply advanced DP services, is not without danger to the smaller party. Safeguards must be in place to prevent the common carrier, after acquiring the basic skills contributed by the VAS, to diversify and provide similar services on its own account. The development of a public E-Mail service with X.400 already represents an intrusion into a domain formerly occupied exclusively by private VANS.

168) Value Added Network *and* Services; see e.g. Wierzewski (1990).

169) A typical network externality effect; refer to section 3.1. It should be noted that it may even for large organizations be advantageous *not* to invest in a private network due to the large up-front investment requirements and the need to employ a minimum staff of telecommunications experts which not only have to be educated and must receive training, but for which career paths have to be developed etc. Therefore, outsourcing telecommunications services may be an attractive alternative

The *fait accompli* created when organizations have grown accustomed to hiring the services of an MDN provider for their *private* long-distance data communication needs generates a natural incentive to use the same conduit for *external* data communication purposes such as EDI. In this way, established communication circuits can be used with the effect that, theoretically, only the network addresses of the new communication partners have to be added while no modification of current technical procedures is required. Thus, organizations that intend to conduct EDI can focus their efforts on resolving potential conflicts regarding the EDI format and subset to be used, send-receive schedules, and operational details. However, neither can such highly favorable circumstances be taken for granted nor are the remaining problems trivial. Particularly when EDI partners belong to different industries, they may have so far been using different MDN providers. As a consequence, either one will have to switch or sign-up with a second network[170)]. And even if both parties are attached to the same network, they might well be using different communication protocols, error recovery mechanisms, etc. Although an EDI user may (e.g. by virtue of its business clout or financial leverage) be able to exert considerable influence on his trading partners and simply dictate the communication standards to comply with, in many cases no single party wields any larger amount of indirect, let alone direct, control over the telecommunication decisions of its business partners. Thus, if it were not for the specialized (value added) interface services of MDN providers or third parties attached to data networks, tedious, multilateral negotiations would ensue to reconcile differing postures between the members of an EDI communications group[171)].

It appears convenient to distinguish between three tiers of value added services VANS are able to supply, that are not necessarily confined to EDI[172)]: Tier 1 refers to services that address basic data transmission tasks, tier 2 consists of services which alter or in some other way affect message format, and tier 3 deals with services targeted on overall operational aspects of EDI communications.

---

compared with the internal supply option, regardless of company size. Cf. Gräber (1990). For the general question of outsourcing information services, see Knolmayer (1991).

170) This underscores the need for a comprehensive, universal communication service, i.e. a service which provides transparent communication between two arbitrary agents.

171) In certain industries, like automotive or aerospace, where thousands of organizations form EDI clusters, just agreeing on a time schedule for sending and receiving messages would be a formidable endeavor.

172) It should be reiterated that EDI *per se* is often considered a value added service similar to E-Mail and others. The view taken here is to assume that these generic type of services can be decomposed into certain basic service elements. Due to the synergy effects involved, VANS usually supply most if not all value added features; see e.g. N.N.(1988a) pp. 107 - 109.

a) Tier 1: Transmission Services

The lowest layer of value added services is comprised of three main functions:

a1) Protocol Conversion

a2) Establishment of Gateways

a3) Establishment of a Clearing Center

a1) Protocol conversion refers to a mapping between network-level technical data communication protocols. If two communication devices are unable to support the same protocol, any attempt to communicate will fail unless a protocol converter bridges the incompatibility gap. Conceptually, there can be protocol converters between arbitrary protocols on any level of the communication systems architecture. With the exception of transmission speed conversion, which evidently requires intermediate buffering, the conversion is invariantly achieved by replacing control information - which has been added to the factual data for transmission purposes - pertaining to the *source protocol* with control information pertaining to the *target protocol*[173)]. The implementation of a protocol converter on level *n* of the communication systems architecture necessitates that a conversion node somewhere in the virtual or physical circuit between the two communicating entities must contain at least the first *n* layers, since the transmission data sent through the circuit must be passed up the hierarchy for conversion, before it can be relayed to its final destination. Unless connection to an MDN is made via leased line, packet assembling/disassembling devices (PAD) must be installed to interface the network infrastructure with continuous communication links. In addition to this sophisticated "(de-)packetizing" type of protocol translation, PADs may also support speed and code conversion which shields VANS subscribers from the adverse effects of incompatible communications equipment. In conclusion, protocol conversion systems are intended to provide (network-level) *protocol independence* to VANS customers[174)].

---

173) Due to the variety of communication protocols found in practice, a large number of protocol conversion systems has been developed. These converters accomplish translation e.g. between different line voltage levels, character codes (e.g. ASCII into EBCDIC or *vice versa*), synchronous vs. asynchronous transmission, packet- vs. line-switched connections, etc. Device emulators may be regarded as another example of a protocol conversion system which is, however, related to the *application layers* of the protocol architecture. An explanatory overview is e.g. given in N.N. (1988b). See further Moshos (1989) p. 240 *et seq.*

174) Stated differently, communication partners do not need to be concerned about resolving potential protocol incompatibility conflicts. The utilization of protocols is fully transparent to the end users since the VANS ensures that the proper transformations are executed.

a2) Another potential obstacle for EDI is caused by the non-universal reach of private MDNs. Organizations that wish to commence exchanging data electronically may find out that they have been using different networks so far. To avoid the inefficiencies of having to maintain (small volume) accounts with several networks simultaneously in order to reach all EDI communication partners[175)], VANS may instead provide network interconnection services for all subscribers[176)]. Such a linkage is usually called a "gateway"[177)]. A gateway will enable a user to successfully invoke a communication session with users on other networks without needing to know which particular networks are involved; VANS ensure proper cross-network routing of the data flows[178)]. Thus, the installation of gateways allows VANS to provide *network (location) independence* to their clients.

a3) Perhaps the most important EDI service VANS can provide is the establishment of a message *clearing center* (or clearing house) to distribute messages among communication partners. In this setting, a network mailbox is assigned to each EDI user which serves as the sole communication conduit for exchanging messages with other network subscribers. Instead of having to initiate multiple bilateral communication sessions between sender and receiver over virtual circuits, users only need to establish a connection to the clearing house and access their own mailbox to *deposit* a single file of *outgoing* messages to possibly more than one addressee and to *retrieve incoming* messages from other subscribers[179)]. Thus, the mailbox system provides an intermediate message storage facility that decouples (desynchronizes) the communication systems of the

---

175) This would also require the creation and maintenance of network tables in order to keep track of communication partner addresses.

176) Connecting VANS has also been called "internetworking" or simply "*interworking*"; see Bidgood (1988), Pope (1988) p. 223, Stallings (1988) p. 447 *et seqq.* While many VANS seem to provide such internetworking capabilities, the problem of how to assess charges for data communication via multiple VANS is yet to be resolved satisfactorily. Until recently, users had to pay regular transmission fees on all networks involved, which is contrary to the tariff structures of PSDNs where charges are based on data transmission volume rather than distance or connection time.

177) Blacker (1988), Emmelhainz (1990) p. 114. More precisely, a gateway is a device that interconnects heterogeneous networks. Devices are usually categorized according to which layer of the communications architecture is used for interconnection. Thus, one can distinguish between, from bottom to top, "repeaters" (for signal amplification within a network), "bridges" (for interconnection between homogeneous networks on the data-link level, primarily between LANs), "routers" (for connecting a company internal LAN with WANs), and finally "gateways" (to link networks with different application level protocols, mostly between WANs). See e.g. Stallings (1988) p. 447 *et seqq.*, Moshos (1989) pp. 241 - 244.

178) A prerequisite for this approach is the availability of unambiguous addressing schemes which enable VANS to determine the correct network and network addresses of all communication partners. This address information must be supplied during the initiation phase of the communication session.

179) The clearing house consists of a computer system that is connected to the MDN but does not necessarily reside on a network node, the service could also be provided by an external VAS supplier; cf. Anner (1990). Mailboxes are dedicated partitions of mass storage devices attached to the clearing house computer system.

communicating entities. Analogous to a post office, the clearing center, periodically or via triggers, invokes a message distribution function which scans subscriber mailboxes for unprocessed mail files. The program decomposes unprocessed mail into individual interchanges which are subsequently distributed to the mailboxes of the intended recipients for future retrieval (refer to Exhibit 2-12). Because of this peculiar processing arrangement, a clearing house is commonly called a store-and-forward system[180].

The establishment of a clearing house system has important ramifications for EDI users due to the separation of a *single* joint communication process into *two* disjoint processes. Even more than protocol converters, a clearing center provides *protocol independence* to communication partners since they can unilaterally connect to the network by their preferred choice of protocol regardless of the communication capabilities of the receiving users. Second, with direct communication, partners need to maintain *network address tables* in order to ensure proper message routing. With a clearing house system, messages are sent only through a single address, the organization's own mailbox, and the VANS assumes responsibility for distributing messages to the intended retrieval points. Thus, users gain the benefit of *address independence*. Third, the intermediate mailbox store obviates the need for a joint communication session. Each party can - within rules dictated by the business purposes pursued with EDI - send and retrieve messages at the most convenient time, a feature which might be called *session independence*.

b) Tier 2: Message Services

Before the establishment of a clearing center, VANS could simply be regarded as more sophisticated suppliers of data transmission networks; by contrast, the clearing house enables VANS to offer customers a range of derivative messaging services as opposed to fulfilling merely a data transmission function. Those services are intended to facilitate and thus stimulate EDI utilization by further reducing the complexity faced by end-users. Two basic tasks can be identified:

b1) Message Format Management

---

180) E.g. Lallande (1986) p. 52, Scott (1988) p. 91, Morris (1989) p. 63, Tate (1989) p. 131, Anner (1990) p. 119. At least equally valid if less common is the expression "store-and-retrieve"; see e.g. Smithers/Willis (1989) p. 38. In fact, the regular connotation of the verb "forward" seems to suggest that received messages are directly transmitted to recipients rather than deposited in their mailboxes. Such a direct delivery option where recipients do not own mailboxes (which implies that they cannot send messages through the clearing house by themselves) has been called "dial-out" mode; see e.g. Akerman (1987) p. 10, Sokol (1989) p. 64, Emmelhainz (1990) p. 113.

b2) Message Flow Management

b1) One additional source of difficulty to overcome arises from the fact that users may have to communicate with correspondents (e.g. in different industries) who are either employing entirely different EDI standards or different subsets of the same format[181]. Regardless of which case applies, the immediate consequences are twofold: First, communications partner *profile tables* must be supplemented by entries indicating the proper EDI standards to be used. Second, either *several* EDI converters will have to be purchased and connected to the internal databases/application systems (perhaps via a programmable software switch to route the data flow communication-partner-dependent to the correct converter), or a *single* converter with the capability of (a) automatically recognizing the respective standards of incoming EDI messages and (b) formatting outbound messages according to the recipients' standard requirements. Similar to the other EDI communication problems, VANS are able to offer dedicated format translation services to relieve users from the task of dealing with multiple formats. Thus, by way of special translation facilities that can not only map messages from one public EDI standard to another, but can also be set up to translate between proprietary and public formats, VANS are providing *format independence* to their customers[182].

Another element of this tier of EDI services commonly supplied by third parties are encryption and authentication support. In cases where the nature of the message exchange requires a particular high level of security (e.g. in Electronic Funds Transfer) message encryption and/or authentication could be requested by users.

b2) A second type of message service sometimes provided by VANS focusses on controlling the flow of messages between correspondents. Since the whole purpose of EDI is to enable autonomous application systems to cooperate by passing messages between them over some communications infrastructure without human intervention, the necessity arises to build safeguards into the system that protect the integrity of user systems,

181) The automotive industry in Europe is a case in point since a supplier located in Germany could well be obliged to accommodate the VDA standard requirements of the domestic vehicle manufacturers, as well as the ODETTE standards when dealing with Scandinavian manufacturers, and EDIFACT when dealing with other parties such as its own supplier organizations.

182) As has been mentioned before, format translation can be regarded as a high-level protocol conversion and would therefore naturally belong into the same class of services. However, since it deals with entire messages and since such a service is yet to become part of current network architectures, treating it as a *sui generis* case may indeed be warranted. Outsourcing the task of converting organization-internal data structures into EDI formats to the EDI third-party has the additional advantage that it effectively shields users from managing the migration process necessitated by standard updates or the introduction of standard modifications which occasionally requires highly specialized expertise; see e.g. Sokol (1989) p. 66.

which could be jeopardized e.g. by processing messages that were received from unauthorized senders or which contain unintended values for data items. To hedge against the ensuing, potentially disruptive effects, VANS offer services such as "closed user groups"[183)] where the exchange of certain types of messages is restricted to a specific cluster of users[184)], *message syntax validation*[185)], and *data element constraint verification*[186)] which ensures that only messages are forwarded into the recipient's mailbox where the entries concerning particular data elements comply with range or domain restrictions specified in advance by the recipient. Of particular importance from an operational standpoint can be the establishment of so called "trade-relations" between EDI communication partners because the feature permits *selective retrieval* of messages by the recipient according to message type, irrespective of the sequence in which the messages were batched when originally submitted to the network[187)].

Another service sometimes provided by VANS, which can be valuable particularly at the beginning stage of an organization's utilization of EDI, addresses the inconvenience caused by not all potential communications partner being already able to receive EDI messages, which entails that arrangements must be made to distinguish between those two groups. In this regard, third party intermediaries sometimes offer a service that may be called *multi-media distribution*[188)]. Irrespective of the recipients' EDI capabilities, a sender transmits all messages to the clearing house where the VANS supplier deposits some into other users' mailboxes, converts the remaining messages into a different media form commensurate with the requirements of non-EDI addressees, and finally

---

183) N.N. (1988a) p. 107.

184) This does not imply that the user is confined to a single cluster; on the contrary, it can be expected that a network subscriber joins several of such groups for as many communication purposes.

185) Also referred to as "compliance checking". Message validation verifies that messages properly comply with the syntax rules of the standard being used. It can be performed by the VANS on request of either party and *inter alia* validates the envelope information, checks the presence and type comformance of all mandatory message data elements, and verifies adherence to segment sequencing restrictions. An overview is given in Akerman (1987) p. 13. See further Sokol (1989) p. 65.

186) A term sometimes found in practice is "special editing"; cf. GEIS (s.a.).

187) For any two users that decide to exchange messages over the clearing house, the third-party establishes a trade-relation. Under this organization, only messages that fall into a particular predetermined category can be exchanged. All other messages, irrespective of whether they are syntactically correct or not, are being rejected by the clearing house until the appropriate trade-relation is opened. Selective message retrieval is akin to *batch independence*.

188) Also called "enhanced routing" or "paper conversion". See Sokol (1989) p. 67 *et seqq*., Emmelhainz (1990) p. 112. This service actually belongs as much into the *message format* as into the *message flow* management category.

forwards the converted messages to the destination. Other conceivable media could be plain paper-based mail, facsimile transmissions or E-mail[189).]

By virtue of this service, VANS provide a unidirectional (simplex mode) form of *media independence* to its clients which eliminates another source of complexity associated with EDI.

c) Tier 3: Auxiliary Services

In addition to enhanced data transmission and message services, VANS suppliers are offering a range of derivative services that address the *operational requirements* of EDI communication partners. Thus far, the analysis of EDI requirements has proceeded in a rather generic way, i.e. no assumption has been made concerning the specific purpose pursued with EDI. Currently, however, EDI is primarily applied to execute commercial business transactions such as ordering, invoicing, etc. In this sense, using the term *electronic business document interchange* (EBDI) would be more appropriate. The auxiliary EDI services were primarily developed in recognition of the nature of the data exchange, giving due consideration to the importance of those electronic commercial documents in the framework of trade transactions. Those operations-oriented services encompass:

c1) Message Status Tracking

c2) Accounting and Reporting

c3) Derivation of Trade Statistics

c4) Marketing and Consulting

c1) The message status tracking service enables the sender of an EDI message to inquire about its present status, i.e. whether it has already been distributed to the recipient's mailbox by the clearing house, and whether (and if so when) the recipient has retrieved it[190)].

---

189) The multi-media distribution service is not necessarily provided at the request of the sender only. In cases of a dominating relationship between sender and receiver, the sender may be able to simply dictate the usage of EDI to its communication partners. If the receiver is unable to meet the given deadline for migration towards EDI, the enhanced routing service could be employed as an interim solution until the receiver's internal systems have been adapted to EDI communication; cf. Emmelhainz (1990) p. 112 *et seq*.

190) Cf. e.g. the remarks in Akerman (1987) p. 14 on the "Sender/Receiver Status Log". Given the realistic assumptions that logging procedures and error-free protocols for submitting messages from

c2) Besides message status logs, other statistical reports, such as a listing of unretrieved documents in clients' mailboxes, are commonly prepared on a periodic basis for billing and auditing purposes.

c3) In certain industries, ordering and invoicing via EDI has already become the norm rather than the exception[191]. Historically, VANS have focussed their marketing efforts on individual vertical industries[192] and have occasionally achieved such high penetration rates, that the message flow through the VANS clearing center represents almost the entire trading activity in that market. Under those circumstances, the VANS supplier is in a unique position to gather comprehensive and highly reliable marketing research information which can be readily extracted from the electronic messages[193].

c4) Finally, the cooperative nature of the EDI concept implies that (the various services of VANS providers notwithstanding) a minimum amount of colaboration between communication partners is indispensable. Since systems installation and integration into the existing hard- and software environment demands some specialized expertise, which might not be instantly available in smaller organizations, VANS frequently offer consulting and/or marketing services to clients and their trading partners in order to facilitate and accelerate the transition process to EDI[194].

To summarize, apart from fulfilling basic data transmission tasks, the whole purpose of VANS with respect to EDI is to shield users from the inherent complexity of establishing a reliable message exchange facility in a diverse environment of organizations

---

EDI users to the clearing center have been installed and that EDI communication partners have, as they are supposed to, signed so called "interchange agreements" that stipulate the operating guidelines for their mutual EDI relationship including commitments to retrieve messages from the assigned clearing house mailbox according to some schedule, and return functional acknowledgements for the messages received, providing a message status tracking service appears to have little more than the psychological foundation of reassuring new EDI users who struggle with the insecurity of dispensing with the proven paper-based forms of data exchange.

191) Cf. e.g. the U.S. wholesale drug industry where most ordering is already performed via EDI; see e.g. Glatzer (1987).

192) Cf. e.g. Dale (1988) p. 53.

193) With few exceptions (e.g. the aforementioned U.S. wholesale drug industry), however, industry participants are adamantly opposed to any kind of message content analysis and demand assurance by the VANS provider that the privacy of their transactions data is safeguarded.

194) Not the least to their own benefit. Cf. the "hub-and-spoke" system, also referred to as the "honey-pot" approach, which represents a special marketing strategy of VANS. According to that strategy, VANS target their marketing efforts on large organizations with many small trading partners as is the case for instance in the automotive sector. If the "hub" can be persuaded to sign a service contract with the VANS provider, it is assumed that the SME trading partners, due to their inferior competitive position, will have no choice but to follow suit. Cf. e.g. Sanders (1988) p. 120, Mulder (1990) p. 654.

with multilateral communication requirements. The clearing house concept may be regarded as the kernel for a variety of services, the general objective of which is to reduce the need for cooperation between EDI users, or, stated differently, to provide as much autonomy to the individual user as possible[195)].

2.3.3.3. Using X.400

The potential for using the public Message Handling System defined in the CCITT X.400 series of recommendations as a delivery mechanism for EDI messages has recently been the subject of intensive discussions[196)]; this applies particularly to Europe where the supposition was made that OSI based messaging systems may be able to "unleash vast growth in EDI"[197)]. The appeal of an X.400 solution to the EDI transmission task apparently derives from suspected synergy effects.

When EDI messages are to be exchanged with more than a few communication partners, direct communication over the PSTN is largely impractical for reasons mentioned before. The anticipated expansion of ISDN networks will mitigate only a fraction of the problems associated with point-to-point connections[198)]. Therefore, even after migration to ISDN, the EDI services provided by VANS, as discussed in the previous section, remain valuable. However, the VANS solution suffers from deficiencies as well. In certain countries VANS may yet to become legally admissible and thus do simply not represent a feasible alternative to direct links. Secondly, given the business interests of VANS suppliers who have a natural incentive to promote their own network at the expense of users rather than competitors in order to recover their large up-front investments in networks and systems[199)], hesitation (or even outright refusal) to participate in VANS interworking, i.e. the unwillingness to establish gateways to other networks, leads to a deliberately non-universal service, in other words the "closed community"

---

195) An overview of EDI service bureaus can be found e.g. in Sokol (1989) pp. 195 - 197, Emmelhainz (1990) p. 120 *et seq.*

196) See e.g. Dawkins (1988), Genilloud (1988), Kenny (1988), Pope (1988), Ross (1988), Plattner et al. (1990) pp. 181 *et seqq.*, to cite but a few of numerous publications on this subject.

197) Dawkins (1988) p. 58.

198) Although, due to digitalization, ISDN provides a higher quality service than is available over the conventional analog telephone system, ISDN e.g. does not provide session independence or transmission error recovery procedures which are important communication service elements for EDI users; cf. Morris (1989) p. *et seq.*

199) After more than five years in operation, the EDI service business of GEIS which is one of the largest international private VANS suppliers is yet to become profitable; see Eickers (1990) p. 8.

syndrome[200]. In conclusion, even in cases where VANS suppliers are available, a *communications gap* exists for EDI message exchange.

Without regard to EDI, CCITT (later joined by ISO) in 1984 released the X.400 series of recommendations which define open standards that govern communication processes between message handling systems. The general objective of the services to be provided by public administrations is to enable a message exchange between subscribers on a store-and-forward basis[201]. The interpersonal messaging system (IPMS), defined in X.420, was to become a vendor-independent, truly public E-mail standard with world-wide reach. The advantages of universal connectivity notwithstanding, it appears as if private households in many cases either lack the need or the necessary equipment[202] for electronic communication. On the commercial side, many large organizations with multiple domestic and foreign subsidiaries or affiliates have their own, proprietary wide-area-networks over which employees conduct E-mail[203]; by contrast, SMEs could capitalize on LAN solutions for most of their E-mail needs. Thus, neither the communication requirements of private households nor those of commercial enterprises for intra-organizational communication represent a huge market for a public E-mail service at this time[204]. As a consequence, current X.400 services appear to suffer from an *applications gap*.

With EDI in need of a universal communications mechanism, and with X.400 services looking for suitable applications, merging the two promises to yield substantial synergies for both[205], not the least by potentially narrowing *diffusion gaps* that stem from the inherent network externality effects associated with communication systems. In order to examine various possibilites for adopting X.400 services for EDI communications, it is necessary to sketch relevant elements of the MHS.

200) Morris (1989) p. 63. Cf. further the discussion in Bidgood (1988).

201) CCITT (1984), the so called 'Red Books'. Cf. Dawkins (1989) p. 147.

202) E.g. a PC in which an X.400 communications card has been installed.

203) E.g. Siemens, IBM, General Electric, Philips.

204) Cf. e.g. Klein (1988) p. 54 who comments on the marketability of MHS services to private households: "Die Dienste, die in näherer Zukunft im Zusammenhang mit MHS X.400 angeboten werden... sind damit für den Privathaushalt weniger attraktiv." It should be noted, however, that the benefits (which ultimately determine demand) of such a service are subject to positive network externalities, giving rise to what may be called a *diffusion gap*. Support for this notion can be obtained from the experiences with the development and diffusion of the highly successful French minitel system; see e.g. Allen (1988).

205) Similar views can be found in the pertinent literature. See e.g. Stranger (1988) p. 7: "Although the major application of MHS standards to date has been for the interconnection of proprietary electronic mail systems, it is already clear that the greatest potential value lies more in the area of structured data interchange (EDI)".

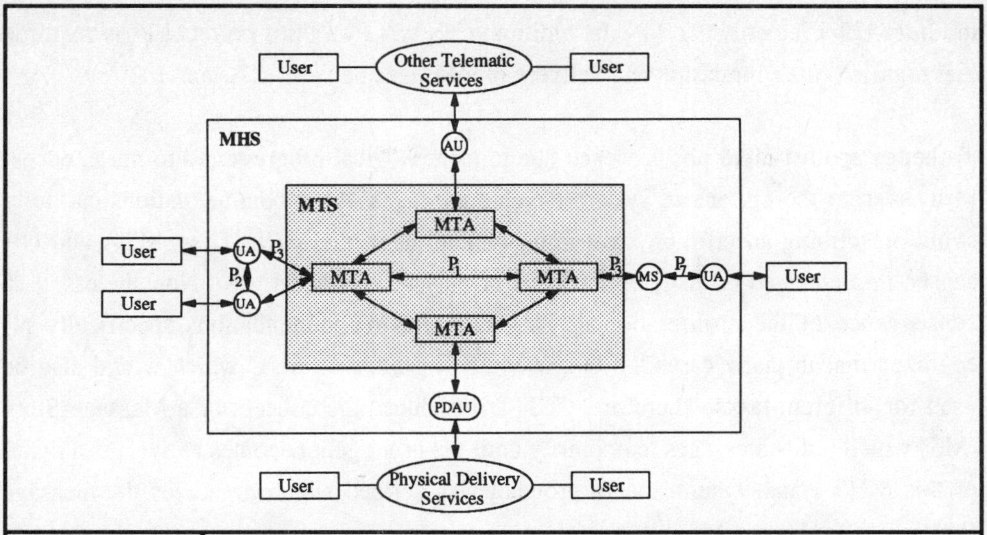

Exhibit 2-14	Message Handling System - Functional Model

Exhibit 2-14 provides a functional overview of the MHS as defined in the X.400 (1988) recommendations[206]. The MHS consists of two primary components: Message Transfer Agents (MTA) and User Agents (UA). The MTAs form the Message Transfer System (MTS) which provides reliable message transport services to network subscribers. The protocol for passing messages between MTAs (which can be separate messaging system operators) is called P_1. UAs assist users in fulfilling basic message management tasks such as creating messages as well as submitting to and receiving messages from the MTS. The only type of UA defined under X.400 until recently was aimed at providing end-to-end messaging services for human users[207] which is why it has justifiably been called the Inter-Personal Messaging System (IPMS). As the objective pursued with the IPMS was to let individuals exchange messages regardless of type (i.e. text, sound, graphics), syntax information needs to accompany a message so that the recipient UA is able to properly present the information to its user. This syntax as well as the aforementioned message management information is contained in a dedica-

206) Cf. CCITT (1988). The original 1984 recommendations have been revised and expanded considerably by CCITT. *Inter alia*, the description of X.400 was formalized and several new objects were added in order to enrich the model with additional functionality. See e.g. Hunt (1988), Plattner et al. (1990) p. 207.

207) X.420 recommendation. This does not imply that the MTS could not be used for different purposes by new types of UAs yet to be defined. In fact, two of the proposals discussed later that have been introduced for adapting X.400 services to EDI communication needs involve the creation of an EDI-specific UA.

ted inter-UA protocol called P_2. In addition to P_1 and P_2 a third protocol P_3 is required that regulates the submission and delivery of messages between UAs and MTAs[208)].

To hedge against rapid obsolescence due to technological progress and to not unnecessarily restrict the options of system developers, the X.400 recommendations carefully avoid prescribing specific physical implementations of the MHS. Thus, MTA and UA can be implemented on different systems or may be co-resident[209)]. Nonetheless, as a consequence of the proliferation of PCs, the 1988 recommendations specifically recognized that in many cases the UA would be installed on a PC which would also be used for different tasks. Therefore, CCITT introduced the concept of a Message Store (MS) which holds messages temporarily until the user agent becomes active. As a result of this MHS enhancement, the P_7 protocol was defined which organizes the message flow between UA and MS[210)].

The respective discussion of how to exploit X.400 services for EDI communication purposes has with few exceptions[211)] dwelled on the four alternative approaches identified in the British VANGUARD Study on EDI and X.400[212)]. Only two of those options cited in the study report are currently available because they are based on existing messaging facilities as defined in the X.400 (1984) or (1988) recommendations. The remaining alternatives rely on the advent of a new EDI-specific UA which is under development by CCITT at the time of this writing[213)].

The first of the currently available implementation options, which is favored in the U.S., makes only use of the *envelope transport services* provided by the MTS. Because it re-

208) Thus, the messaging process requires that a user initiates access to the assigned UA and enters the data to be transmitted into the system. The UA attaches a header to the message body according to the information provided by the user, wraps the message content (comprised of message body and header) into a protocol envelope and submits the whole message (that consists of envelope, header and body) to the MTA for transmission. If the recipient's UA is not linked to (or does not reside in) the same MTA, the message must be forwarded via the MTS.

209) Various alternative system designs are presented e.g. in Hunt (1988) p. 120 *et seq.*

210) The 1988 recommendations contain other extensions depicted in Exhibit 2-14. In due recognition that addressees may be incapable of receiving messages via X.400 protocols, the model provides for Access Units (AU) that perform conversion to and from other telematic services (e.g. fax, telex); moreover, Physical Delivery Access Units (PDAU) have been defined that enable paper conversion. Those conversion services are fairly analogous to the multi-media distribution facilities provided by VANS.

211) Cf. Genilloud (1988a,b).

212) Most of the arguments presented in this section are based on Pope (1988). Cf. also Ross (1988).

213) So called *draft recommendations* have been submitted for approval by the CCITT Associate Rapporteur Group for EDI and X.400 in mid 1990; those are the recommendations F.435 (services) and X.435 (systems or protocol), respectively. However, products are, as usual, not expected to become available on a widespread basis for quite some time.

quires that a process maps EDI interchange control information onto the MTS envelope - introduced earlier as the P_1 protocol - and submits the complete message to the assigned MTA, this solution has been referred to as the P_0 approach. Alternatively, EDI messages could be forwarded by utilizing the service elements of the IPMS, i.e. the UA P_2 protocol. Here, EDI interchanges are transmitted as IPMS *body parts* with the required header information to be extracted (copied) from the EDI message.

The proposed functional extensions to the (1988) recommendations envisage the definition of a new UA specifically designed for EDI communication; the respective protocol is therefore called P_{EDI}. According to those proposals, envelope contents will consist of a *body part*, containing the factual information for the ultimate recipient, and a *header part* that carries the necessary control information for the recipient's user agent. Depending on whether only the header part (and the interchange is carried transparently in the X.400 message body) or header and body are defined in terms of ASN.1, like the other X.400 protocols, two versions of the P_{EDI} solution emerge that have been named "P_{EDI} TRANSPARENT" and "P_{EDI} ASN.1", respectively[214].

A comparative assessment of the merits of all four alternatives involves an investigation of the extent to which each solution fulfills the operational demands of EDI users. In order to determine the relevant EDI messaging requirements, the authors of the VANGUARD study conducted semi-structured interviews with personnel in a sample of twelve organizations that were either users or providers of network services and came up with a total of 28 requirements that were clustered into the six categories "Message Transfer", "Message Store", "Interworking", "Security and Audit", "Acknowledgement", and "Other"[215]. Since X.400 defines a store-and-forward system and since it is based on OSI standards, most of the important lower-level (i.e. Tier 1) value-added communication features provided by VANS such as protocol, location[216], and session independence are 'automatically' provided by the MTS. The major differ-

214) Pope (1988) p. 21. The X.435 draft recommendations fall somewhere in the middle between the P2 and the P_{EDI} Transparent approach; a comprehensive treatment of the services defined within the context of X.435 P_{EDI} is given in Hill (1990).

215) Pope (1988) pp. 4 - 6, 22. "Other" in this context refers to (a) the need of being able to distribute the same interchange to several recipients (e.g. in order to update product information or price lists), (b) to translate between syntaxes, and (c) interchange prioritization.

216) Due to the goal of universal connectivity, X.400 *ex definitione* provides interworking between private and public communication networks, the so called Private and Administrative Management Domains. The functionality of a globally distributed address database is defined in the X.500 (directory systems) recommendations, which, by virtue of a hierarchical addressing scheme, organizes the unequivocal allocation of X.400 addresses to users. A short introduction into X.500 services is e.g. provided by Brabner (1989), for a theoretical treatment of OSI addressing cf. Jakobs (1986). A comprehensive overview can be found in Plattner et al. (1990) p. 279 *et seqq*.

ence between the four alternatives is related to their capability to support *selective message retrieval.* From an economic perspective, batching EDI messages into functional groups and functional groups into interchanges, and transmitting each interchange as a single X.400 message to the recipient is more efficient[217)]. The recipient, however, frequently desires to retrieve messages selectively by type, so that they can be processed in a single batch run of the application system; moreover, sometimes a user would like to process received EDI messages in a different sequence, for example urgent messages first, etc.[218)]. Since there is no X.400 equivalent to the "trade relations" of VANS, selective retrieval from an MS is only possible when messages somewhere contain the necessary control information.

Selective message retrieval is impossible in the P_0 approach as the MTS envelope protocol does not provide sufficient message content identification. The P_2 approach, where EDI messages are transmitted as IPMS body parts, allows for selective retrieval when the IPMS header contains a respective indicator, e.g. in the Subject Clause, but only if X.400 messages consist of single EDI messages or at least single functional groups. Thus, the possibility for batching is seriously eroded with detrimental impact on message overhead requirements. Furthermore, as no international standards exist that unambiguously stipulate which elements of an EDI message should be mapped onto the IPMS header and how they should be represented, EDI communities would be obliged to resort to their own standard definitions (profiles), which is contrary to the objective of universal applicability. According to the analysis of the VANGUARD study, either one of the P_{EDI} solutions would rectify the problems introduced by the natural mismatch between the services provided by the IPMS UA and the commercial needs for EDI communication[219)]. Implementation of P_{EDI} ASN.1 would have the additional advantage

---

217) This approach eliminates redundancies with respect to message control information and is therefore more economical under a transmission-volume based tariff system. Note further the awkwardness introduced by the multiple meanings of the term "message" in this context. An *X.400 message* is defined as consisting of an address envelope and an envelope content, the latter of which may be (in the case of the IPMS) further devided into header with predefined structure and arbitrary body part; by contrast, an *EDI message* does not contain a transmission envelope yet the message itself has a predetermined structure.

218) Cf. also Pope (1988) p. 223.

219) Some of the IPMS services may even be harmful because, if not carefully avoided, they may lead to (inadvertant) security breaches. An example would be the *blind copy recipient* service. Cf. further Ross (1988) p. 255. Occasionally, the problems associated with the P_2 approach appear somewhat exaggerated. It has been claimed, for instance, that the allegedly highly useful *receipt* and *delivery notifications* are of dubious value since they do not represent the X.400 equivalent of an ANSI X12 functional acknowledgement; Pope (1988) p. 224. One could argue in response that these services were never intended to provide such functionality, because it is completely outside the scope of the IPMS. Thus, they are simply a device for message status tracking which is valuable but obviously cannot substitute for a recipient's successful message processing indication.

of allowing selective EDI transaction set retrieval by virtue of a structured message body part[220].

Choosing between the currently available options, it may come as no surprise that, due to different circumstances concerning the diffusion of private communication networks, the U.S. has favored the P_0 approach while the IPMS solution is more common within the European environment. Despite its deficiencies, systems implementation of the P_2 solution has already progressed well beyond prototype stage and has successfully been utilized by various industrial user groups[221]. It can be anticipated that during the absence of a stable P_{EDI} definition, P_2 (or a derivative) will remain the preferred choice of X.400 users in Europe.

In conclusion, given the similarities (but not congruency) between EDI messaging requirements and the MHS, it seems clear that X.400 can be a generally suitable mechanism for the delivery of EDI messages, particularly due to its universal connectivity. Some performance related limitations do apply, however, including the lack of support for *interactive EDI*, as a consequence of the store-and-forward system, and restrictions on message sizes which could pose a problem for high-volume users. Nonetheless, it is beyond dispute that public X.400 services providers will be able to play an important role in stimulating the use of EDI. PTOs are going to compete in some market segments (Tier 1) with private VANS suppliers who will be forced to capitalize on their innovativeness advantage against the inherent inertia of public services providers[222] and continue to develop higher-level (Tiers 2 and 3) and custom-tailored, as opposed to commodity-type services to protect their future viability[223].

---

220) "Only by use of Interchanges encoded in ASN.1 can a fully integrated approach to EDI and X.400 be achieved meeting all the requirements of EDI. In particular, delivery of an Interchange to multiple recipients... and retrieval of functional groups from within interchanges... is only supported by this approach." Pope (1988) p. 23.

221) A case in point is the European EDIFICE group, abbreviation for EDI For Companies with Interest in Computing and Electronics. Further information can be found e.g. in Hill (1989). Moreover, the influential customs organizations in Europe are actively involved in pursuing the P_2 EDI approach.

222) Public services providers, by institutional design, cannot exclude any member of the public from using those services under non-discriminatory conditions. The PTO's frequently ridiculed inertia at least partly stems from this universality obligation which requires a commitment of resources which is incomparable to private suppliers who can be much more selective and therefore flexible in choosing particular market niches. Nonetheless, due to externality effects private organizations likewise have a rational incentive to expand their service offerings indefinitely.

223) Cf. Dawkins (1988) p. 72, Hill (1989) p. 155 *et seq.*, Eickers (1990) p. 8. See further the description of typical VANS activities in Wierzewski (1990).

2.3.4. Operational Requirements

The foregoing discussion dwelled (with some exceptions) on generic requirements of EDI, i.e. requirements which are independent of a particular purpose or the circumstances present. This section introduces contingent prerequisites of EDI in relation to specific (commercial) applications, namely, for *trade data interchange*.

2.3.4.1. Object Identification

In addition to data structure definitions and transport protocols, messages used in commercial applications have to contain unique identifiers in order to allow both communicating agents to reference at least one particular object (or class of objects) in a transaction[224]. Thus, identifiers can be regarded as values of variables which correspond with and represent specific entity instances. Examples include customers, suppliers, certain types of documents, such as e.g. orders and products[225]. An attribute that uniquely identifies entity instances is commonly called a *primary key* of that entity[226].

For efficiency reasons, it is customary in organizations to identify relevant objects by means of artifical attributes. The set of all artificial identification attributes establishes a *numbering system*[227]. Due to the importance of numbering systems to manage an organization's resources and to effectively monitor and control organization-internal processes, it is usually taken for granted that enterprises develop and maintain proprie-

---

224) Cf. also Canright (1987) p. 44.

225) It is with respect to products where the terminology often becomes imprecise; see e.g. Hammel (1977) p. 81. In all but the most unusual circumstances, trade transactions do not refer to a particular instance of a product, i.e. a physical representation which would be an object of reality, but rather to any instance of that product, which implicitly assumes that all instances carry the same attributes and attribute values that are relevant to the transaction partners. Thus product identifiers actually do not represent physical objects but rather *classes* of objects with particular characteristics which is different from, say, a customer number that refers to a particular individual or organization. The importance of product attributes in economic transactions was emphasized by Lancaster (1971).

226) Cf. e.g. Hansen (1986) p. 99. A key may well consist of several attributes in which case it is called a concatenated key. Cf. further the taxonomy of key types in McFadden/Hoffer (1988) p. 166 *et seq.*

227) This does not presuppose, however, that only numbers are used as primary key values, which may be the norm but is certainly not mandatory. Car license plate identifiers, for example, frequently consist of alphanumerical character-strings. Devising effective numbering systems for organizations that meet current and anticipated needs in terms of flexibility, expandability, and analysis options can be a rather demanding task and is often poorly executed in practice; cf. e.g. Grupp (1987) p. 1. Cf. further Kunerth (1974).

tary systems which are both well-adapted to their idiosyncratic needs and provide them with indispensable flexibility in comparison with the adoption of external standards[228].

While many organizational identifiers are either completely irrelevant for other organizations (e.g. employee ID) or are always transformed into a standardized format to meet the requirements imposed by the message delivery mechanism[229], some refer to entities that are the subject of business transactions (e.g. products), which implies the existence of *synonyms*. Assuming *m:n* supply/demand relationships between trading partners, the number of converters necessary to translate between proprietary product codes can again be limited to a linear[230] rather than quadratic increase by the establishment of a standard code, quite analogous to solving the incompatibility problems caused by different telecommunication protocols. The by far most successful international standard used in practice is the 13-digit EAN-code of the retail industry which is a superset of its American precursor, the Uniform Product Code (UPC)[231].

2.3.4.2. Legal Certainty

The inherent riskiness of business transactions for both partners has led to the creation of a complex web of security features, partly involving third parties such as banks, to ensure the legal enforceability of existing contracts as well as the proper execution thereof. While the conclusion of contracts does not necessarily rest upon mandatory paper documentation as a statutory requirement[232], especially for international transac-

228) See e.g. Wieland (1980) p. 131, Hagen (1987) p. 3.

229) It is e.g. perfectly feasible for two organizations to bilaterally agree on a 2-digit addressing scheme for their mutual communication needs. The public mail service, however, would not be able to deliver the messages based upon the proprietary code, unless it is transformed into the standard public address code prior to submission. An alternative option would be to ask the messaging service to perform the necessary code conversion in which case both users enjoy *address independence*.

230) The coefficient of proportionality being 1 (or 2, respectively); cf. formula (2.11).

231) The structure of the code as well as some advantages and disadvantages are e.g. explained in Hansen (1986) pp. 157 - 161, Grupp (1987) pp. 170 - 175. An interesting side aspect of using the EAN codes relates to the maintenance of product master data. Since the integrity of the master data file represents a necessary condition for error-free trading, there seemed to be a need to automate the expensive and error-prone manual maintenance procedures. The solution found was to establish a large data center for customer-independent product (and supplier) master data that is accessible to suppliers and customers alike, similar to an on-line catalog. Thus, suppliers are no longer obligated to transmit updates individually to perhaps hundreds of customers nor are those required to manually enter that data into their systems. Whenever the need arises business organizations can access the data center and either update or retrieve the desired data. For obvious competitive and data modeling reasons no price information is stored in the central database. Cf. Sternberg (1988), Suzuki (1988). See further Marshall (1989), especially p. 52, and Petri (1990) p. 64 *et seqq*.

232) However, the conclusion of contracts (i.e. offer and acceptance of a legally enforceable promise; cf. Metzger et al. (1986) p. 130) *inter absentes* is normally accomplished by exchanging paper-based documentation. Differences in writing requirements are discussed in Bergsten/Goode (1989) p. 136 *et seq*. Much of the present discussion regarding the legal problems created when electronic

tions (that possibly involve multiple customs, transport, and insurance agencies as well as banks), paper-based documents pertaining to the contract trigger the various processes needed to conclude the transaction until all parties have properly performed their contractual obligations. Thus, besides their primary function as a data carrier ("informative function"), traditional paper-based trade documents fulfill important secondary functions ("evidential", "symbolic") and represent an essential part of the legal relationship between business partners[233]. Therefore, the question arises whether and how this functionality can be preserved with the intended replacement of such documents by electronic means, e.g. EDI.

Disregarding the problem of *negotiability*[234], much attention has been devoted to the *authentication* of electronic messages. Any suitable means of authentication serves a twofold purpose: (1) Identification of the message sender and (2) verification of the information content so as to render a document "legally admissible in evidence"[235]. Authentication of paper documents is usually performed by handwritten signatures which cannot be directly attached to electronic messages. However, they may still be used by sending (in parallel) a signed hardcopy of the message to the recipient, which does not reduce the amount of paper circulating between trading partners but at least preserves the advantages of automatic data entry. A variety of more sophisticated technical alternatives[236] has been developed but, with the exception of high-security applications such as in banking, they are currently not in wide-spread use. Especially interesting

---

communication media such as E-mail are being used for contracting purposes is based on the seminal paper by Newman and Harvey (1984). Their detailed analysis largely applies to EDI as well. Cf. further Nogossek (1986), Schneider (1988), and especially Amory (1989). The foregoing descriptive analysis of what constitutes EDI shows that much of what is commonly regarded as contracting - the exchange of views and proposals in a negotiation process until agreement between the parties has been reached - is completely outside the scope of EDI in its present usage. In fact, contracts formed via EDI have been exhaustively preconceived to handle well-structured situations. While gaining economic benefits in terms of lower data entry and error correction costs, the EDI user still bears the full amount of transaction costs with respect to searching for information and negotiating the terms of future business transactions, which can be significant especially when several intermediaries are involved. To attenuate this problem, artificial intelligence extensions to EDI have been proposed to enable systems to conduct a "formalized contracting conversation"; see Lee (1990).

233) Thomsen (1989) p. 33.

234) Concerning possible substitutes to the negotiability feature of certain trade documents, such as a bill of lading, which cannot be replicated with EDI, refer e.g. to Ramberg (1989), Wheble (1989). Other important issues not dealt with explicitly here include e.g. the legal relationship between users and suppliers of VANS or public providers of MHS; refer to Schneider (1988), Sundblad (1989), Thunis (1990) and Walden (1990) pp. 249 - 251.

235) Thomsen (1989) p. 19 *et seq.*, cf. Amory (1989) p. 13.

236) Such means *inter alia* consist of call-back procedures, system access protection through personal identification codes (e.g. passwords) / devices (e.g. smart cards) or verification of specific physical user attributes through biometric devices (e.g. fingerprints, retina patterns), and cryptography; cf. Nogossek (1986) p. 358, Amory (1989) p. 27, Sherick (1989) p. 67 *et seq.*

from the perspective of EDI seem asymmetric methods of cryptography based on the *private* (secret) and *public key* concept[237)] since they can be used to generate the electronic equivalent of a signature.

The law typically lags behind business practice in adapting to technological innovations[238)]. While this lag may in many cases be desirable since it provides for a grace period during which the most effective implementation alternative is determined by means of a trial-and-error process, it also temporarily creates a legal vacuum, which could have a detrimental impact on business because entering contractual relationships becomes more hazardous, and forming contracts is therefore more difficult. In the absence of legally enforceable default rules, organizations have been counseled to bridge the legal uncertainties by using their freedom to contract, i.e. the liberty to bindingly define their mutual obligations within certain bounds; parties who are interested in conducting trade transactions via EDI should stipulate the precise terms of their EDI trade relationship in a (bilateral) contract, a so called "interchange agreement"[239)] (IA), in order to limit their risk exposure at least until stable business conventions have been established and accepted as such by legal authorities[240)].

Due to the inefficiency of having to enter into multiple bilateral agreements, developing a standard interchange contract that is legally binding for all users would be desirable. While this has been feasible in various closed user communities, such as airlines and banks, the diversity of needs encountered in practice has obstructed initial attempts by the UN/ECE to devise a universally applicable EDI communication agreement. However, in retracting from that objective, a generic code of conduct - referred to as UNCID, acronym for Uniform Rules of Conduct for Interchange of Trade Data by Teletransmission - was defined that was intended to serve as a legal umbrella for private IAs. The UNCID code consists of eleven articles covering relevant security aspects of EDI communication[241)]. User groups have already expressed their appreciation of UN-

237) One possibility would be to employ the RSA algorithm; cf. Rivest/Shamir/Adleman (1978). See further Cooper (1989) p. 330 *et seqq.*, Stolz (1991).

238) See with respect to EDI e.g. Marsh (1988) p. 88, Thomson/Wheble (1989), p. 7, Walden (1990) p. 240.

239) E.g. Amory (1989) p. 26.

240) The stipulation of legal responsibilities should not be confined to EDI users, but should also consider the liabilities of the network services supplier; cf. *supra* note 233, especially Walden (1990) pp. 249 - 251.

241) The UNCID articles begin with defining subject and scope of the code and then continue with establishing norms of what should be included in IAs. Those norms specifically address questions concerning message authentication, acknowledgement, confirmation of content (the latter two of which are difficult to resolve due to the problem of *infinite regress*), data protection, maintenance of complete transaction logs (Write-Once-Read-Many devices may be particularly interesting in this

CID because of the guidance provided in otherwise fairly uncertain territory[242)]. Nonetheless, by creating merely a flexible foundation for binding IAs, it must be regarded as of uncertain legal authority for the time being. It can be suspected, however, that, by virtue of introducing the notion of a professional "norm of behaviour", the code may eventually evolve into a readily available yardstick in court proceedings[243)].

Notwithstanding their theoretical importance, claims that the legal uncertainties created by the use of EDI are of serious concern to potential users appear somewhat exaggerated[244)]. EDI by conception was developed to automate the execution of a specific class of highly standardized, repetitive inter-organizational transactions of comparatively low value in well-established, ongoing business relationships. It is ill-suited for singular transactions between casual business partners. Thus, it appears hardly conceivable that a party would jeopardize the long-term profitability of a trade relation because of a disagreement concerning a single, insignificant transaction[245)].

2.4. Business Implications of EDI

2.4.1. Overview

Evaluation of EDI from a cost/benefit perspective is a rather difficult endeavor as a consequence of the intangible (strategic) nature of many effects commonly ascribed to EDI[246)]. Methodologically, EDI should be treated like any other investment project, i.e. it should be evaluated by means of a capital budgeting (discounted cash flow) analysis which meticulously ascertains the various cash in- and outflows over time. Although this has been attempted[247)], the major difficulty encountered rests, as usual, with quantifying the observed or assumed effects. Since those effects can be suspected to depend largely on idiosyncratic circumstances, the economic implications of EDI tend to differ substantially across organizations and thus, EDI investments can only be appraised on a

---

regard), and arbitration in cases of dispute; cf. Thomsen (1989b). See further Wheble (1988) pp. 132 - 137.

242) Thomsen (1989b) p. 168. A normative view concerning IAs may also be found e.g. in Amory (1989) p. 26 *et seq.*, Walden (1990) pp. 245 - 248.

243) Cf. Thomsen (1989b) p. 172 *et seq.*

244) Similar views are expressed e.g. in Marsh (1988) and Sarich (1988) p. 46.

245) As one interviewee during the field study (see section 4.2.) put it: "If you want to start with EDI you have to search for trustworthy communication partners among your most important business relationships, since you need someone to phone a technician rather than a lawyer when things go awry."

246) Cf. Picot (1990).

247) Cf. Finch (1988).

case-by-case basis. For this reason, a pragmatic approach is chosen here, which intends to identify the major cost/benefit categories, summarizes the respective experiences of EDI adopters as reported in the available literature, and evaluates the plausibility of some frequently made assertions regarding the business implications of EDI.

Prior to contemplating various direct and indirect effects, it is necessary to make a careful distinction between the concept of EDI as it was defined in section 2.2. and other means of electronic integration between businesses. In particular, EDI should not be confused with what has been called "inter-organizational systems"[248)] (IOS). IOS, defined as "automated information systems shared by two or more companies"[249)], has been portrayed as a general term for electronic linkages between organizations, under which EDI should be subsumed[250)]. According to the dissenting view of this thesis, IOS are entirely different from EDI: The term IOS has probably been coined in appreciation of the success of early remote data entry systems such as the well-known ASAP system of Baxter Travenol (previously American Hospital Supply) in the U.S. health care industry, where customers were provided with data entry terminals to place orders electronically[251)]. Due to the specificity of the system, those dumb terminals could serve no other purpose and must therefore be regarded as dedicated hardware components pertaining to a distributed system. Specificity is contradictory to the independence philosophy intrinsic to the concept of EDI as explained in sections 2.1. and 2.2. With EDI, there is no single IS with identifiable, distributed components, but rather a loose federation of autonomous systems which have been designed as to permit the exchange of a restricted set of messages between them.

Likewise, EDI may be related to, yet does not fit into the categories of "electronic markets and electronic hierarchies"[252)]. The relative advantage of markets vis-à-vis hierarchies as the two alternative governance mechanisms for executing economic transactions has been analyzed extensively in the works of Williamson[253)]. It is hypothesized that means of electronic interconnection *ceteris paribus* reduce coordination costs and

---

248) Barrett/Konsynski (1982).

249) Cash Jr./Konsynski (1985) p. 134. See further Cash Jr. (1985).

250) See Benjamin/de Long/Scott Morton (1990).

251) See e.g. HBS (1985). The interesting question whether the success of Baxter Travenol (or AHS for that matter) can actually be attributed to the possibility of receiving orders electronically, or should instead be credited largely to a significant effort to provide customers with materials management know-how in order to reduce costs, is of no concern here.

252) Cf. Malone/Yates/Benjamin (1987). See also e.g. Griese (1989).

253) Cf. e.g. Williamson (1975).

should therefore favor markets over hierarchies as the preferred choice of coordination mechanism[254]. Both electronic markets and hierarchies imply the existence of a database to which transaction partners jointly have *read access*; with respect to electronic hierarchies there exists a *1:m* relationship between provider and users of the database[255]; in the case of electronic markets an *m:n* relationship holds[256]. Again, those characteristics are inconsistent with the (primitive) view of EDI advanced here. EDI ultimately entails a data exchange between autonomous databases; the mode of database manipulation is *write-only* (store) with no ability of remote systems to unilaterally extract (retrieve) local data. Thus, no single party has exclusive control over the communications process; the decision how to respond is always at the disposal of the message recipient.

Non-specificity and *shared control* have far reaching consequences for the strategic implications of electronic linkages between organizations: With non-specificity of system components, erecting market barriers based on switching costs becomes impossible; shared control on the other hand thwarts any attempt to obtain a superior bargaining position as a result of more profound information about trading partner operations[257].

2.4.2. Direct Effects

2.4.2.1. Costs

Prima facie, the costs of implementing EDI can be more easily determined than its benefits. Supposing that a fully integrated EDI system is to be installed from scratch, investment costs may consist of expenditures for

- a dedicated EDI hardware platform (e.g. a multi-tasking PC to perform all communication tasks),

---

254) Cf. Malone/Yates/Benjamin (1987) p. 489; Picot (1989) p. 367. Cf. further Malone/Yates/Benjamin (1989).

255) See Malone/Yates/Benjamin (1987) pp. 493 - 496.

256) For a similar view on electronic markets, see e.g. Mertens/Schumann/Hohe (1989) p. 129 *et seqq.*

257) This is why usage of the term "integration" in the context of EDI is rather unfortunate. It has a connotation of inescapability, i.e. integrated entities observe the restrictions imposed by the system purpose, regardless of dynamic preferences; cf. Lehman (1980) col. 977. *Per contra*, the goal of EDI is to make entities compatible so as to allow coordination of activities while preserving their individual autonomy/independence. Thus, integration in EDI is only by choice and can be revoked at any time.

- converter software and the initialization of converter tables,
- establishing a link to the corporate databases and applications systems as well as possible modification thereof[258],
- the training and possible hiring of personnel.

Moreover, less quantifiable, ancillary project costs, such as modifying administrative processes, negotiating interchange agreements with trading partners, etc., need to be budgeted for, since they can account for a significant proportion of the overall costs. Besides those initial investment expenditures, a number of recurring operating cost categories exist, including systems maintenance, maintenance of the converter software and tables (which may be called 'syntax maintenance'), trading partner incentive programs, and, above all, telecommunciation costs.

While the essential elements of one-time and recurring EDI expenditures can be readily identified, some of those elements (e.g. the adjustment of internal processes) may be rather difficult to measure. The measurement task becomes even more formidable with respect to long-term organizational restructuring effects that are only to some unknown degree attributable to EDI. In those cases it is virtually impossible to provide an accurate estimate of the costs involved, let alone what fraction of the overall costs is caused by EDI. Therefore, it may be advisable for organizations to completely disregard those strategic aspects within the context of a capital budgeting analysis of EDI and focus only on its investment and operational ramifications.

2.4.2.2. Benefits

2.4.2.2.1. Reduced Transaction Costs

The most apparent category of benefits accruing to EDI adopters are the savings derived from automating repetitive administrative processes. As mentioned above, it has been estimated that up to 70% of the transactions data exchanged between organizations is computer generated and destined for a computer system on the receiving side. Rekeying that data manually into interactive application systems is a likewise inefficient

258) Databases may have to be adapted to store and retrieve data that are mandatory in public EDI standards but which previously were not used internally. Applications systems in practice have often been exclusively designed for interactive data entry and may therefore require significant maintenance work to accommodate the external communication constraints imposed by EDI.

(redundant) and error-prone task[259]. Thus, automation does not only reduce the amount of clerical labor required to enter data but also virtually eliminates the 2 - 5% transcription and other data-entry errors, the rectification of which can become very costly[260]. For example, if an order for 1000 items of a particular product was received but the order quantity entered into the order processing system was merely 100, the error would not be realized until delivery and might then cause disruptive ripple effects when rush orders need to be pushed through the manufacturing system, and lead to additional costs when special express transportation services are hired to make up for the shortfall[261]. Similar adverse effects occur with material sent to the wrong address, or delivery of non-ordered items that must be shipped back, with a subsequent rise in premium freight charges.

Furthermore, empirical investigations have shown that a single business transaction gives rise to the exchange of anywhere between five and twelve (up to 30 for international trade) business documents[262]. Organizations not only incur the costs of preparation, handling, and archival, but those documents must also be reconciled with each other, which can be exemplified by the need to verify an invoice against shipments received and past orders. Those costs can be quite substantial; one wholesaler in the U.S. reports annual savings in clerical labor of $ 600'000.- merely by automating a few reconciliation processes[263].

Finally, a number of incidental savings accrue with respect to (a) office supplies, such as paper forms, envelopes, etc., to (b) storage and archival space, such as file cabinets, and to (c) postage expenditures. To be more specific about the extent of potential transaction cost savings, the listing below shows some practice reports[264]:

- Service Merchandise projects a reduction in order processing costs due to EDI from $ 50.- to appr. $ 13.- [265]

---

259) Cf. e.g. Dearing (1990) p. 5.

260) Cf. Lallande (1986), Malone/Yates/Benjamin (1987) p. 495.

261) Cf. Emmelhainz (1990) p. 32. Navistar Inc., for instance, reports a reduction of 90% of premium freight charges in the aftermath of the transition to EDI; cf. Dearing (1990) p. 5.

262) See e.g. Emmelhainz (1990) p. 30.

263) Cf. Dearing (1990) p. 5.

264) The selected citations are intended to provide only an indication of the range of transaction processing economies experienced with EDI in practice. Values differ substantially across industries and applications as should be expected. For more examples, refer to Emmelhainz (1990) p. 29.

265) Canright (1988a) p. 104.

- Motorola and Siemens estimate savings of DM 20.- per business transaction when using EDI[266].
- Data Design Associates claims a reduction in average order processing costs from $ 49.- to $ 1.- due to EDI[267].
- DEC reports a reduction in average transactions cost from $ 125.- before to $ 32.- after implementing EDI systems[268].
- PMI Food Equipment contends that its average order processing costs shrank from $ 25.- to $ 5.- with EDI[269].
- Dow Chemical estimates savings due to EDI of $ 12.- per order[270].
- According to the findings of a survey among business organizations in the U.S., savings in transactions cost due to EDI average about $ 5.- per document[271].

2.4.2.2.2. Improved Cash Flow

The result of combining EDI with Electronic Funds Transfer (EFT) to accelerate the payment cycle of trade transactions is not so much a benefit to be derived from EDI than it is a vehicle to overcome a trading partner's resistance to adopt EDI, which is evidently a prerequisite for being able to capitalize upon its advantages[272]. The source of this resistance is peculiar to North America where payments, even between geographically dispersed trading partners, are predominantly initiated by check. This situation has led to some 'creative liquidity engineering' whereby the delays of the mail system are exploited to temporarily improve the cash position of the buying organization beyond what has been agreed upon in the payment terms[273].

Trade credit terms stipulate the financial settlement details pertinent to a business transaction. In order to provide an incentive to the buyer to remit payment on the invoice early, fast payment is usually credited with a price discount (e.g. 2% for payment within 10 days). Naturally, buyer and seller have diamatrically opposed interests in completing the payment cycle and therefore become engaged in a zero-sum game called "playing

---

266) Ebers (1991).

267) Joyce (1989) p. 62.

268) Kemezis (1987b) p. 5.

269) Stevens (1988) p. 53.

270) Jenkins (1988) p. 72.

271) Hill/Ferguson (1987) p. 21.

272) An example which occurred in the automotive industry is mentioned in Stevens (1988) p. 56.

273) Cf. e.g. Brealey/Myers (1984) pp. 673 - 675.

the float"[274]. Since the buyer wants to defer actual debiting of his account to the very last moment, he could try to cheat on the date when the invoice had been received, and he would at any rate mail a check to the seller which is drawn on the most remote bank he maintains an account with in order to earn undue interest during the time the check is in the mail or is being cleared through the banking system; this time period is sometimes called "collection float"[275]. The seller desires to credit his account as soon as possible and may for this purpose keep an outlet in the vicinity of the buyer to which the latter is instructed to send the check. This arrangement minimizes the mail float and allows for a fast clearing of the check[276].

If the seller proposes to use EDI/EFT for executing transactions the buyer might object since instantaneous transmissal of invoice and payments would deprive him of collection float profits[277]. The idea presented by Hill/Ferguson[278] is to point to the mutual transaction processing economies offered by EDI. They suggest several alternative schemes of splitting the proceeds from EDI between the two trading partners based on a renegotiation of payment terms such that both parties gain. Provided the negotiating range is positive (which depends e.g. on the extent of the processing efficiencies derivable from EDI and the parties' cost of capital), and EDI is in fact installed, additional benefits would most likely accrue since faster financial settlement reduces the uncertainty of the cashflows and might thus permit a more efficient cash management[279].

2.4.2.2.3. Reduced Inventory Levels

The notion that the use of EDI allows organizations to "significantly" reduce inventory requirements is among the most widely held beliefs about EDI and frequently proclaimed by EDI advocates as one of its most important merits[280]. Even a casual perusal

---

274) Cf. here and in the following Brealey/Myers (1984) p. 672 *et seqq.*

275) Cf. e.g. Hill/Ferguson (1987a) p. 22. Note the somewhat different definitions of payment and collection float than those provided by Brealey and Myers.

276) This scheme has been referred to as "concentration banking". Alternatively, the seller, could establish a purpose-specific local mailbox ("lock-box") and ask a local bank to act as an agent on behalf of the seller to collect the mail and deposit the checks received; see Brealey/Myers (1984) p. 673, Canright (1988a) p. 105.

277) Cf. Grimaldi (1988), Joyce (1989) p. 64.

278) See *supra* note 275.

279) Cf. in this regard also Butler Cox (1987) p. 2, Canright (1987) p. 42.

280) Cf. e.g. Stern/Kaufmann (1985) p. 56, Meyer (1987) p. 415, Milbrandt (1987) p. 7, Anderson/Bovet (1988), Belitsos (1988), Canright (1988a) p. 102, Finch (1988), Norris (1988) p. 718, Schumann/Hohe (1988) p. 519, Stevens (1988), Turnbull (1988) p. 13, Webb (1988), Boland (1989), N.N. (1989) p. 4, Sokol (1989) p. 18, Thomas (1989), p. 28, Dearing (1990) p. 5, Emmelhainz

of the available literature on business aspects of EDI yields an array of practice reports according to which inventory costs have been reduced as a result of adopting EDI. To cite some popular examples:

- Navistar was able to lower inventories by $ 167 million. Including suppliers, inventories were reduced by approximately 80%[281)].
- Digital Equipment Corporation reduced inventory levels by 75% [Ebers (1991)] and for some components by 90%[282)].
- Perkins Engines was able to double inventory turnover which implies inventory reductions of 50%[283)].
- Daimler Benz AG achieved a reduction in average parts inventory from a twelve day supply in 1980 to less than seven days in 1986[284)].

This seemingly conclusive evidence notwithstanding, it appears a worthwhile endeavor to complement case study data with some conceptual analysis in order to evaluate the consistency between those practice reports and theoretical considerations. The analysis presented in Hill/Hansen (1989) will be used as a starting point for the subsequent discussion.

The basic rationale usually presented to support claims of EDI inventory effects rests on the assumption of a shorter order cycle time when orders are transmitted to suppliers via EDI rather than via the traditional, paper-based mail. Thus, under certain conditions (such as the availability of appropriate means of transportation) EDI allows an increase in the frequency of placing orders, i.e. to replace one occasional large transaction with several smaller ones, diminishing the average amount of inventory held over the planning period. For instance, GE Transportation Systems, Inc. reported a fivefold increase in the number of orders sent to suppliers due to the introduction of EDI, with a consequential decline in warehouse stock levels[285)]. The extent of the achievable inventory benefits therefore appears primarily dependent on the relative advantage of EDI over conventional transmission methods in terms of time savings for transmitting and pro-

---

(1990) p. 31, Oswald (1990) p. 138, Petri (1990) p. 263, Schumann (1990) p. 308, Picot/Neuburger/Niggl (1991) p. 27, to name only a few of numerous.

281) Milbrandt (1987), p. 7 *et seq.*

282) Kemezis (1989) p. 5, Jasany (1990) p. 26.

283) Lallande (1986) p. 52.

284) Meyer (1987) p. 414.

285) Cf. Dearing (1990) p. 5. Although the author does not quantify the amount of reduction achieved, it must be in the vicinity of 80%: Assuming constant demand and instantaneous inventory replenishment, the average amount of inventory held is half the order quantity. If the order quantity is reduced by 80% so must the average period inventory.

cessing orders, which is obviously most distinct when EDI replaces paper-based mail procedures. Because orders can, however, also be sent by other means of instantaneous communication, e.g. by telephone, or telex, which have been available for quite some time before the advent of EDI, the delays associated with conventional mail could be easily circumvented by organizations and therefore do not represent a very cogent explanation for pursuing EDI[286].

Inventory can basically be separated into two categories: Firstly, *regular stock* which balances inventory carrying costs against ordering costs and covers the expected demand between two adjacent ordering points; secondly, *safety stock* which is being held in excess of the expected demand during the lead time to hedge against the possibility of stock-outs, due to either higher than expected demand, or longer than expected lead time, or both if lead time is non-deterministic. If neither demand nor lead time are subject to uncertainty, the traditional *economic order quantity* (EOQ) can be used to determine that order quantity which minimizes the sum of ordering and inventory carrying costs[287]:

$$EOQ \equiv q = [2\,C_o D / C_c]^{1/2} \quad , \tag{2.12}$$

with

C_o := ordering cost per order,
C_c := carrying cost per unit of inventory and time,
D := demand during the planning period.

Assuming that EDI lowers order processing costs, *ceteris paribus*, the average amount of inventory held $q/2$ declines because

$$\partial q / \partial C_o = [D / (2\,C_c C_o)]^{1/2} > 0 \quad . \tag{2.13}$$

Evidently, the amount of inventory savings is dependent on the degree of ordering cost reduction achieved. It is possible to determine the implied efficiency effect of EDI in the previously cited example, where the frequency of placing orders quintupled. Assuming overall demand D and carrying costs C_c did not change, the order quantity after implementing EDI q_{EDI} must be one fifth of the previous quantity:

286) Cf. also Norris (1988) p. 718.
287) Cf. Harris (1915).

$$q / q_{EDI} = 5$$

Substituting the EOQ formula for q and q_{EDI} immediately yields

$$C_o / C_o(EDI) = 25 \quad ,$$

which implies that EDI led to a reduction of ordering costs by about 96%. Even if one were to commit the same mistake as Hill/Hansen and equate 'order processing costs' with 'ordering costs', such a large efficiency gain as a result of using EDI seems *utterly unrealistic*[288)].

Obviously, ordering costs not only derive from data processing tasks associated with placing orders. It is also necessary to prepare the goods receiving area and warehouse space, the goods must be physically handled, undergo quality control, etc., all of which is not affected at all by automating certain data processing functions[289)]. Furthermore, for lack of activity-based costing systems[290)], the arbitrary nature of conventional overhead cost allocation methods so prevalent in practice renders it at least difficult to obtain precise ordering cost data[291)]. For the sake of argument, assuming that order processing accounts for one half of the ordering costs[292)] and that EDI reduces that amount by 80%, average inventory would decline by only about 22.5% which, however, would still yield considerable opportunity cost savings[293)].

To complement the preceding discussion, the implications of EDI for safety stock under the more realistic assumption of non-deterministic demand shall be analyzed next. To

---

288) *Nota bene*, there can be no doubt that GE in fact introduced EDI and they actually increased the number of material releases sent to suppliers fivefold with a concomitant large reduction of warehouse requirements. Only the reduction cannot be exclusively attributed to EDI. Very likely, the situation prior to the introduction of EDI was characterized by a rather inefficient materials management with substantial surplus inventory. When this situation was realized, an efficiency program was initiated in the course of which EDI came into being. The concurrency of both events led to the unwarranted conclusion that the introduction of EDI was entirely responsible for the reduction in inventory. This example illustrates the main point of this section: *The uncritical dissemination of 'success stories from current practice' spawns exaggerated claims about the benefits derivable from EDI which is rather unfortunate since the ensuing disappointments of many new adopters will tend to impede the EDI diffusion process.*

289) A fairly comprehensive discussion of the carrying cost principle in materials management can be found in Bernard (1989).

290) Cf. e.g. Cooper (1988a,b, 1989), Cooper/Kaplan (1988), Bromwich/Bhimani (1989), Horvath/Mayer (1989). See further Pfeiffer (1990a).

291) Cf. e.g. Gardener Jr. (1980).

292) According to practicioners, the upper bound is more likely to be in the vicinity of 25%; cf. e.g. Dearing (1990) p. 5.

293) The fact that speeding up the flow of transactions data yields only marginal inventory economies was already demonstrated in simulation studies conducted by Forrester (1961); cf. e.g. p. 33.

simplify the exposition, it is assumed at the outset that only the demand during lead time is stochastic and follows a normal distribution, while the lead time itself remains a non-random, endogenous variable. Intuitively, the savings of EDI should be positively related to the shortening of the lead time.

Let

d	:=	one time period demand; $d \sim N(\mu_d, \sigma^2_d)$
$D(L)$	:=	lead time demand; $D(L) = \Sigma d_i$; $D(L) \sim N(\mu_{D(L)}, \sigma^2_{D(L)})$
ζ	:=	permissible stockout ratio (e.g. $\zeta = .05$)
Z_ζ	:=	value of the Standard Normal Distribution: $\{P(Z) \geq Z_\zeta\} = \zeta$
SS	:=	safety stock

Given these definitions, the amount of safety stock required to incur stockouts in $\zeta * 100\%$ of all cases can be computed as

$$SS = \sigma_{D(L)} Z_\zeta \quad . \tag{2.14}$$

It is therefore necessary to determine $\sigma_{D(L)}$. Given the plausible assumption that all n one period demands d_i are equal

$$d_i \sim d \qquad \forall i \qquad \{i = 1,...,n\} ,$$

the variance $\sigma^2_{D(L)}$ is calculated as[294)]

$$\sigma^2_{D(L)} = Var(\mathbf{1}'\mathbf{d}) = \mathbf{1}'\Sigma_d\mathbf{1} \ .$$

Assuming further that all covariance terms in Σ_d are zero as a result of the independent distribution of all d_i, yields

$$\sigma^2_{D(L)} = n\,\sigma^2_d$$

which leads immediately to the following conclusion:

$$SS = (n)^{1/2}\,\sigma_d Z_\zeta \quad . \tag{2.15}$$

Hence, the safety stock required after the introduction of EDI becomes

294) Vectors are column vectors by default. Similar to matrices they are printed in boldface type.

$$SS_{EDI} = (n_{EDI})^{1/2} \sigma_d Z_\zeta \quad . \tag{2.16}$$

It is thus possible to determine the proportion x of safety stock reductions due to EDI. After setting SS_{EDI} equal to $SS * (1 - x)$, substituting for SS_{EDI} in (2.16), and a few algebraic transformations, the following solution obtains:

$$x = 1 - (n_{EDI} / n)^{1/2} \tag{2.17}$$

The relative reduction in safety stock is solely dependent on the ratio of the lead times *after* and *before* the implementation of EDI[295]. For instance, supposing lead time can be reduced from eight to two days, safety stock requirements will drop by 50%.

The analysis becomes more complex when additionally the assumption of deterministic lead time is abandoned. Supplementing the notation introduced before:

μ_L	:=	mean lead time
σ^2_L	:=	lead time variance

Under certain assumptions regarding the distribution and independence of the random variables, $\sigma^2_{D(L)}$ can be derived as follows:

$$\sigma^2_{D(L)} = \sigma^2_d \mu_L + \sigma^2_L \mu_d \tag{2.18}$$

This formula is cited in Hill/Hansen[296] who subsequently apply (2.18) to an example in order to show the influence of EDI on safety stock levels. While the formula is correct, the example presented unfortunately is not, because it is based on the tacit presumption that, irrespective of the modified conditions, D continues to follow a normal distribution which is generally unfounded. As Eppen/Martin demonstrate, simply multiplying σ_D by a suitable Z_ζ to determine safety stock levels can lead to "egregiously" erroneous stockout predictions[297]. Eppen/Martin also derive a straightforward solution for this problem which, however, requires *a priori* information concerning the lead time distribution. In order to avoid 'guestimating' such distributions and going through the cumbersome calculation process, the concept is not further pursued here. Suffice it to say that the effectiveness of EDI under these conditions depends on how it influences the lead time distribution.

---

295) Or any other cause of a lead time reduction.

296) Cf. Hill/Hansen (1989) p. 57.

297) Cf. Eppen/Martin (1988).

Finally, it should be noted that lead time reductions or more frequent deliveries do not necessarily induce organizations to lower the amount of capital tied up in inventory. A retailing outlet, for example, whose storage capacity is identical with its limited shelf space, will hardly see any incentive to leave some precious shelf space idle. Instead, product variety will be increased which should have a positive impact on inventory turnover and profitability. Due to changing consumer purchasing habits (e.g. preference for one-stop shopping), being able to offer a greater variety of products within space restrictions may in some cases be a matter of essential (competitive) importance, since the viability of the business can hinge on such a service aspect. Under those circumstances, the implementation of EDI may be considered to provide a strategic (i.e. customer service oriented) benefit.

2.4.3. Indirect Effects and Opportunities

2.4.3.1. General Remarks

Much of the attention EDI has recently attracted stems from the notion that EDI can become a source of competitive advantage[298]. Arguments to support this notion have frequently referred to the value chain concept[299]. The value chain has been generally recommended as a fruitful device to evaluate the strategic potential of IT applications[300]. While the productiveness of this approach with respect to EDI appears limited to the customer and supplier interfaces, the discussion below nonetheless has a tripartite structure, in the sense that potential impacts on *customer relation*, *supplier relation*, and *internal operating efficiency* are examined separately.

To complement the value chain perspective, it may also be helpful to deduce business implications of EDI from a different point of reference, i.e. by analyzing its functional role within the organization. Exhibit 2-15 sketches the dependency relationship between EDI and other major components of the organization's IT resources which, according to a normative view, should be designed so as to ultimately support the organization's business strategy[301].

---

298) Cf. e.g. Keen (1988), Boland (1989), Schwab (1989), Sokol (1989), Weid (1989), Emmelhainz (1990) p. 33 *et seqq.*, Walden (1990) p. 239, Ebers (1991).

299) Cf. Porter (1985), p. 33 *et seqq.*, Meffert/Benkenstein (1989). For an attempt to apply the value chain concept to EDI, see e.g. Boland (1989) p. 139.

300) See e.g. Porter/Millar (1985), Clemons/McFarlan (1986).

301) For the alignment between IS and business strategies, refer e.g. to Hanker (1990).

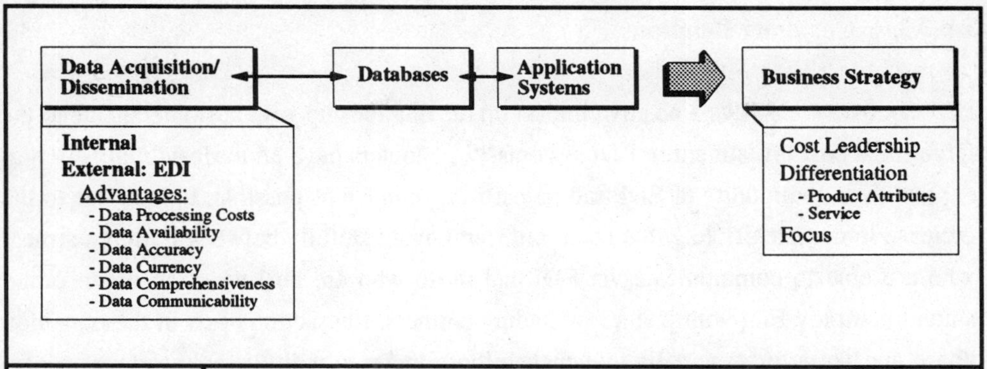

Exhibit 2-15	Framework for Analyzing the Impact of EDI on Business Strategy

Conceptually, EDI can be subsumed under the category of technologies which support the data acquisition/dissemination tasks. The distinguishing feature of EDI in comparison to other technologies falling into the same class (e.g. manufacturing data acquisition systems) is its external orientation. EDI offers at least six types of improvements over conventional (manual) data acquisition/dissemination procedures: (1) It lowers data processing (transaction) costs[302)]; (2) it makes transactions data available for electronic processing; (3) it improves the *accuracy* of the organization's data resources; (4) it improves the *currency* of the organization's data resources; (5) it can widen the *scope* of the organization's data resources, if data are being collected with EDI that were previously not captured under manual operating procedures[303)]; (6) it improves the *communicability* of the organization's data resources, i.e. the relative ease with which data can be selected, extracted, transmitted to, and processed further by external recipients. Given the above analysis framework, the strategic relevance of EDI may be amenable to diagnosis by evaluating those six effects with respect to the three generic strategies that businesses can pursue: *cost leadership*, *differentiation* and *focus*[304)]. Thus, the question is how EDI can assist organizations in reducing costs, differentiating products and services (as perceived by customers), and in targeting market/industry segments.

302) Cf. preceding sections.

303) This argument is particularly stressed in Norris (1988) p. 718.

304) Cf. Porter (1980) p. 34 *et seqq*., Porter (1985) p. 11 *et seqq*.

2.4.3.2. Customer Relation

EDI can *ipso facto* have a positive impact on the relationship with customers. Due to the large fixed cost investment in EDI systems[305)], adopters have an intrinsic motivation to expand their community of EDI trading partners as much as possible. In fact, due to the increase in complexity (e.g. the need to differentiate carefully between trading partners who are able to communicate via EDI and those who are not) when an organization starts to employ EDI with just a few trading partners, transaction costs in the transition phase are likely to be actually higher than those incurred with the conventional paper-based system. Thus, simply being able to communicate via EDI may be a customer service advantage over competitors during the initial stages of the diffusion process[306)]. However, as soon as the majority of organizations within the relevant trading community have adopted, the competitive advantage temporarily enjoyed by early adopters vanishes; instead, laggards will face a competitive disadvantage as a consequence of their inability to conduct transactions electronically[307)]. Indeed, a consensus is emerging in the more recent literature on EDI according to which the pure 'feasibility value' of EDI will eventually degenerate into a "cost of doing business"[308)].

Another major customer service aspect of EDI frequently cited is the reduction in order lead time which supports a customer's JIT inventory management strategy[309)]. By reducing the length of the order cycle, as a consequence of instantaneous communication and (more importantly) instantaneous processing, customers are able to limit their risk exposure with respect to purchased inventory. This increase in customer responsiveness seems particularly valuable in industries that are characterized by a comparatively large variety of products and erratic demand patterns such as in the apparel industry. Faced with continuously shifting fashion trends, retailers prefer to keep low inventories since unfashionable items can only be sold through markdowns with a detrimental impact on the profitability of the operation. It is therefore hardly surprising that the apparel industry was one of the earliest advocates of EDI as an essential element of the "Quick

---

305) Cf. e.g. Mertens/Schumann/Hohe (1989) p. 122.

306) See e.g. Canright (1988b) p. 84.

307) According to practice accounts, a large number of EDI users seems to have adopted out of fear of being unable to match a service supplied by competitors. See e.g. Joyce (1989) p. 64. See further Emmelhainz (1990) pp. 25 - 27.

308) Benjamin/de Long/Morton (1990) p. 39. Cf. further Mertens/Schumann/Hohe (1989) p. 123 *et seq.*, N.N. (1989) p. 5, Knolmayer/Pfeiffer (1990) p. 34, Schumann (1990) p. 309, Ebers (1991).

309) Cf. sections 2.4.2.2.3. and 2.4.4.

Response" (QR) strategy[310]. Similar to JIT, the philosophy of QR resembles the Japanese Kanban system[311] in that manufacturing of products is controlled primarily by 'demand pull' instead of the conventional push-through system. It has been estimated that pursuit of QR will be able to reduce the annual loss to the U.S. apparel industry of $ 25 billion due to markdowns by no less than 50%[312].

Finally, EDI may provide customers with timely information regarding products, prices, promotions, etc. which enhances the transparency of the market for the buying organization. At the same time, transmission of status information on orders and shipments in transit reduces planning uncertainty and permits goods receiving and internal distribution tasks to be performed more efficiently. Collecting and storing information about the shipment of materials also provides opportunities to monitor and compare the performance of logistics intermediaries such as shippers, third-party warehouses, and distribution agents.

2.4.3.3. Internal Efficiency

In addition to improving customer service and responsiveness, EDI provides a number of internal advantages for adopting organizations. For example, by being able to quickly analyze up-to-date sales information the manufacturer is in a better position to early realize demand trends and adapt production plans accordingly[313]. Thus, customers' QR and JIT programs can be accommodated without incurring a proportionate increase of finished goods inventory levels[314]. Furthermore, staff responsible for selling and buying activities is relieved from time-consuming manual paper processing chores and can therefore spend its time more productively on primary activities[315].

In general, as a result of the more timely status of the organization's databases, it should be possible to exert tighter, i.e. real-time, control over many (sequentially dependent)

---

310) Cf. White (1985). See further Monczka/Carter (1988) p. 4.

311) Cf. e.g. Wildemann (1988, s.a.).

312) Cf e.g. White (1985) p. 40, Jenkins (1988) p. 66.

313) This presupposes the ability for fast retooling. In fact, the potential of EDI to increase the responsiveness of organizations is constrained by the flexibility of the manufacturing system. See Bruns Jr./McFarlan (1987) p. 93, Davis (1989).

314) Even without the possibility of improved forecasting, aggregation of less than perfectly correlated random demand sources *ceteris paribus* always yields safety stock economies. Cf. the analysis in section 2.4.2.2.3.

315) See e.g. Emmelhainz (1986).

operating activities, the better coordination of which tends to reduce the amount of slack resources (e.g. all kinds of inventories such as supplies, finished goods, cash, etc.) required to protect against activity interruption due to the temporary failure of preceding operations[316)].

2.4.3.4. Supplier Relation

The impact of EDI on the relationship with suppliers (upstream) is in many respects the mirror image of the impact on customer relation[317)]. Thus, efficiency gains such as lower transaction costs and JIT inventory management apply accordingly. Differences arise mainly from the specificity of supplies. On the retail side, *brand effects* may prevent or at least diminish the possibility of switching to alternate supply sources by end-consumers. The situation for component manufacturers may be different as a result of the higher *product standardization* which tends to reduce switching costs for their industrial customers. Combined with an improved supply market transparency due to EDI, the degree of service-based competition in supplier industries may increase[318)].

2.4.4. EDI and Just-In-Time

The objectives commonly pursued with JIT programs are twofold: First, the gradual elimination of slack resources throughout the organization frees working capital for more productive usages and thereby contributes to improve return-on-equity[319)]. Second, the lack of buffer inventories in "lean production systems"[320)] reveals inefficiencies of or imbalances between organizational activities, shortcomings which can subsequently be redressed. A *ceteris paribus* reduction of safety buffers tends to increase the organization's susceptibility to unintended work stoppages. This risk exposure can be alleviated by a catalog of measures to adjust organizational activities to the modified operating conditions[321)]. With a shrinking margin for error, quality defects or

316) For a discussion of the information processing ramifications for organizational design, refer to Galbraith (1972, 1973).

317) Cf. e.g. Mertens/Schumann/Hohe (1989) p. 123.

318) See e.g. Picot/Neuburger/Niggl (1991) p. 28.

319) Empirical research by Wildemann (1990a) on a sample of 172 European corporations revealed that with JIT, inventory levels may be reduced by some 40% (Range: 10% - 70%), cycle time by more than 50% and total costs by between 8% and 12%.

320) Krafcik (1988).

321) Cf. e.g. Arnold (1989), Fandel/François (1989).

delivery disruptions can no longer be tolerated which manifests itself in a soaring attention devoted to quality control. To offset the cost disadvantage of smaller lot sizes and more frequent transactions, which could make a JIT program prohibitively expensive, it is necessary to enhance the flexibility of manufacturing operations (e.g. through the installation of flexible manufacturing systems) and to reduce transaction costs[322]. The latter goal can be attained by standardizing and automating organizational processes and by eliminating redundant activities along the entire value chain, including coordination with channel partners.

EDI can become an important element (tool) of a JIT strategy mainly for two reasons: (1) It lowers transaction costs and (2) it reduces the frequency of communication errors that impair the coordination of dependent activities[323]. Both aspects indicate why EDI is so ubiquitous in industries where JIT is strongly entrenched such as the automotive sector. However, the concurrency of EDI and JIT should not lead to misguided perceptions about the existence of causal relationships between the introduction of EDI and other elements of JIT strategies. For example, Scheer[324] describes in great detail how the redundancies of traditional inter-organizational transactions can be eliminated, apparently by implementing EDI which improves transaction efficiency. In support of this hypothesis, the author refers to a method that has elsewhere been called "evaluated receipts settlement"[325]. According to this method, the supplier does not submit any invoice to the customer, because payment conditions have been agreed upon prior to the transaction and stipulated in a medium-term frame contract. As soon as the shipment reaches the premises of the customer, payment is initiated after the contents of the shipment have been found to be in compliance with outstanding orders[326]. Thus, the customer's administration is relieved from order-shipment-invoice reconciliation, while the supplier is still obliged to match payment data against the implicit invoice concealed either in the advance shipment notice sent prior to arrival of the goods, or in the shipment itself. Given the obvious efficiency gains to be derived from evaluated receipt

---

322) The general desirability of ever smaller lot sizes is very often uncritically taken for granted. Knolmayer/Lemke (1990), for example, show by means of an extensive simulation study that smaller manufacturing lot sizes, the *conditio sine qua non* of low (zero) inventory levels, cannot be regarded as a virtue *per se*, as so often portrayed in the contemporary literature. The benefits are very much contingent upon certain environmental conditions, especially capacity utilization.

323) Given the existence of alternative means of instantaneous communication, the error reduction advantage of EDI may well be its most important aspect with respect to supporting JIT; see also Sadhwani/Sahran (1987) p. 27, Knolmayer/Pfeiffer (1990).

324) Cf. Scheer (1987b).

325) Cf. e.g. Canright (1988a) p. 102.

326) Payment could be triggered even earlier, e.g. when the advance shipment notice has been received from the supplier's warehouse, itemizing the contents of the shipment.

settlement, the system has been widely embraced particularly in the automotive industry. However, the compelling logic why it can only be implemented on the basis of EDI systems is neither intuitively obvious nor explained in the paper. The same benefits would accrue by sending the advance shipment notice via telex or facsimile or even without any information transfer, since the goods *ipso facto* carry all required information. Even more astonishing than this example must be deemed the reference in the paper to quality control. The author correctly points out that conducting a quality control check on the same goods twice (by supplier and customer) is inefficient and he argues convincingly that the supplier should therefore assume the sole responsibility for guaranteeing the dispatch of defect-free items[327]. Again, while the reasoning appears sound, the imputed causality with EDI is - cautiously formulated - very difficult to follow. Nonetheless, this did not prevent other researchers from adding this "effect" to the list of EDI virtues[328].

2.4.5. Conclusions

EDI offers adopters a variety of direct and indirect benefits the most important of which seem to be (a) the enhanced JIT capability as a result of savings in transactions cost and the reduction/elimination of errors, and (b) improved management control over operations due to the real-time availability of important logistics data in electronic format which can be instantly analyzed. From a strategic perspective, the ability to communicate via EDI can temporarily become a source of competitive advantage; but since the technology is non-proprietary by definition, competitors will catch up sooner or later and the advantage will give way to a strategic disadvantage for laggards. For industries that are characterized by thin sales margins and intensive price competition, implementing technologies that reduce administrative costs may be the *conditio sine qua non* of long-term viability[329]. In other industries such as textiles and apparel, the ability to early detect changes in consumption patterns and quickly adjust production accordingly (in order to avoid costly mark-downs on a large inventory of outfashioned items) renders EDI particularly attractive. It is only by the laborious and time-consuming process of realigning organizational acitivites, and by devising business applications that har-

---

327) Due to the shipping costs involved, it is obvious that quality checks should be conducted *before* the shipment is dispatched.

328) Cf. Petri (1990) p. 260 *et seq.*, Schumann (1990) p. 310.

329) A case in point is the wholesale drug industry in the U.S. where sales margins are on average less than 1%. This industry was one of the first to introduce EDI systems. See e.g. Sokol (1989) p. 103 *et seqq*. Monczka/Carter (1988) p. 4 mention other typical circumstances under which EDI opportunities may exist.

ness the increased wealth and timeliness of logistics data, that organizations will be able to more fully exploit the opportunites offered by EDI and achieve a less perishable business advantage[330].

A fundamental aspect of capitalistic societies is the freedom of decision making of independent agents. If organizations need to trade-off some amount of independence in order to capitalize on technological innovations, they will do so only temporarily and strive hard to regain their full independence, for example by standardization in order to reduce the specificity of the technology. This is the reason why proprietary inter-organizational systems are doomed to eventual failure, while open standards based EDI and electronic markets can be expected to prevail since they cater to basic needs of agents who wish to execute economic transactions[331].

2.5. Utilization of EDI in Practice

2.5.1. Evolution of Standards

Due to their large variety, it must be deemed virtually impossible to give a comprehensive overview of EDI applications in practice[332]. However, because multi-lateral EDI presupposes the existence of non-proprietary standards, as was explained in previous sections, the evolution of standards should be a fairly accurate indicator of EDI usage, except where message exchanges based on private communication standards are concerned. Therefore a brief review of important stages in the international development of EDI standards is given below.

---

330) The frequency of fairly dubious assertions about the great variety of organizational and strategic implications of EDI warrants a rather trivial note of precaution: Concurrency of events must not lead one to jump to unfounded conclusions about the existence of causal relationships. Inferring causal effects from single-shot case studies, which "have such a total absence of control as to be of almost no scientific value", must be avoided at all costs; cf. Campbell/Stanley (1963) p. 6. Causality can only be deduced from experimental or quasi-experimental research. Anything else is either empirical exploration or desk-work hypothesizing and should be formulated as such. This problem is intrinsic to business informatics and most other branches of the social sciences since their preferred objects of examination - organizations, economies, countries, etc. - are often very difficult to experiment with. The ubiquity of descriptive/explorative studies (of which this study is unfortunately no exception despite the best intentions at the outset) provides ample evidence of the almost intractable difficulties involved.

331) For a similar view, see Malone/Yates/Benjamin (1989) p. 166 *et seq.*

332) For snapshot-like, non-exhaustive listings of EDI projects in various countries refer to Mertens (1985), Hitchcock (1988), Sarich (1988) p. 35 *et seqq.*, Petri (1990) p. 178 *et seqq.*

It has been stated that EDI was initially conceived to facilitate the airlift supply operation during the blockade of Berlin in 1948 at the start of the cold war[333]. According to most accounts, however, the beginnings of EDI in multi-lateral form can probably be traced to the formation of the Trade Data Coordinating Committee (TDCC) by members of the transportation industry in the U.S.[334] It was not until 1975, however, that the first set of sectoral standards for rail transportation was published by TDCC[335]. During the 1970s, coinciding economic interests among business partners within various industries precipitated the emergence of a number of other industry-specific standards in several countries. Those standards were in most cases of domestic scope only, with such exceptions as the international banking network SWIFT which was launched in 1978. In the same year, ANSI initiated a project to develop cross-sectoral standards in order to stimulate the use of EDI in the U.S. The Accredited Standards Committee X12 was established in 1979 for that purpose.

Standard development in Europe was strongly influenced by the activities of the ECE Working Party on the Facilitation of International Trade Procedures which produced the first international standard for trade data elements UN/TDED in 1980 that was bound to become ISO Standard 7372. One year later, the GTDI were published with the explicit intention to define a mandatory set of EDI syntax rules to be employed by all users. The advantages of universal compatibility notwithstanding, national and sectoral idiosyncracies led to the further development of non-universal standards not only in the U.S. but also in several European countries such as France and the U.K.[336] The growth of EDI was especially strong in the U.K. after the introduction of the highly successful TRADACOMS standards (a GTDI derivative) in 1982 which were originally developed to address the needs of the retail industry but later diffused into other industrial sectors as well[337].

In recognition of the dire prospects for companies with international business interests of having to support a multiplicity of national and sectoral standards, an initiative was undertaken in 1985 under the auspicies of the UN to find a way to merge the two predominant sets of syntax standards ANSI X12 and GTDI. As a result of the development

333) Cf. Ioannou (1990) p. 60.

334) Cf. Canright (1988a) p. 108, Meier (1989) p. 58, Emmelhainz (1990) p. 63. Cf. especially Laidet (1990) p. 66.

335) A review of the TDCC work is given in Notto (1990).

336) Cf. Roos (1989) p. 49.

337) Cf. Moore (1987) p. 554, McGuffog (1988).

work conducted by the Joint Electronic Data Interchange (UN/JEDI) group, the EDIFACT syntax rules came into being and were, after gaining approval from the ECE, eventually adopted by ISO in 1987 as Standard 9735[338].

The preceding short historical review of important stages in the evolution of EDI standards seems to suggest that the scope of standards continuously expanded over time. Initially, innovative users had to resort to private communication conventions for lack of publicly available standards. With the use of EDI becoming more ubiquitous, the proliferation of proprietary standards within the same industry could not continue indefinitely. This gave rise to the development of industry-wide standards for so called "vertical applications", i.e. EDI applications between business partners in a customer-supplier relationship. From this point onwards a pattern of two parallel evolutionary trajectories emerged. On the one hand, existing standards were extended or modified to be applicable across different industrial sectors (horizontal applications). This approach was pursued particularly in the U.S., which is not unexpected given its comparatively small fraction of international trade. The other trajectory called for the creation of international industry-specific standards such as ODETTE in the European automobile industry. The logical conclusion of this process is the formulation of the universal EDIFACT syntax rules which are supposed to become the common EDI denominator for all industries and countries[339], raising two important questions about the likely success of EDIFACT:

(1) To what extent will the advantage of universality be compromised by the development of EDIFACT subsets by private user groups?

(2) To what extent will EDI users try slowing down the migration to EDIFACT in order to protect their investments in applications based on other domestic or sectoral standards?

The first problem has been emphasized before[340]; it is already apparent in the context of national cross-industry standards such as ANSI X12[341] and is bound to become even more severe with respect to EDIFACT. The second question relates to a problem refer-

---

338) A more detailed account of the history of EDIFACT is provided e.g. by Walker (1988), Warner (1989). Cf. further Meyer (1988a) p. 35 *et seq.*

339) A similar assessment is given in Mackintosh/Lewin (1990) p. 12. Cf. also Exhibit 2-6.

340) Cf. section 2.3.1.3.

341) Cf. Canright (1988a) p. 111 *et seq.*

red to as "excess inertia" where switching costs prevent the adoption of superior standards (or goods) among a group of potential adopters[342)].

2.5.2. The Diffusion of EDI in Practice

Considering the many advantages regularly attributed to EDI[343)] and the fact that the basic technological prerequisites, namely DP systems and a telecommunications infrastructure, have been available for several decades by now, the low penetration level of EDI even by the most optimistic assessments of market research agencies is rather intriguing. Table 2-2 below shows a summary of published data of actual or predicted diffusion levels[344)]:

Year	U.S.	U.K.	Europe (incl. U.K)
1986	3000	-	-
1987	3000	800	-
1988	3500-6000	1500 - 1600	2350
1989	5500-9000	-	1500 - 4000
1990	10000-14000	2500 - 4000	5000
1991	10500	-	-
1992	18000	-	-
1993	-	-	-
1994	100000	-	20000

Table 2-2 Summary of EDI Diffusion Data/Estimates

With millions of business organizations as potential EDI users, those statistics indicate the still rather embryonic stage of EDI utilization in practice which is not expected to change significantly any time soon, even if growth forecasts averaging about 50% per year turn out to be accurate[345)]. Moreover, 68.1% of the 1094 respondents of a tele-

342) Farrel/Saloner (1985) p. 71; see further with respect to EDI Picot/Neuburger/Niggl (1991). Cf also section 3.3.

343) Cf. section 2.4.

344) Cf. Schindler et al. (1987) p. 20, Keefe (1988) p. 50, Meyer (1988b) p. 19, Schatz (1988) p. 56, Mason (1989) p. 110, Meier (1989) p. 60, Wigglesworth (1989) p. 165, Clark (1990) p. 76, Ioannou (1990) p. 60, Mackintosh (1990) p. 10, Mulder (1990) p. 660, Thomas (1990) p. 170. Distinguishing between forecasts and estimates was considered superfluous due to the general unreliability of those numbers. Suffice it to say that many initially 'rosy' forecasts have since then been revised downward.

345) Cf. e.g. Müller-Berg (1991) and *supra* note 332. Underscoring the low penetration figures of EDI, Mulder (1990) p. 660 reports that in 1988 there were about 1500 active EDI users in the U.K., 400 in France, 200 in Germany, 150 in Sweden, and 100 in Italy.

phone survey among U.S. enterprises conducted in 1988 either did not have any plans for implementing EDI or were postponing a decision[346].

2.5.3. A Sample EDI Application[347]

The previous section on the evolution of EDI syntax standards has demonstrated that due to the business interdependencies along the logistics chain, vertical, i.e. sectoral, applications preceded the use of EDI between organizations having horizontal, i.e. cross-industry relationships (mostly service-based). A typical example of a horizontal EDI application concerns the cooperation between customs authorities and customs agents. As can be seen from Table 2-2, in comparison to the United States, EDI usage in the European Community - with the noticeable exception of the U.K. - lags behind. It seems plausible to suspect that this lag can at least partially be attributed to the higher complexity in European trade as a consequence of market fragmentation, language barriers etc. Compared to the situation in North America, a larger proportion of business transactions pertains to a flow of goods and services across borders[348]. Thus, in addition to having to coordinate the activities between the two primary transaction partners (and intermediaries such as banks, transportation agencies, etc.), the customs authorities of at least two countries become involved, which substantially adds to the administrative overhead already incurred.

It is not only that paperwork preparation and processing requirements associated with international trade on average accounts for almost 10% of the entire transaction value[349], but another adverse side effect is that processing delays tend to slow down the transaction considerably. Studies have shown that while goods can be moved between any two locations literally within but a few hours (by air transportation), clearance of the goods at the final destination is "averaging a week"[350]. In due recognition of the current trend towards the implementation of JIT concepts in the business community, which - as was pointed out in section 2.4.2.2.3. - entails the break-up of *one* infrequent large transaction into *several* smaller transactions spread over some period of time in order to reduce inventory levels, customs authorities in Europe have undertaken

346) Cf. Ferguson/Hill (1989a) p. 22.

347) For further details on this case refer to Pfeiffer (1990c).

348) Review e.g. the statistics provided in OECD (1991) p. 32 *et seqq.*

349) Cf. e.g. Sarich (1988) p. 8, Thomsen (1989a) p. 13.

350) Thomsen (1989a) p. 13.

various efforts to streamline their operations[351]. Cases in point are the development of the Single Administrative Document (SAD) and the adoption of simplified declaration procedures for major traders[352].

The EDI system described briefly below falls into the category of horizontal systems and, while representativeness may be difficult to establish, it provides at least some insights into the technical and procedural aspects of EDI implementations which may be deemed typical. Moreover, it illuminates the interaction between EDI systems and a messaging network.

The customs EDI system, whose basic architecture is depicted in Exhibit 2-16, was implemented by a wholly owned subsidiary of a major European electronics manufacturer. The exclusive task of the subsidiary is to provide customs brokering services for the domestic affiliates of the group in France.

The system can basically be decomposed into the three subsystems Customs Office, Customs Broker and VAN. The flow of messages between both locations through the network is controlled on either side by multi-tasking workstations running under Xenix, each of which is equipped with a printer to produce transaction logs. In order to initiate a transaction, a customs broker employee prepares a customs declaration message on a PC either by entering the information interactively or by retrieving it from a datafile. Based on that data, the PC application generates a flat file in proprietary format and sends it over the LAN to the workstations where it is translated into EDIFACT format and stored as a message in a database. At the request of some operator, the message is retrieved from the database, wrapped into a protocol envelope (X.400) and transmitted to the VAN.

351) The JIT/competitiveness argument is frequently advanced to show the need for automating customs procedures. It implicitly suggests that without the proper systems in place no international JIT partnership between supplier and customer is feasible. This is evidently not the case, and even with automated customs systems, it would seem hardly conceivable that a JIT supplier would voluntarily expose himself to the risk of a systems failure and completely dispense with a delivery warehouse in the vicinity of his customer's premises; see e.g. Morrin (1989) p. 80 who aptly describes the many dilemmas faced by customs organizations in fulfilling their diverse responsibilities on the one hand and supporting the needs of the business community on the other.

352) Simplified procedures are commonly based on period entry schemes, according to which (in parallel with trade transactions) only a limited amount of data for basic control purposes is being sent to customs at first. The comprehensive set of data pertaining to recent transactions is provided *ex post* in periodic recapitulations. See e.g. Sarich (1988) p. 47 *et seq.*, Tweddle (1988), Holder/Halstead (1989).

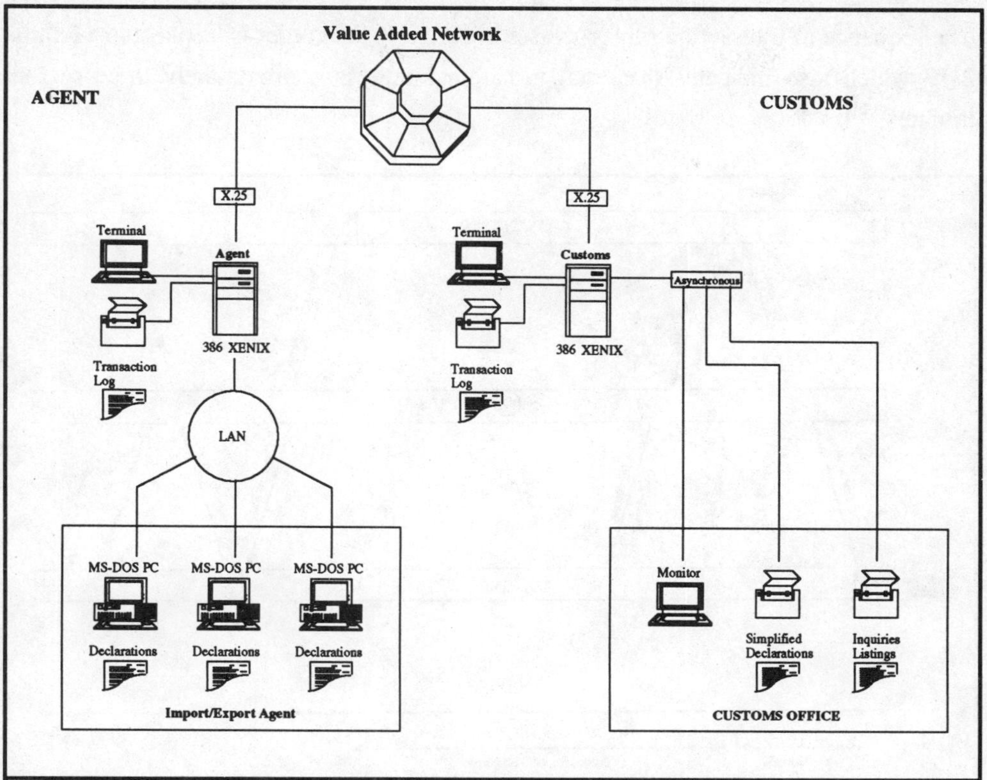

Exhibit 2-16	Systems Architecture of a Customs EDI Application

While the network always operates in store-and-forward mode, the forced delivery option does not wait for the customs office to retrieve the message from a clearing house mailbox, but rather transmits it instantly upon receipt to the customs office workstation. The received message is verified for compliance with EDIFACT syntax rules and, in case no violation was found, a functional acknowledgement is sent back to the originator. Furthermore, a subset of the declaration's data is displayed on a screen (and printed off) for customs personnel to decide about the appropriate action to take. If a physical examination of the imported or exported goods is deemed necessary, the broker is sent a response message to hold the goods for inspection. Otherwise, the workstation automatically generates a clearance message and sends it via VAN to the agent[353].

353) The message is generated automatically after a prespecified length of time since reception of the declaration has elapsed. A status flag is being maintained in the agent's workstation database to trace and check the status of each transaction. The VAN time-stamps all messages submitted and generates a reference number so that sender and receiver can identify messages based on the same attributes. It also provides both communication partners with acknowledgements in order for them to keep track of their transmissions.

The sequence of transaction sub-processes in chronological order is displayed in Exhibit 2-17 which also indicates that total turnaround time is approximately three to four minutes[354].

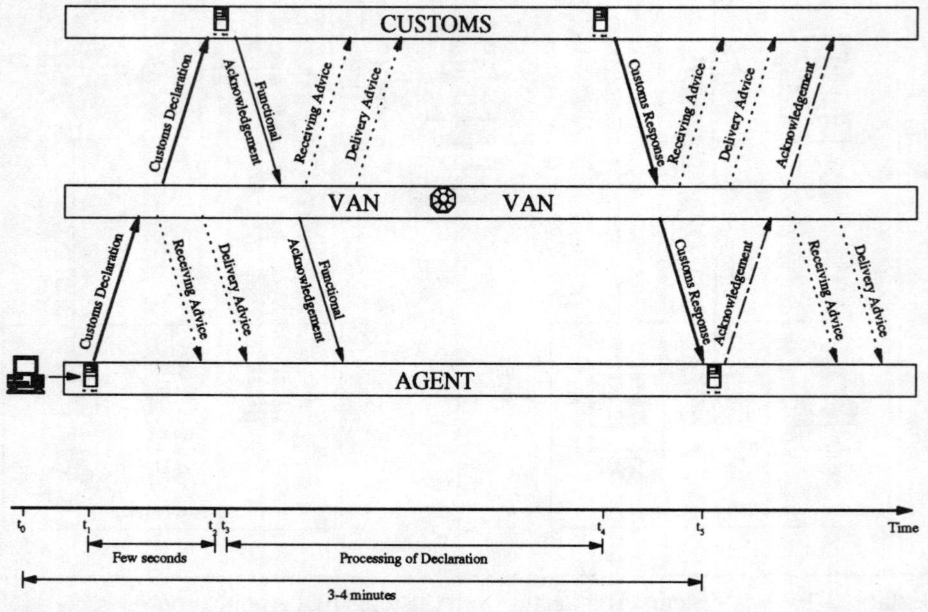

Exhibit 2-17	EDI Transaction-Process Diagram

According to the management of the brokerage, the system has improved the productivity of operators by between 200 and 400% with considerable implications for staffing requirements. Within one year, staffing levels have been cut in half. While the system is of proprietary nature and must therefore be regarded as a pilot project only, the envisaged implementation of large-scale EDI systems at customs can be expected to raise similar problems.

354) Evidently, the arrows indicating message transmission should be perfectly vertical. They were deliberately tilted for the sake of presentational clarity only.

3. The Aspect of Diffusion

3.1. Network Externalities

The diffusion data and estimates presented in section 2.5.2. above show that EDI has not yet reached a large penetration level. Since EDI is foremost bound to replace an obsolete transaction processing mode, any efficiency gains should be positively correlated with the degree of replacement achieved. In other words, individual users have an intrinsic motivation to expand usage of EDI once the basic decision has been made to implement EDI systems[1]. The general desirability of more efficient operations notwithstanding, conducting EDI presupposes a willingness on the part of the organization's trading partners to reciprocate. Hence the *circulus vitiosus* that EDI may not yet be in widespread use because it is not widely used, which follows from a peculiar feature of certain goods or services that has been labeled "network externalities"[2]. Network externalities express the fact that the total utility a consumer derives from the use of a good or service is not only dependent upon its functional characteristics and specific demand conditions, such as idiosyncratic environmental circumstances (e.g. time, location, purpose of usage), but also upon the number of other consumers using the same, a compatible, or a complementary good or service.

Network externalities are most obvious where communication technologies (interactive media) such as the telephone, facsimile or E-mail are concerned[3]. Users of such technologies directly benefit from others joining the network. However, network effects are not necessarily confined to interactive media. They are also said to arise indirectly in cases of complementary goods and services. One frequently cited example in this regard refers to the interdependence between hard- and software in the computer industry. Given the intuitively plausible assumption that the development of compatible software is contingent upon the installed hardware base, current users would prefer others to

---

1) Cf. e.g. Dearing (1990) p. 6.

2) Also called "externality", Buchanan/Stubblebine (1962); "network consumption externalities", Rohlfs (1974); "positive demand externality", Oren/Smith (1981) p. 467; "adoption externality", Dybvig/Spatt (1983); "positive external consumption benefits", "positive consumption externalities", Katz/Shapiro (1985) p. 424; Katz/Shapiro (1986) p. 823; "positive externalities", Cabral (1990) p. 299.

3) Apparently, the owner of the only existing telephone set would derive no utility from the device until at least one other (connected) set is installed at a different site and accessible to an individual with whom the first owner desires to communicate. While such an extreme case would never occur in practice (early telephone systems were installed in pairs linked by direct line rather than via switched services; see e.g. Rohlfs (1974) p. 36, Markus (1987) p. 501.), it illustrates that rational users of public communication technologies should favor diffusion of the system until universal access has been achieved. Cf. further the discussion in section 3.2.2.

purchase similar equipment. Such a mutual dependency relationship is so ubiquitous in practice that it has been called the "hardware-software paradigm"[4]. Network externalities also arise in the context of standards and innovations[5]. While standards have a number of other advantages, such as the reduction of transaction costs[6], the externality effect ultimately stems from the economies of scale accruing when similar purpose equipment is deliberately designed for compatibility, thus, effectively extending the relevant network of users by integration[7]. The adoption of innovations can be subject to network externalities in the case of significant training or set-up costs[8]. The last example underscores the diversity of network effects in practice and provokes the conclusion that any technological innovation is affected to some extent. Furthermore, the importance of the social system's behavioral characteristics should not be overlooked; it is those characteristics that are claimed to make the concept applicable even to such non-technical innovations as the establishment of information centers and the use of computer-aided-software-engineering (CASE) methodologies[9].

To summarize, the question of diffusion is an important aspect of innovative communication technologies in general and of EDI in particular[10]. It seems logical therefore, to

---

4) Katz/Shapiro (1985) p. 424. Other examples falling into the same category include all systems where information processing devices are physically distinct from information carriers which can thus be sold separately, such as (video) cassettes, records, video games, etc. Even the availability of automobile service networks is said to provide a positive consumption externality for the sale of automobiles; see e.g. Katz/Shapiro (1985) p. 424, recited in Wiese (1990) p. 2. It is somewhat surprising that the quoted literature on this phenomenon fails to emphasize the obvious *systems property* of the given examples as the source of the network externalities. For instance, the consumer is certainly not interested in purchasing just a physical PC unit simply because the utility of the mere hardware is *nil*. Only the entire system composed of both hardware and software is relevant from a demand perspective. Thus, only when the (artificial) supply-side distinction between system components is being made, indirect network effects occur, the degree of which is determined by the individual importance of the complementary components with respect to the utility of the entire system (more precisely, the *expected* utility over the system's period of usage as immediately follows from the aspect of insurance).

5) Cf. Dybvig/Spatt (1983) pp. 231 - 233, Cabral (1990) p. 299.

6) See e.g. Kindleberger (1983). Disadvantages of standards are e.g. the reduction in variety. See further Farrell/Saloner (1985) p. 70 *et seq.*, Cullen/Defraigne (1990) pp. 536 - 540.

7) See e.g. Esser/Leruth (1988) p. 251

8) Cf. Dybvig/Spatt (1983) p. 232, Katz/Shapiro (1986) p. 823. This implies that later adopters are able to capitalize on learning curve effects while innovators may benefit from special introductory prices (e.g. as "pilot users"). Providing efficiency gains are passed on, it may be considered a special instance of the case of sharing fixed costs among a larger group of consumers; see e.g. Chou/Shy (1990).

9) Cf. Gurbaxani (1990) p. 74.

10) Cf. the argument in Clemons/Row (1990) p. 346: "Network externalities exist when the value of a system is dependent on the number of participants in the system. Systems that handle interactions between customers and suppliers may exhibit such economies, because the value of the system to the customer may depend on the range of products or suppliers participating." See also Sokol (1989) p. 68: "In fact, benefits attributable to EDI are realized in direct proportion to the amount of business transacted electronically. In effect, more partners, more benefits." Cf. further Pi-

examine some results of the vast literature on innovation diffusion in order to identify factors that in previous studies have been found to impinge upon diffusion processes. Special attention will be dedicated to those determinants that could be manipulated by decision makers in practice in order to control (stimulate) the rate of adoption. Moreover, differences in the diffusion between 'conventional' innovations and those exhibiting particularly strong network externalities need to be carefully considered and analyzed with respect to their relevance for the spreading of EDI.

3.2. Diffusion of Innovations

3.2.1. Diffusion of Conventional Innovations[11)]

3.2.1.1. Introduction

According to the most widely accepted definition, "diffusion is the process by which an innovation is communicated through certain channels over time among the members of a social system"[12)]. Due to the presumed impact on industrial competitiveness[13)] and social welfare, the socioeconomic phenomenons *technological change* and the *diffusion of innovations* have been studied intensively for several decades[14)]. While despite all efforts the dynamic processes underlying *invention* and *innovation* are still apparently less well-understood[15)], the concept of diffusion, i.e. the spread (adoption) of novel techniques, practices, products, or ideas over time, has - in the course of several thousand research publications on the subject matter - gradually evolved into a theory of its own[16)]. Besides the (in this context exclusively relevant) diffusion process itself, the conceptual foundations of diffusion theory encompass *inter alia* the innovation decision process, the categorization of adopters according to the relative time of adoption, the

---

cot/Neuburger/Niggl (1991) p. 24: "EDI beziehungsweise ein EDI-Standard ist ein typisches komplexes Gut, bei dem Netzeffekte auftreten".

11) "Conventional" in this context refers to innovations where network effects are either absent or of negligible impact.

12) Rogers (1983) p. 5.

13) Cf. e.g. Gold (1981) p. 247, Albach (1989). The same view with respect to the introduction of IT was expressed by Gurbaxani et al. (1990).

14) The roots of pertinent research can at least be traced back to the early 1900s. For a review of past research on the diffusion aspect, see e.g. Brown (1981) p. 3 *et seqq.*, Rogers (1983) p. 38 *et seqq.*, and Gatignon/Robertson (1985).

15) Cf. Sahal (1981) p. 3.

16) Cf. Rogers (1983).

roles of mass media communication, opinion leaders, and change agents[17]. Most generalizations of diffusion theory have been derived from investigations conducted in the framework of consumer research where adoption decisions are usually being made by private individuals or households. However, there is also a considerable body of research on organizational innovations[18], and it is claimed that "...the diffusion processes for each of these two types of innovation are more similar than is generally recognized."[19]

Diffusion processes can be described in terms of at least four dimensions[20]: (1) The shape or pattern of the diffusion curve, which shows the temporal characteristics of the process and provides clues as to the underlying behavioral causes that govern it; (2) the rate of diffusion or adoption, which measures the velocity with which the innovation spreads among adopters; (3) the potential penetration level, which describes the maximum level of diffusion an innovation is likely to achieve within some community; (4) the extent of utilization (or implementation) of an innovation, which explicitly takes into account that - especially in the case of technological innovations - the diffusion process cannot be adequately characterized by a sequence of simple binary-choice decisions of adoption vs. non-adoption. Instead, it is necessary to determine and analyze the implementation of the technology, i.e. how it is being used by adopters[21]. Since the potential penetration level is largely irrelevant for the purpose of this study, only the other three dimensions are examined further in the following sections.

---

17) For a comprehensive listing refer e.g. Gatignon/Robertson (1985) p. 850 who also provide an integrated diffusion model. Cf. further Rogers (1983).

18) Publications on diffusion in industry date back to the early 1960s. The seminal contribution by Mansfield (1961) is frequently quoted as the beginning of dedicated research in the field. For an assessment of past research and suggestions for future studies, see e.g. Gold (1981).

19) Brown (1981) p. 2 *et seq*. The conventional diffusion paradigm, as described in the works of Rogers, primarily focusses on the *adoption aspect* of the diffusion process, or the *demand side*. Brown (1981) in particular has striven to complement Rogers' model by adding a market and *infrastructure perspective* which is supposed to represent the missing *supply effects*. Cf. also Robertson/Gatignon (1986) who advance the notion that the competitive environment of technology-supplying and technology-adopting industry influences the diffusion process. Due to the broad acceptance of the Rogers model, however, this text will basically follow the propositions of the conventional diffusion paradigm and supplement them where deemed necessary.

20) The first three dimensions listed are also mentioned e.g. in Gatignon/Robertson (1985) pp. 858 - 861.

21) The question of implementation is said to be particularly relevant for interactive media as a consequence of their "tool" character; cf. Rogers (1986) p. 121. The importance of implementation in the context of innovation diffusion is also emphasized in Sahal (1981) p. 4, Tornatzky/Klein (1982) p. 29, Robertson/Gatignon (1986) p. 3.

3.2.1.2. The Pattern of Diffusion

Diffusion curves generally plot the cumulative number or proportion of innovation adopters against time. It is probably fair to say that in the majority of empirical investigations a *sigmoidal* diffusion pattern has been postulated or observed, which means that the diffusion process follows an S-shaped curve[22]. The "contagion effect" present in "epidemic" models, which describe the spread of an infectious disease among a population[23], is frequently cited as the theoretical underpinning for the assumption of a sigmoidal cumulative diffusion pattern. The basic premise of this model is that the hazard rate, i.e. the rate at which agents catch the disease, depends linearly on the number of uninfected agents multiplied by the proportion of the population already infected at any instance in time[24]:

$$\partial m_t / \partial t = \beta (n - m_t) m_t / n \quad \Leftrightarrow$$

$$\partial m_t / \partial t = \beta (n - m_t) f_t \tag{3.1}$$

With

n	:=	Size of the population
m_t	:=	Number of agents infected at t
β	:=	Constant reflecting the propensity to become infected
f_t	:=	Fraction of the population infected at t: $f_t = m_t / n$

The solution to the differential equation (3.1) is the familiar logistic function presented below which, when plotted, shows a symmetrical S-shaped pattern.

$$f_t = [1 + e^{(-\alpha - \beta t)}]^{-1} \tag{3.2}$$

or, alternatively:

---

22) Cf. e.g. Rogers (1983, 1986), Gatignon/Robertson (1985) p. 859. Besides the empirical evidence cited in the references, there seems to be some intuition behind the assumption of a sigmoidal diffusion pattern. During the early stages of diffusion a considerable amount of uncertainty is likely to prevail with respect to the innovation's functionality and reliability, exacerbated by a tendency to reveal a number of design or manufacturing deficiencies that can only gradually be eliminated. As a consequence, the initial diffusion process will be fairly slow. As soon as the technology has matured, its attractiveness soars and diffusion proceeds more rapidly, until most of the implementation opportunities are exhausted. For a similar viewpoint see e.g. Sahal (1981) p. 81 *et seq.* who contemplates the diffusion process from the common perspective of technological substitution.

23) Cf. e.g. Davies (1979) p. 9 and the references cited there.

24) Cf. e.g. Davies (1979) p. 10, Sahal (1981) pp. 77 - 78, 83 - 84, Trajtenberg/Yitzhaki (1989) p. 36.

$$f_t = [1 + a\, e^{-\beta t}]^{-1} \tag{3.3}$$

The parameter *a* reflects the prevailing conditions at the start of the contagion process, i.e. the *initial* diffusion.

There are several *pendants* to the epidemic model in the economic realm, such as the "bandwagon"[25)] effect which refers to the tendency of consumers to purchase certain goods for conformity reasons only, i.e. not for their functional utility but because others have acquired them as well. Contagion effects are also said to arise in the dissemination of information or due to increasing competitive pressure e.g. when innovations are adopted by competitors[26)].

The perhaps most attractive property of the logistic function for researchers, besides the relatively straightforward application to statistical regression techniques, is its capability to condense information. If the model correctly describes the diffusion process, its entire information content can be summarized by only two parameters, α and β, where the former has previously been explained as a measurement of starting conditions and the latter indicates the rate of diffusion. However, indiscriminate use of the logistic function as a model of the diffusion process - even if it follows a sigmoidal pattern - has been criticized sharply on several grounds[27)]. For this reason, a number of alternative S-shaped functions have been proposed, such as the Gompertz function or the cumulative log-normal distribution function, which have the desirable property of asymmetry and should thus provide a better fit with asymmetric empirical diffusion data[28)]. Moreover, the exponential diffusion function, which is concave over the entire interval, was introduced as a principle alternative to the family of S-curves[29)]. Given the fairly large number of available choices, with probably similar goodness-of-fit values when matched against empirical data, any preferential treatment of one pattern over the others is either

---

25) Leibenstein (1950); see especially p. 189. Cf. also e.g. Sahal (1981) p. 77.

26) Cf. e.g. Brown (1981) p. 155, Trajtenberg/Yitzhaki (1989) p. 36.

27) See e.g. Davies (1979). Arguments presented against the use of the logistic curve include e.g. the ad hoc nature of its theoretical basis and the unrealistic symmetrical shape with the point of inflexion at the 50% penetration level. It can be suspected, that some of the criticism is also due to the deceptively high coefficient of determination R^2 obtained when regression analyses are performed with the logistic function. Simulation studies have shown that fitting a logistic function to any monotonic growth pattern will usually lead to R^2 values which exceed 0.90 which can therefore not be interpreted as "confirmation" of the assumption of an underlying logistic process; cf. e.g. Trajtenberg/Yitzhaki (1989).

28) Cf. Sahal (1981) p. 78.

29) For a comparison between different sets of conditions that either lead to a sigmoidal or an exponential diffusion pattern see Gatignon/Robertson (1985) p. 859.

based on *a priori* theoretical assumptions about the nature of the underlying dynamic process or must be qualified as *arbitrary*[30].

3.2.1.3. The Rate of Diffusion

Given the aforementioned presumed positive impact of technological innovations on competitiveness and social welfare, it is obvious that policy makers, whose defined *raison d'être* is to further the well-being of their constituents, should be interested in determining factors that facilitate or impede the spread of innovations in order to foster the establishment of environmental conditions that are conducive to a rapid dissemination of new ideas, technologies, etc. Before research can provide any guidance in this endeavor it is necessary to develop a measurement concept for the diffusion rate.

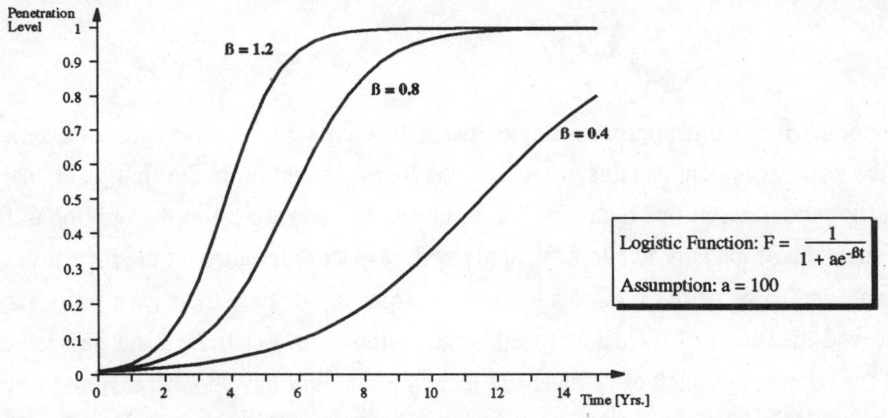

Exhibit 3-1	Comparison of Logistic Curves

Evidently, there is a wide variety of possible constructs that could be used as proxy measures of diffusion speed, such as e.g. the time elapsed until a 50% penetration level is reached, or the time lapse between the 10% and 90% penetration levels and so on[31]. One, mostly for statistical convenience, frequently chosen growth indicator is the β-

30) Interestingly, some authors have begun to express serious reservations about the usefulness of searching for the 'correct' diffusion growth model. For example, technological innovations are typically characterized by continuous functionality enhancing development which may well lead to a significant expansion of the set of prospective adopters. Under those circumstances, the fraction f of actual adopters may in fact decrease for some time period even with a growing user base. A postulated pattern of monotonic increase in the proportion of adopters, which seems to be the common denominator of all diffusion models, is clearly contradictory to a temporarily declining f-value. Hence the futility of the entire endeavor; see e.g. Gold (1981) p. 248 *et seqq.*

31) Cf. e.g. Davies (1979) pp. 11, 26.

parameter of the logistic function. It was already mentioned that this parameter can be regarded as a measure of diffusion speed. The point is illustrated in Exhibit 3-1 above which depicts a comparison of three logistic curves with the same *a* yet different β values. Clearly, the greater β the more rapidly a high penetration level is achieved.

Now, given a set of empirical diffusion data, it is a straightforward exercise to obtain a parameter estimate of β. All it takes is (a) to perform a simple logarithmic transformation of equation (3.2.) which yields[32)]

$$ln[f_t / (1 - f_t)] = \alpha + \beta t \ , \qquad (3.4)$$

and (b) to conduct a linear regression analysis with the thus transformed data set to determine α- and β-estimates. Adding a disturbance term ε, the regression equation (3.5) becomes[33)]:

$$ln[f_t / (1 - f_t)] \equiv y = \alpha + \beta t + \varepsilon \qquad (3.5)$$

The popularity of this approach may be partially ascribed to its analytical convenience, yet the same arguments against the use of the logistic function in the first place, namely the stringent assumptions regarding the stability of β over time and the unimodal distribution of the propensity to adopt[34)], apply with respect to reliance on the β-parameter as the sole indicator of the rate of adoption. In order to advance their own proposals for improved measures of diffusion speed, some authors have criticized the pervasive use of β for its apparent lack of "a clear-cut meaning that will have conceptual and descriptive appeal"[35)]. This, however, seems to be an unnecessarily negative view since it can be shown that β is the reciprocal of the Gini measure which "represents the expected time difference between any two adoptions over the whole diffusion process"[36)]. Thus,

---

32) When based on equation (3.3.) the following equivalent result obtains:
$ln[(1 - f_t) / f_t] = ln(a) - \beta t$

33) This type of regression analysis of the logistic function is fairly typical and has even been applied to administrative innovations; cf. e.g. Teece (1980). It should be noted, however, that due to the *ex ante* logarithmic transformation of the empirical data, those parameter estimates merely represent approximations since they presuppose multiplicative disturbance terms which seems not easy to justify on theoretical grounds; see e.g. Harvey (1990) p. 38 *et seq*. For this reason, non-linear curve fitting is generally preferable as will become evident in the empirical section of this text. Cf. also Knolmayer (1980) p. 260.

34) Cf. Davies (1979) p. 11 *et seq*.

35) Trajtenberg/Yitzhaki (1989) p. 37.

36) Trajtenberg/Yitzhaki (1989) p. 37 *et seq*. While the Gini seems to offer some advantages compared to other diffusion speed measures, it is quite intriguing that the authors, by proclaiming the superiority of the Gini and deriving such a simple relationship with the β-parameter of the logistic function, effectively invalidate their own semantics-based argument against the use of β.

both measures are just inversely related to each other. Based on the preceding discussion, the conclusion seems warranted that in many situations the consistent application of the selected measure (perhaps on different data sets) is probably more important than its actual choice.

According to the findings of the meta-research conducted by Rogers as well as Tornatzky and Klein[37)], the speed of the diffusion process or the rate of adoption associated with an innovation is determined by *subjective perceptions* on the part of decision makers regarding five, respectively ten generic attributes of the innovation. Rogers identifies the following characteristics[38)]:

(1) Relative advantage, defined as "the degree to which an innovation is perceived as being better than the idea it supersedes", is presumed to be positively related to diffusion speed.

(2) Compatibility, defined as "the degree to which an innovation is perceived as consistent with the existing values, past experiences, and needs of potential adopters", is presumed to be positively related to diffusion speed.

(3) Complexity, defined as "the degree to which an innovation is perceived as relatively difficult to understand and use", is presumed to be negatively related to diffusion speed.

(4) Trialability, defined as "the degree to which an innovation may be experimented with on a limited basis", is presumed to be positively related to diffusion speed.

(5) Observability, defined as "the degree to which the results of an innovation are visible to others", is presumed to be positively related to diffusion speed.

Tornatzky and Klein add the categories *cost, communicability, divisibility, profitability*, and *social approval.* The value of those supplemental criteria remains suspect, however, since the disadvantage of such a large set of attributes evidently arises from semantic similarities between the various dimensions. For instance, a difference between the definitions of trialability and divisibility ("extent to which an innovation can be tried on a small scale prior to adoption") is barely recognizable[39)]. Moreover, there is inconclusive evidence concerning the predictive power of the explanatory variables mentioned. While Rogers reports that the five variables extracted for the conventional model ac-

37) Cf. Rogers (1983), Tornatzky/Klein (1981).

38) Cf. Rogers (1983) p. 210 *et seqq.*

39) Cf. the references given in Tornatzky/Klein (1981) p. 37. To be sure, the innovation attributes mentioned suffer from many deficiencies. A case in point is their "unenlightening" superficiality; Gold (1981) p. 257. This applies in particular to the relative advantage criterion which is frequently regarded as a "garbage can" variable into which ultimately any presumed explanatory diffusion characteristic can be dumped; cf. Tornatzky/Klein (1981) p. 34.

count for an impressive 49 to 87% of the variance found in empirical studies on adoption rates[40], the meta-research by Tornatzky and Klein revealed that only three of the ten variables displayed a statistically significant or near-significant relationship with the diffusion rate (judged on a 5% rejection level): The attributes *compatibility* and *relative advantage* were found to be positively related to the diffusion rate and the characteristic *complexity* was negatively so[41] which is consistent with predictions. In light of those results, it would seem advisable to keep diffusion models as parsimonious as possible, and empirical studies, that tentatively gather data on tens of different variables that are *a priori* presumed to exert some influence on diffusion speed, should capitalize on available data reduction techniques (e.g. factor analysis) to condense the voluminous inventory of variables into fewer underlying constructs whenever feasible.

Besides characteristics pertaining to the innovation itself, other sources of adoption rate variance have been proposed, namely, organizational and environmental attributes such as the size of the organization, its willingness to absorb risks, the degree of competition in the industry, the activities of change agencies, type and extent of authoritative intervention, etc.[42]

Finally, it is important to emphasize again the inherent *subjectivity* of the generic factors that has been deliberately designed into the implied causal relationships. Adoption decisions are generally taken by management which constantly evaluates alternative investment options that compete for scarce resources. Therefore, managerial perceptions (expectations) about the relative attractiveness of those options - on the basis of the organization's specific internal and external situation, its objectives and strategy - govern the outcome of the decision processes, which has considerable ramifications for practical research. In lieu of e.g. pursuing the hopeless objective of trying to estimate the implementation-specific, *actual* value of technological innovations, researchers, endowed with a naturally transient interest in the subject matter, should rather strive to elicit the more accurate perceptions of the adopters themselves (supposedly specialists in their field) regarding the extent of the benefits conveyed[43].

---

40) Rogers (1983) p. 232.

41) Tornatzky/Klein (1981) p. 40.

42) See e.g. the competitive behavior paradigm in Robertson/Gatignon (1986) p. 2. Cf. further Brown (1981) p. 158, Gold (1981) p. 255.

43) Cf. Gold (1981) p. 265. The author apparently deemed it necessary to comment on dissenting opinions: "In view of the endless disagreements among R & D, Engineering, Production, Marketing and other groups in taking credit for favorable firm performance and disavowing blame for any unfavorable results, one cannot but be astonished at the naïveté of claims to measuring the specific proportion of profits attributable to innovations which usually affect only narrow segments of total

3.2.1.4. The Implementation Aspect of Diffusion

It was argued before that particularly for technological innovations with *tool character*, where the innovation is not an end *per se* but rather a means to achieve some objective, dichotomous adopt vs. non-adopt decisions do not adequately reflect the full complexity of the diffusion process[44]. Due to a fair amount of customization (re-invention) associated with tool technologies, e.g. the installation of software on a PC according to the user's idiosyncratic needs, basic adoption data must be augmented and enriched by information concerning the site-specific implementation of the technology, e.g. the extent and purpose of its utilization.

Prima facie such a statement seems unobjectionnable if not trivial. Nonetheless, it is probably easier said than done. The major obstacle that needs to be overcome is to devise generally applicable measures for the empirical construct 'implementation' which would allow comparisons across industries and other types of adopter groups or even between different innovations. One possibility would be to differentiate between (a) the functional scope of innovations, indicating the number of distinct usages to which the technology can be applied, and (b) the maximum potential degree of utilization in each usage category. With those two yardsticks it would subsequently be feasible to develop implementation profiles, e.g. in terms of the proportion or number of usage categories actually employed and the percentage of maximum utilization achieved per category. The evolution of those profiles over time could then be subjected to further diffusion-type analysis[45].

3.2.2. Diffusion of Innovations with Significant Network Externalities

The property of conferring network externalities that distinguishes some technologies/concepts from others has direct implications for their diffusion which is usually described by the notion of a "critical mass"[46]. The analogy with nuclear fission does

---

firm operations within a setting involving many other concurrent changes." Gold (1981) p. 261. See also Sutton (1980) p. 192 *et seq.*

44) See e.g. Rogers (1986) p. 121 *et seq.*

45) A fairly similar idea is e.g. formulated in Tornatzky/Klein (1982) p. 42.

46) Rohlfs (1974) p. 18, Oren/Smith (1981), Oliver/Marwell (1985), Rogers (1986) p. 120, Markus (1987), Allen (1988). The term "critical mass" has apparently been taken from nuclear physics where it specifies a minimum amount of radioactive material necessary to sustain a chain reaction; cf. e.g. Lindner (1973) pp. 232 - 238.

have some appeal, yet the chain reaction ensuing from a *social critical mass* - defined as "a small segment of the population that chooses to make big contributions to the collective action while the majority do little or nothing"[47] - differs substantially from its nuclear twin in complexity and refers to the possible incapacity of a group of perfectly rational individuals to initiate action in order to further the collective welfare (the "common interest") of the group[48]. While other sources of network externalities have been mentioned in section 3.1., the critical mass effect is usually illustrated with the example of a telecommunications service or network, because establishing a network, whose inherent purpose is to provide universal access to the members of some community, can be viewed as similar to the provision of a public good[49].

Given the assumption of significant network externalities, a "start-up problem"[50] arises at the zero diffusion point as the utility for the initial subscriber is *nil*, unless group members somehow coordinate their actions (e.g. because of coercion by some authority), or one member of the community alone is sufficiently interested in providing the entire public good (in this case the telecommunication service) all by himself which *ex definitione* cannot be withheld from any member of the community[51]. Without collective action or a single provider, the success of the service hinges on three factors: (1) The shape of the service production function, (2) heterogeneity of interest in providing the service and disposable resources[52], and (3) expections of group members regarding the behavior of their colleagues[53].

In contrast to the sequential interdependence of conventional innovation adoption decisions, where individuals base their actions primarily (if not exclusively) on the observed experiences made by previous adopters, adoption decisions concerning innovations with network externalities are subject to reciprocal interdependence[54] which directly leads to the *critical mass effect*: Some members of the community 'join' (establish) the net-

---

47) Oliver/Marwell/Teixeira (1985) p. 524.

48) This intriguing proposition was first forcefully suggested by Olson Jr. (1965), see especially pp. 9 - 16.

49) Cf. Artle/Averous (1973).

50) Rohlfs (1974) p. 18.

51) Free-rider problem, or, in the terminology of Olson Jr. (1965) p. 29, the "exploitation of the great by the small".

52) Intuitively, a positive correlation between both would be conducive to the success of the service; cf. Oliver/Marwell/Teixeira (1985) p. 530.

53) See Oliver/Marwell/Teixeira (1985) and Allen (1987).

54) Cf. Thompson (1967) cited in Markus (1987).

work initially at a loss[55] in the expectation that their contribution will increase the utility provided by the service to induce marginal non-users to follow suit which in turn increases the utility of the network again and the process continues until some equilibrium state is reached (e.g. universal access, i.e. full interconnection). If this strategy is successful, the *initial subscriber set* is said to constitute a critical mass. If, on the other hand, non-users do not reciprocate because their utility threshold levels are too high, the pioneers will eventually discontinue their tentative efforts, in which case the attempt to establish the service fails, even if the welfare of the community suffers[56]. For the purpose of the empirical analysis presented in the next chapter it is important to note that, given the assumption of normally distributed threshold values, it can be shown that the service will succeed and the resulting diffusion pattern is the familiar sigmoidal-curve, very similar to the diffusion of conventional innovations[57].

In recognition of the difficulties encountered when launching a new telecommunications service from scratch, various strategies have been devised to surmount the start-up problem. Much of the literature on the diffusion of new interactive media focusses on determining the appropriate pricing strategy in order to reach critical mass[58]. Most schemes involve *temporal price-discrimination*, i.e. either zero or heavily discounted prices during the launch of the service hoping that, as soon as the bandwagon effect emerges, the endemic start-up losses can be recovered later which leads to a *prima facie*

---

55) This implies that the initial user-set is not viable which means that it cannot be profitably served. Cf. Rohlfs (1974) p. 18.

56) A special case of the prisoners' dilemma; cf. e.g. Owen (1968) p. 139.

57) Cf. Gurbaxani (1990) p. 66. However, the author refuses to assume the *onus probandi*, quoting instead a pre-announced publication by Rogers. Even without the benefit of that analysis, the asserted diffusion pattern must be based on certain assumptions concerning the shape of the production function. Without further elaboration: It is straightforward to see that the boundary condition for achieving universal access requires that if one superimposes the curves of production and cumulative threshold distribution function in the same diagram, beyond critical mass, the former must always be greater than the latter. Cf. in this respect also the dynamic model described in Cabral (1990) where it is shown that network externalities can lead to discontinuous diffusion patterns. According to the analysis presented, diffusion may initially remain (close to) zero, unchanged by the contributions of early adopters. As soon as some critical point has been reached, the model predicts an instantaneous (quantum leap type) upward adjustment in the number of adopters. The derived discontinuous equilibrium adoption path may, however, be approximated by a steep S-curve since the middle section of the graph is quasi-concave. A similar proposition is provided in Williams/Rice/Rogers (1988) p. 73 who also analyze the implications of network externalities for diffusion theory and compare two diffusion curves in a conceptual diagram. The curve which represents the diffusion of an interactive communications technology exhibits a steeper ascent in its middle section than the curve depicting the diffusion of a conventional innovation. Yet both curves follow a sigmoidal pattern. Thus, with all due caution, there seems to be some theoretical basis on which to ground the assumption of S-shaped diffusion patterns which has been so frequently claimed in empirical studies.

58) Cf. Rohlfs (1974), Oren/Smith (1981, 1982).

bizarre shape of the demand curve[59]. Apart from this form of subsidy and besides the obvious strategy of *coercion* (e.g. government intervention) mentioned before, another possibility put forth in the literature refers to the provision of a *failure insurance* that reimburses early adopters for their initial investments in case the establishment of the service does not succeed. While the concept may be difficult to operationalize due to intractable measurement problems, the idea must be deemed (at least conceptually) ingenious: Due to the complete elimination of adoption risk, "many agents adopt, so there are never any insurance claims, and the insurance is costless to provide"[60].

To summarize, the property of network externalities which is particularly strong with respect to telecommunication services can pose significant problems during the start-up phase. Without coordination, rational decision making on the part of individual group members may well lead to suboptimal outcomes on the community level. To overcome the initial inertia, various strategies of intervention, involving direct and indirect subsidies, have been proposed.

3.3. Implications for the Diffusion of EDI

It was shown in section 2.4.2.1. that organizations which intend to implement EDI systems incur comparatively high costs in terms of converter software and systems development/maintenance. As a communications technology, EDI is subject to network externalities and if network effects were indeed strong, the start-up problem could pose substantial difficulties. While the "embryonic"[61] state of the overall EDI penetration level has already been commented on, the very existence of EDI suggests that either the network externalities may not be as severe as conceivable or, alternatively, certain

59) As shown in the synopsis presented by Allen (1988), with network externalities, the conventional macroeconomic analysis of a static supply and demand equilibrium no longer applies and must be replaced by a framework containing the 'heretic' assumption of an (at least within a certain range) upward sloping demand curve. While this may look strange, it is nonetheless logical since the principal idea of prices is to reflect value which is low during start-up and soars with diffusion. The importance of universal access of interactive media is further emphasized and elaborated in Markus (1987) who proposes that with interactive media there are only two equilibrium states in a community of users: "all or nothing"; Markus (1987) p. 500. Markus' Proposition 1 is, however, subject to debate. The outcome of the diffusion chain reaction again depends on the distribution of individual threshold values and the production function; see *supra* note 53. The empirical evidence presented in support of the proposition is scant ("meager") by his own admission and hinges very much on the definition of what constitutes the relevant community. The reasoning presented almost seems to suggest the tautological solution whereby the relevant community of users is defined as that group of individuals that eventually adopt, an obviously trivial definition which presupposes the desired result of universal adoption.

60) Dybvig/Spatt (1983) p. 232. Those and alternative means to overcome the start-up problem, such as the manipulation of consumer expectations, are discussed in Wiese (1990) p. 47 *et seqq*.

61) Joyce (1989) p. 65.

mechanisms are effective that mitigate the extent of the start-up problems. As it turns out, both reasons apply simultaneously.

The first thing to note is the fact that studying the overall diffusion of EDI does not constitute the appropriate level of analysis. As has been pointed out[62], the (for ease of analytical treatment) often made assumption of a "uniform calling pattern", which postulates that current users experience a utility gain anytime an arbitrary non-user joins the network, implying that externalities are derived independently of the identity of network members, seems hardly realistic for most telecommunication services. Since EDI was conceived to automate repetitive inter-organizational transactions between longtime business partners rather than for occasional use between more or less alien organizations, the uniform-calling-pattern assumption must be considered especially invalid in the case of Electronic Data Interchange. It appears more congruent with actual EDI implementations in practice to postulate the existence of *special interest communities* (e.g. trade groups) where the majority of transactions are executed *within* as opposed to *between* communities. Moreover, most of the community members will "typically have a few principal contacts who alone account for a substantial part of their communication"[63]. This seemingly innocuous change of the previous situation, which was characterized by the member identity-independence with respect to externality effects, has far reaching implications:

- Network effects are restricted to the interior of the community. Since members derive no incremental utility from community-external organizations which make use of EDI, overall (*macro-level*) diffusion of EDI is by and large irrelevant and can therefore be disregarded by decision makers. What matters instead is the diffusion of EDI *within* the community (henceforth referred to as *micro-level* diffusion) where externalities are particularly strong[64].

---

62) Cf. Rohlfs (1974) p. 18.

63) Cf. Rohlfs (1974) p. 18.

64) It should be noted that acknowledgement of the importance of micro-level diffusion as opposed to overall diffusion represents an essential cornerstone of this thesis. Without this premise there would neither be any hope in gathering a pool of meaningful empirical data nor would the findings be overly relevant anymore for decision makers, at least not with respect to the case of EDI. The problem of (for policy purposes) outdated results is obviously an inherent property of any diffusion study. See e.g. Trajtenberg/Ytzhaki (1989) p. 39.

- The comparatively small size of the relevant group facilitates the coordination problems required for any form of collective action considerably[65]. The early development of proprietary and sector-specific EDI standards, described briefly in section 2.5.1., is not only consistent with this assumption but also supports the previous idea that attention should be directed towards the diffusion of EDI within communities of interest rather than on the macro-level[66]. The existence of so called "self-sufficient user sets"[67], which are characterized by an intensive flow of messages between a small number of interacting agents that renders the use of EDI viable, permits a much more gradual macro-level expansion because organizations do not have to adopt virtually at the same time but can do so in a (batch-) sequential fashion.

Secondly, notwithstanding the necessity of closing bilateral agreements between trading partners, to define the standard subsets to be used, to stipulate the legal terms of the EDI relationship, etc., EDI remains essentially a set of communications standards which can be considered a public good that has already been provided, reducing in effect the size of the contribution required by prospective EDI users[68].

---

65) To reiterate the arguments put forth by Olson Jr. (1965), in virtually all cases large groups will be at a disadvantage compared to small groups when it comes to initiating collective action, due to the coordination problems and the rational presumption of group members that their individual contribution will have no palpable effect on achieving the objectives pursued by the group as a whole. By applying his analysis to an example from industrial economics, Olson is able to show that while large groups will frequently fail entirely to provide themselves with a desired public good, small groups tend to produce only a suboptimal amount, if any at all.

66) While small group sizes are advantageous in the context of the start-up problem, the co-existence of various EDI standards also creates inefficiences for those organizations that belong to several communities, due to the burdens associated with supporting redundant standard sets. This raises the (for practical and theoretical reasons) interesting problem faced by EDI user communities of whether and when to migrate from proprietary to public standards. As mentioned in a previous section, standards *per se* can be regarded as a source of externalities and thus the benefits accruing from compatibility may prevent the changeover to a superior standard. The phenomenon of a group of agents being trapped into an obsolete standard unable to coordinate a joint transition has been called "excess inertia"; Farrell/Saloner (1985) p. 71. By means of a game theoretic approach the authors demonstrate that innovation success (i.e. migration to the new standard) is determined by agents' unanimity of preferences and completeness of information. See also Cullen/DeFraigne (1990) pp. 538 - 540, Picot/Neuburger/Niggl (1991). It would merit an investigation of its own to find out, to what extent the problem of excess inertia applies to EDI communities and how it is being resolved. The current literature on the subject is rather scarce and epitomized by statements such as the following: "If eventually there are good business reasons to merge domestic EDI standards with international EDI standards then business will decide to do so." Warner (1989) p. 131.

67) Rohlfs (1974) p. 31.

68) Adoption of standards, which in effect signals trading partners the readiness to conduct EDI, is another form of providing a public good since it yields externalities; cf. Dybvig/Spatt (1983) p. 232.

Thirdly, the conventional assumption of independent decision making by rational agents is hardly commensurate with the realities of the business environment. As the success of the so called "hub" or "honeypot" marketing strategies of VANS indicates[69)], under *oligopolistic* or, in the extreme case, *monopsonistic* demand conditions, purchasers are able to influence the behavior of their suppliers either by outright coercion[70)] or by subsidies that can take a variety of forms including side-payments, assumption of systems development costs, etc.

To summarize, the preceding discussion has argued that while there are significant network effects associated with EDI, the macro-level diffusion process is not inordinately hampered by the usual start-up obstacles due to a variety of factors that diminish the extent of the inherent coordination problems. Most importantly, the critical mass effect is relevant only *within* a community of interest group, which is why research efforts should focus on the intra-community (micro-level) diffusion of EDI. Moreover, the success of EDI does not depend solely on finding a solution to the critical mass problem[71)]. The decision to adopt, the specific form of implementation (i.e. the systems design), and the rate of diffusion among business organizations will also be contingent on the perceived attractiveness of EDI with respect to a number of core attributes, which is determined by the interaction between functional properties and intra-organizational circumstances. Finally, the fact must not be neglected that organizations are inherently open systems, i.e they do not operate in isolation[72)]. Organizations are embedded in a sociotechnical environment which on the one hand creates opportunities for the pursuit of business and other objectives but, *per contra*, also imposes restrictions on the number and types of choices for action available to decision makers. Thus, characteristics of the supersystem, such as e.g. the availability of standards, will likewise have an influential bearing on the diffusion of technological innovations such as EDI.

3.4. EDI Diffusion Reseach Framework

The identification and analysis of factors that are presumed to exert influence on the diffusion of EDI in the preceding section allows integration of those findings into a re-

---

69) Cf. e.g. Sanders (1988) p. 120.

70) In most cases this means the thinly veiled threat to loose supplier status if compliance is refused. Cf. also the well-known competition analysis framework of industrial economics by Porter (1980) p. 3 *et seqq.*, especially pp. 24 - 26.

71) See also Allen (1988) p. 258.

72) See e.g. Grochla (1971) p. 563.

search framework which models the hypothesized causal relationships between the micro-level diffusion of EDI and composite determinants in a comprehensive, yet not necessarily exhaustive way. The research framework depicted in Exhibit 3-2 may be regarded as a specialization of more generic causal diffusion models proposed elsewhere[73]. It is deliberately restricted to describe the diffusion of Electronic Data Interchange as perceived within the context of this study and simply serves as a map to guide the empirical research presented in the next chapter, for instance by allowing to deduce hypotheses that can be subjected to empirical testing.

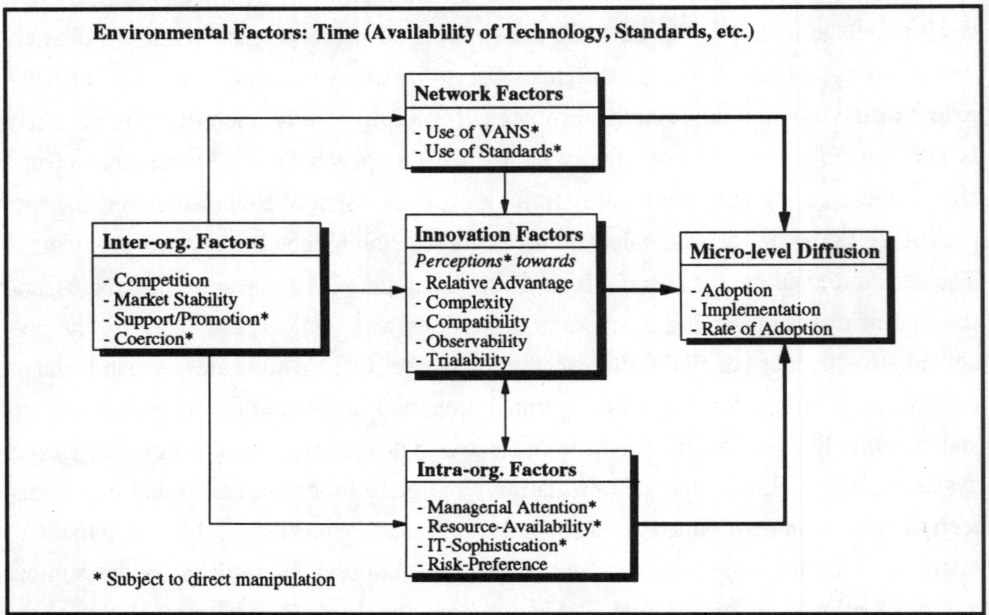

Exhibit 3-2 Research Framework for the Adoption/Diffusion of EDI

The normative framework consists of five major elements, one dependent and four independent or exogenous modules. Arrows indicate the direction of the hypothesized effects and convey an idea of the relative strengths (ordinal scale); for reasons of parsimony, feedback loops have been intentionally suppressed. Variables which are be-

73) To name only a few of many, see e.g. Rogers (1983) p. 233, Gatignon/Robertson (1985) p. 850, and Robertson/Gatignon (1986) p. 2. Those diffusion models have frequently been introduced with the label "paradigm" perhaps to underscore their importance, and it seems as if a consensus has emerged that the framework described by Rogers deserves of this title. While an increasing number of paradigms may be indicative of the rapid progress achieved in a given branch of science, there may also be less awe-inspiring interpretations for this phenomenon. There is no intention to suggest any generality at all of the research framework advanced here (even if the model would, with only minor modifications, turn out to be applicable to other network technologies).

lieved to be (within bounds) subject to direct manipulation by organization-internal or -external agents are marked with an asterisk.

The dependent module contains those three variables that were previously singled out as proxy measures for the micro-level diffusion of EDI: *Adoption* measures whether an organization implements EDI systems and signals its willingness to business partners to exchange data electronically. *Implementation* refers to the site-specific way how EDI is utilized. Surrogate indicators may include *inter alia* the types of messages used, the choice of hardware-platform, the degree of integration with other internal systems, the contents of interchange agreements, and the establishment and integration of organizational EDI subunits. *Rate of adoption* summarizes the dynamic development of the number of EDI relationships between an organization and its business partners.

The other four modules represent factors which either directly or indirectly affect the dependent variables just described. Firstly, there are those parameters that have direct implications for the size of the potential set of communication partners and thus yield network externalities. By choice of a communications network and a syntax standard, an organization at least in principle gains access to all other organizations on the same network or standard. At the same time it makes itself available for communication, thereby increasing the utility for other subscribers. Secondly, micro-level diffusion is partially determined by the already introduced innovation attributes pertaining to the extant diffusion paradigm. Thirdly, intra-organizational factors, such as the amount of attention decision makers in upper echelons of the organization's hierarchy devote to EDI, or the amount of risk the organization is willing to absorb in (tentatively) modifying sensitive business processes, are presumed to impact the diffusion of EDI. Falling into the same category are the experience and capability of the organization in utilizing IT for business purposes, as well as the availability of required resources, not only in terms of obtaining a budget but also with respect to personnel and cross-departmental authority[74)].

Part of the difficulty in explaining the diffusion of EDI stems from the non-hierarchical nature of the relationship between dependent and explanatory variables. It is therefore

74) This last point is generally regarded as an important prerequisite of any successful EDI project. As the data sent and received via EDI (e.g. procurement information) originate in and are processed by various departments, a fair amount of interdepartmental coordination and sharing of responsibility will be necessary to achieve a smooth migration from paper-based procedures; cf. Robinson/Stanton (1988) p. 125. Some thoughts on the management of EDI projects can be found e.g. in Monczka/Carter (1988), Payne (1989), Sokol (1989) p. 79 *et seqq.*, Emmelhainz (1990) p. 125 *et seqq.*, Petri (1990) p. 153 *et seqq.*

important to emphasize the diverse interdependencies between network, innovation, and intra-organizational factors. For example, many of the various services provided by VANS are designed to bridge the multidimensional incompatibility between any two EDI communication partners in a community of users with multilateral business relationships[75]. By establishing a buffer layer between systems, VANS are able to effectively reduce the complexity confronted by EDI users and mitigate vexing incompatibility problems. Thus, in addition to the direct impact mentioned before, there is an indirect linkage between VANS and micro-level diffusion of EDI via some of the innovation factors[76]. Similarly, the perceived attractiveness of EDI should be positively related to the amount of managerial attention devoted to it as well as the abundance of available resources. The arrow between innovation and intra-organizational factors is double-pointed, however, due to the existence of reverse effects. For example, experience in using IT can be expected to reduce the perceived complexity of EDI, and so on.

Finally, a number of inter-organizational antecedents can be important in determining the spread of EDI. However, the impact will mostly be indirect through the other three factors. The linkage between certain competition characteristics, e.g. the degree of price competition or the importance of responsiveness, and the relative attractiveness of EDI have been discussed before[77]. Moreover, diffusion will be mediated by structural characteristics of the industry. Circumstances such as those prevailing in the automotive sector, where a small number of influential multinational companies deal with thousands of marginal suppliers, are conducive to EDI since those large organizations can harness their economic leverage to enforce a rapid introduction of EDI systems. Besides coercion, diffusion of EDI can be stimulated by providing support to prospective communication partners. This support may come in various forms ranging from organizing EDI seminars, where the basic concepts and requirements of EDI are conveyed, over reimbursements for telecommunications costs incurred, through selling EDI converters at discounted prices, or even temporarily providing systems development resources.

---

75) Cf. the discussion in section 2.3.3.2.

76) Evidently, the indirect effect is not necessarily positive. VANS service charges may be high enough to more than offset any perceived gains in terms of complexity reduction and increased compatibility by diminishing the relative advantage attributed to EDI.

77) See section 2.4.

Promotional activities of industry associations[78] and public institutions[79] acting as change agents are also falling into the same category[80].

Last but not least it seems worth mentioning that the micro-level diffusion of EDI presumably depends also on a large number of inextricable environmental conditions which elude any attempt of quantitative measurement. However, in order to at least capture the dynamic changes of those conditions in the model, the variable *time of adoption* has been included as a crude surrogate measure. Obviously, time is devoid of any explanatory power and can only serve as a descriptive device. Nonetheless, it has some intiuitive appeal since the readiness of other agents to communicate via EDI should improve over time as a result e.g. of the growing sophistication in the use of IT or the availability of public standards and of low-cost converter software[81].

---

78) A case in point is the study by Arthur D. Little about the opportunities offered by EDI for the U.S. grocery industry conducted on behalf of the Grocery Industry Trade Association. See ADL (1980). See also Thomas/Steen (1987) p. 40.

79) Cf. the TEDIS program of the EC.

80) Cf. also Rogers (1983) p. 234.

81) For a similar viewpoint concerning the importance of including time in such a model, compare the organizational diffusion framework proposed in Robertson/Gatignon (1985) p. 2.

4. Empirical Investigation on Electronic Data Interchange

4.1. Project Overview

4.1.1. Introductory Remarks

One cannot help but feel a little bit discouraged when preparing a proposal for research in the midst of all the confusion and controversial debate about the current status and future viability of business informatics as a new ("young") scientific discipline[1]. This search of identity has been widely commented on in the MIS literature with equally widely divergent conclusions, pitting pro-positivists, calling for increased discipline and enrichment of the field by "substantive theories"[2] and paradigms, against advocates of a "pluralistic", multiple method, "free-for-all"[3] approach to research. Juxtaposing these well-known positions has so far failed to produce a consensus among researchers as to whether the field rightfully belongs to the engineering or the administrative disciplines

---

1) See e.g. Kaplan/Duchon (1988), Banville/Landry (1989), Seibt (1990), and Teng/Galletta (1990). The adjective 'young' is often advanced as an implicit excuse for the field's current level of immaturity when compared e.g. to physics. The suggested improvement in the future seems a little naïve. There has probably been more research effort expended on MIS over the last 20 years than in the first 200 years of active research in physics, ever since the beginning of Enlightenment, without any comparable progress in terms of the development and empirical (in)validation of theories. Due to the intrinsically fickle and idiosyncratic nature of its technology driven research objects, there is little hope that the science of MIS will ever reach the same precision and predictive power than the natural sciences. The question remains, however, whether this apparent weakness matters; as long as the research is directed towards socially important problems, slow progress in little incremental steps is better than nothing.

2) The "severe lack" of which has "hampered scientific progress in the field"; Farhoomand (1987) p. 55. See also e.g. Bariff/Ginzberg (1982).

3) Banville/Landry (1989) p. 58 *et seq*. This approach may also be tellingly labeled the 'anything goes' doctrine. Cf. further Kaplan/Duchon (1988) pp. 571 - 575, and e.g. Vogel/Wetherbe (1984) as one representative of the 'MIS taxonomy papers'.

of scientific endeavor[4)], let alone produced a solution to the vexing epistemological problems of the field.

The empirical investigation conducted in the framework of this study intends to take a neutral position in this ongoing debate. Rather, the study epitomizes a *pragmatic approach* to research in its quest to find an explanation for and possible solution to a problem of current practical relevance[5)]: Having clarified the meaning of some key expressions within the ever changing vocabulary of IT parlance, which, due to the rate of technological progress, is characterized by a rapid succession of new terms with often transient and partly overlapping semantic, the analysis thus far aspired (a) to present practicioners with a more comprehensive picture of the alternatives at their disposal in terms of the relevant action parameters for implementing EDI, and (b) to provide decision makers with a framework of the consequences to be expected. The objective of the research elaborated in this section was to corroborate at least some aspects of the proposed framework, which reduces the uncertainty involved and thereby facilitates the decision process. At the same time, gathering empirical data allows one to explore actual experiences and views of EDI user organizations on a larger scale than the ordinary single site case study, which promises to yield more profound insights towards the extent and relevance of problems and concerns encountered in practice than any theorizing or literature review could provide.

4.1.2. Research Objectives

The chain of arguments leading to the main research questions of this study and which provides a rationale for the need to collect empirical data is rather straightforward. The

4) In the context of distinguishing business administration from other scientific fields, Chmielewicz (1970) p. 30 *et seq.* identifies "die wirtschaftlichen Aspekte beliebiger Entscheidungen" as defining characteristics of the field. If one were to subscribe to this view, business informatics may be dichotomized into two branches one of which may *arguendo* be called 'information systems engineering' which - as an engineering discipline - would deal with the design, development, implementation, and maintenance of IS in terms of the arrangement of hardware components, the design of databases and software as well as with communication systems. The second branch, for the sake of argument called 'information systems management', will be part of administrative science and only deal with the management of organizational IT resources, assessing the business implications of information technology, and planning for its proper exploitation in the pursuit of economic goals. Up until other educational institutions (engineering schools or computer science/informatics departments) allocate the necessary resources, business administration may *nolens volens* have to temporarily fill the gap between supply and demand of systems personnel. However, as Seibt (1990) p. 9 admonishes, similar to other branches of administrative science, business informatics should *address* yet *not be dominated by* technological issues: "Das Primat der nichttechnischen Ziele steht aber immer dann in Gefahr verlorenzugehen, wenn die konstruktiven Aufgaben der Entwicklung und des Betriebs der Technologie-Anwendungssysteme zu stark verselbständigt...werden."

5) For pragmatism as a scientific objective in organizational research, see e.g. the remarks in Grochla (1976) p. 632.

original motivation to conduct a study on Electronic Data Interchange, besides the general reason of a conspicuous lack of research on telecommunications in the context of business informatics despite the importance attributed to this topic in practice[6], was to illuminate and try to resolve an apparent contradiction that arises from two assumptions and two observations:

Premise 1: Organizations with primarily economic purpose pursue a strategy of (long-term) profit-maximization.

Premise 2: The socio-technical prerequisites of EDI, such as standards, SW, HW, and a telecommunications infrastructure, are readily available[7].

Observation 1: As its advocates fervently argue, EDI offers adopters a range of business benefits with substantial direct and indirect impact on profitability.

Observation 2: Overall, EDI is currently not in widespread use.

Given both premises, the observations are obviously contradictory to each other. Two potential explanations are conceivable; either at least one of the observations or premises is plain wrong or, alternatively, validity is context-specific, i.e. depends on the circumstantial values of auxiliary (secondary) factors. Even though estimates and forecasts by market research organizatons about the diffusion levels of EDI in various geographical areas differ significantly in absolute terms[8], the validity of Observation 2 - extremely low overall penetration level of EDI - is not threatened by a dispute over a few percentage points. Similarly, it was shown in section 2.3. that the essential requirements of EDI, at least for its proprietary version, have been available to potential adopters in one way or another for several years. Therefore, non-adoption can *exceptis excipiendis* hardly be justified by pointing to alleged technical deficiencies. As it must be deemed a futile if not dangerous undertaking to argue with Premise 1[9], the only remaining candi-

---

6) A review of respective research efforts can be found e.g. in Adams/Lacity/Mullins (1990).

7) Given the discussion about the present state of the technological requirements of EDI in previous sections of this text, Premise 2 may have alternatively been called Observation 3.

8) Cf. the data presented in Table 2-2.

9) Disregarding problems introduced by agency relationships [cf. e.g. Jensen/Meckling (1976)], assumptions to the contrary would effectively invalidate the Fisher separation theorem which - in connection with the existence of (perfect) capital markets - provides the theoretical underpinning for the ability of individuals with non-congruent consumption preferences to pool resources in order to achieve common economic goals, a *conditio sine qua non* of professionally managed large-scale organizations; cf. e.g. Copeland/Weston (1983) p. 17 *et seqq.*

date for debate about its validity is Observation 1 which deserves careful scrutiny indeed, considering the fact that this observation merely summarizes the subjective views of EDI proponents whose ability for impartial assessment may be somewhat compromized by intrinsic role-specific precepts.

The plausibility of claims regarding the extent of pecuniary benefits associated with the introduction of EDI systems has already been evaluated in section 2.4. A sober reflection about the theoretical potential of EDI to lower operating costs and boost turnover due to improved customer service reveals that many claims regarding the advantageousness of EDI are dangerously exaggerated and appear to be the result of a confusion between EDI and organizational programs to improve efficiency. The merits of a theoretical assessment notwithstanding, pure theoretical treatment, for ease of mathematical analysis, frequently rests on simplifying assumptions that do not adequately take the complexity of decision situations encountered in practice into account. Recognition of the need for triangulation[10)] immediately leads to the *first* conclusion with respect to the research objectives of the empirical study:

- Objective 1: In order to gain a more comprehensive and accurate understanding of the advantages associated with EDI, it seems imperative to complement the literature review and the conceptual appraisal of the costs and benefits involved with empirical data obtained from a sufficiently large sample of user organizations.

In so doing, preference should be given to user perceptions rather than questionable attempts to quantify effects by objective measurement, primarily for two reasons: One, due to the partially intangible nature of the benefits provided, estimating those in monetary terms would most likely lead to highly unreliable data. Thus, nothing would be gained by striving for a largely fictitious precision. Two, even if reliable figures could be provided, adoption decision would still be based on users' (categorical) perceptions of those benefits[11)].

---

10) See the earlier citations in section 1. Cf. also the discussion in Cook/Campbell (1979) p. 59 *et seqq.*, and especially Jick (1979).

11) Cf. e.g. Sutton (1980) p. 192: "However, in all cases it is the potential user's estimate of benefit which is important, not a quasiobjective estimate made by the supplier, or even by an impartial observer....[Estimates] will depend upon the quality of the available information, which is usually sparse and sometimes contradictory."

Secondly, since EDI is subject to network externalities, the question arises, which measures can and should be taken in order to stimulate the diffusion process until the typical start-up problems vanish. Providing guidance for institutional intervention efforts requires the specification of a conceptual model which shows the causal linkages between diffusion and its endogenous determinants. Commensurate with this requirement, the initial idea of the research conducted here was to construct (specify) such a causal model by building upon relevant elements of innovation diffusion theory - properly modified for the presence of network externalities - and then try to identify the model by collecting empirical data on the measurement variables and using the LISREL approach[12)] to estimate respective path coefficients[13)]. Given the fully identified model, showing decision makers which of the endogenous variables to manipulate in order to achieve the largest possible intervention effect would become possible. Dividing path coefficients by the costs of antecedent variable manipulation would then allow one to determine the most cost efficient alternatives of action.

The research framework depicted in Exhibit 3-2 represents a sizeable step towards the development of a causal diffusion model; while it falls short of specifying in detail the full set of variables and their empirical indicators, further decomposition would not be too difficult to accomplish. Due to the ability of LISREL to model latent variables and cope with measurement errors of the variable indicators, its application seemed particularly appropriate in the context of this study where most of the variables defined in the research framework, such as *degree of competition*, *observability* or *managerial attention*, cannot be measured directly. However, since LISREL was not readily available, further refinement of the research framework into a fully-fledged causal model would have been to no avail. Instead, it was necessary to moderate the initial objectives and resort to the less sophisticated, conventional methods of hypothesis testing (e.g. t- and F-tests in the context of regression analysis or ANOVA) to explore the possibility of causal effects between dependent and independent variables, with the familiar detrimental consequence of having to analyze model components individually rather than simultaneously. Irrespective of the data analysis method chosen, however, the need to broaden the scope of the study, by collecting data on other potential determinants of the EDI diffusion process as well, is evident. Whether those factors are believed to affect diffu-

---

12) Cf. e.g. Jöreskog (1982). The LISREL approach is also explained e.g. in Förster et al. (1984).

13) Confirmatory application of LISREL as opposed to exploratory analyses where LISREL is being used to specify the causal model that provides the "best" fit with the data; cf. e.g Weede/Jagodzinski (1977), Jöreskog (1978). See further Homburg/Dobratz (1991).

sion directly or function as intervening variables that constrain the advantageousness of EDI could not be controlled for, but this may be of only secondary importance anyway.

- Objective 2: In addition to gathering data about the benefits of EDI, it appears necessary to further examine to what extent the concept's diffusion is influenced by supplemental factors that out of theoretical considerations are presumed to impact the diffusion process of EDI.

It is interesting to note that empirical data *ipso facto* can have a contributory effect on diffusion, as a result of reducing the uncertainty about the benefits of EDI confronted by potential adopters. Whether this change in perception results in a modified decision towards the adoption of EDI is dependent on given circumstances and the decision maker's risk attitude. If the individual is strongly risk-averse[14)], the advent of additional information may lower the perceived downside risk of an investment in EDI systems and may thus induce him to reverse a previously negative attitude towards EDI, *even if the additional information leads to a sharply reduced expected value of the benefits*[15)].

Finally, the occasion of a data gathering project offers the opportunity to elicit the perspectives of EDI users not only regarding the impediments to rapid diffusion and possible remedies but also with respect to a number of other important issues germane to EDI, such as which type of data communication services provided by intermediaries are considered most valuable, the proliferation of EDIFACT, future application areas of EDI, and the like[16)]. Thus, a third, "informative" research objective can be defined[17)]:

---

14) Empirical investigations have provided some indication that organizational reward systems are wittingly or unwittingly often designed so as to reinforce a conservative, i.e. risk-averse behavior by decision makers; see e.g. Kerr (1975).

15) This can be illustrated by means of an example: Suppose that prior to gaining access to the research information a decision maker anticipates only two possible outcomes if a decision is made to implement EDI: (1) There is a 20% chance that the benefit of EDI turns out to be a (present value) net loss of 20 currency units and (2) there is an 80% chance for a net gain of 100. Apparently, the expected benefit value E(B) is
$E(B) = .2 * (-20) + .8 * 100 = 76.$
After the above mentioned research information about EDI becomes available the decision maker's perceptions change such that he now expects a net gain of 10 with probability .4 and a gain of 50 with probability .6 . Thus, the expected benefit value becomes
$E(B) = .4 * 10 + .6 * 50 = 34.$
Now, even though the expected value of the benefit that may obtain in case EDI is adopted drops by more than 50% as a consequence of the additional information, the initial opposition to EDI may nonetheless be reversed if the decision maker's behavior is guided by the imperative to minimize his risk exposure to being responsible for a loss to the organization.

16) Cf. the remarks given in section 1.3. on the merits of a *formative evaluation* during the early stages of an innovation's life cycle where the innovation undergoes constant refinement (by trial-and-error) until the most suitable design has been determined; see further Williams/Rice/Rogers (1988) p. 117 *et seqq*.

17) Grochla (1976) p. 633. See also Grochla (1982) p. 70.

- Objective 3: The opportunity of gaining access to the experiences of knowledgeable practicioners in the course of the empirical investigation should be exploited to collect and analyze data about other aspects of EDI that are currently of considerable practical interest, although they may only be marginally related to the main subject of this research project.

To summarize, the apparent contradiction between the benefits attributed to EDI and its very limited degree of utilization in practice cannot be resolved without recourse to empirical data. After deriving a conceptual explanatory framework for the diffusion of EDI, the necessity of empirical confirmation arises regarding completeness of the overall model structure (holistic view), and with respect to dependency relationships between individual model components (partial views). The opportunity of a primary research study promises to yield important side-benefits beyond the elucidation of the diffusion question, in that first-hand data about other interesting aspects of EDI can be collected as well. Analysis and dissemination of study findings are valuable contributions of this research project not only for informative but also for practical reasons, because a concomitant reduction of the uncertainty confronting potential adopters may accelerate the pace of diffusion which would be beneficial due to the externality effects involved.

4.1.3. Research Hypotheses

This section itemizes the specific hypotheses that were chosen to be tested empirically. They have been organized into three different categories according to whether they relate to *business implications* of EDI (A), to *communication aspects* of EDI (B), or to the *adoption*, *implementation* or *diffusion* of EDI (C). Evidently, the hypotheses listed represent only a small subset of the universe of hypotheses that could be formulated concerning EDI. The primary selection criterion used was relevance with respect to the stated objectives of the research project[18]. Further information on various other aspects

18) Also applied were a number of normative filtering criteria that research hypotheses should observe in general, such as the derivability of empirical referents, simplicity, and predictive power; see e.g. Stone (1978) p. 20. Thus, for example, the question of whether organizations located in the U.S. or the U.K. began to use EDI earlier than their counterparts elsewhere may be the subject of (heated) dispute but is not explicitly mentioned as a test-hypothesis here due to the absence of future relevance. Exclusion, however, does not imply that no commentary can be given on this question in the description of the study's exploratory results. Furthermore, some care was exercised to avoid falling prey to the typical tendency of empirical research in administrative science in general and business informatics (MIS) in particular to formulate trivial hypotheses. That this laudable intention is frequently impossible to realize can be illustrated by the following example which cites a hypothesis proposed by a group of very experienced authors, who aspired to develop a normative framework of MIS research [Ives/Hamilton/Davis (1980) p. 923]: "The amount of vendor supplied support (external environment) will positively influence the time it takes to implement an information

of EDI can be obtained from the description of explorative study findings presented in sections 4.2. and 4.3.

For simplicity of understanding, only the Alternative Hypotheses, *Hypotheses*$_{[A]}$ (of which confirmation is desired), rather than the actually tested Null Hypotheses, *Hypotheses*$_{[0]}$ (of which refutation is desired), are being formulated; the *ceteris paribus* assumption always applies even though it has been deliberately suppressed in the proposition statements. Each hypothesis shown is accompanied by a brief rationale which was taken either from respective contentions in the literature or derived from the analysis or the research framework developed in the preceding chapter[19)]. A discussion of empirical referents chosen for those variables mentioned in the hypotheses which are not intuitively obvious is provided in section 4.1.4.2.

4.1.3.1. Hypotheses Relative to Business Implications of EDI

Hypothesis A1: The cost of systems implementation is negatively related to the lateness of adoption.

In addition to learning curve effects, the rationale behind this hypothesis relates to the assumption that the increasing stability of EDI standards over time fosters the development and commercial availability of standard EDI software packages which should be more cost effective than custom-tailored solutions.

Hypothesis A2: The perceived utility of EDI is positively related to transaction volume.

Economies of scale effect. This hypothesis is based on the idea that setting up EDI systems requires a certain amount of fixed cost investment. Thus, the more transactions are being conducted via EDI the lower the average costs per transaction.

Hypothesis A3: The use of EDI is perceived to have a significant positive impact on transaction costs.

---

system". It is not only subject to question whether the actual intention was not to say 'negatively influence' in terms of the implementation time lapse, but also the gain accruing from corroboration or refutation of this hypothesis seems minimal since only the direction of the effect is examined and, understandably so, not the extent, yet only the latter would be relevant in a practical decision situation. For a similar critique, see e.g. Martin (1987) p. 217 *et seq.*

19) See Exhibit 3-2.

It has been argued in section 2.4. that by virtue of standardizing and automating administrative tasks, the use of EDI displaces clerical labor.

Hypothesis A4: The use of EDI is *not* perceived to have a significant impact on lowering inventory levels.

The discussion of possible inventory effects of EDI in section 2.4.2.2.4. has shown that many such claims in the literature appear exaggerated and may be the product of a confusion with JIT programs. Therefore, in light of the theoretical considerations presented in the same section, it is hypothesized that EDI has only a negligible impact on stock levels.

Hypothesis A5: The use of EDI is perceived to have a positive impact on customer service.

Given the desire to leverage fixed investment costs and the complexities associated with the need to maintain parallel systems, the ability to offer customers the option to communicate via EDI may be perceived as a valuable service *per se*.

Hypothesis A6: The use of EDI is perceived to have a positive impact on customer responsiveness.

Instantaneous, low cost, and error-free communication is a prerequisite to support a customer's JIT program. Additionally, trading partners can be almost instantly provided with timely information regarding product availiability, prices, the status of shipments etc.

Hypothesis A7: The use of EDI is perceived to have a positive impact on internal control.

EDI enhances the ability of organizations to more quickly realize contingencies in the form of changing environmental conditions, such as a shift in demand patterns. Thus, improved operating transparency allows to better co-ordinate the various organizational activities with less need for slack buffer resources.

Hypothesis A8: The use of EDI is perceived as allowing organizations to avoid competitive disadvantage, irrespective of the lateness of adoption.

Inability to communicate via EDI may become a disadvantage in a market environment characterized increasingly by response competition. Therefore, adoption of EDI at least prevents a service deterioration vis-à-vis competitors.

Hypothesis A9: The use of EDI is perceived by early adopters as providing competitive advantage.

Early adopters may derive a competitive advantage from EDI by offering a unique customer service.

Hypothesis A10: The use of EDI is not perceived by late adopters as providing competitive advantage.

The competitive advantage mentioned in the preceding hypothesis will be short-lived due to the fact that competitors can easily acquire similar technological capabilities.

Hypothesis A11: The use of EDI is *not* perceived by adopters as increasing their dependence on certain suppliers.

It has been argued that EDI tends to lock an organization into business relationships with only a few EDI-capable suppliers[20]. However, the trend towards open standards based EDI should allay fears of increased switching costs which is why the opposite hypothesis was formulated.

Hypothesis A12: The adoption of EDI is expected to induce modifications of organizational processes.

Migration from a paper-based to an electronic exchange of transactions data should lead to a modification of some organizational processes due to the elimination of certain manual tasks such as data entry and reconciliation.

---

20) Cf. La Londe/Emmelhainz (1985) p. 7, Butler Cox (1987) p. 3. For the hazards associated with "transaction-specific" investments, see Williamson (1979).

Hypothesis A13: The adoption of EDI is *not* expected to induce modifications of organizational structures.

While the impact of EDI on processes appears plausible, any change in organizational structure due to EDI is difficult to foresee, despite frequent claims in the literature to the contrary.

4.1.3.2. Hypotheses Relative to Communication Aspects of EDI

Hypothesis B1: The perceived utility of VANS is positively related to the number of EDI communication partners.

It was shown in section 2.3.3.2. that the general service offered by VANS is to decouple (insulate) the systems of EDI trading partners. By virtue of establishing a flexible communications interface, VANS effectively shield subscribers from the many complexities of data communication, especially in a multi-lateral trading environment. Because without an intermediary, the number of interfaces required that must be developed, implemented, and maintained may increase quadratically with the number of communication partners, the benefits derived from VANS in terms of compatibility, independence, and transparency should be positively related to the micro-level diffusion of EDI[21).

Hypothesis B2: According to the perceptions of EDI user organizations, the services provided by VANS can be grouped into the three categories "Transmission Services", "Message Services", and "Auxiliary Services".

The various services provided by VANS have been categorized accordingly in section 2.3.3.2.

Hypothesis B3: VANS transmission services are considered more valuable by EDI user organizations than message or auxiliary services.

---

21) Cf. e.g. Schatz (1988) p. 62, Joyce (1989) p. 64, Sokol (1989) p. 62 *et seqq.*, Emmelhainz (1990) p. 108.

As EDI is still at a very early diffusion stage, with most organizations having but a few EDI trading partners, the conclusion seems warranted that VANS subscribers are more concerned with solving basic problems, such as being able to simply reach each other, rather than with gaining access to more sophisticated services like message syntax translation, etc.

Hypothesis B4: Organizations located in Continental Europe tend to expect a larger positive impact of X.400 on the diffusion of EDI than those located in North America and the U.K.

X.400 can be regarded as a substitute for the services provided by private VANS. Since VANS are more prevalent in the U.S. and the U.K., the need for X.400 based communication services for EDI communication appears particularly urgent in Continental Europe.

Hypothesis B5: Organizations located in Continental Europe tend to expect a larger positive impact of EDIFACT on the diffusion of EDI than those located in North America and the U.K.

The availability of open standards is one prerequisite for the rapid diffusion of EDI. Both the U.S. and the U.K. have had national EDI standards (ANSI X12 and TRADACOMS) for quite some time. Domestic standards are less important in Europe where more trade transactions are conducted across borders. Therefore, the advent of the international EDIFACT standards can be expected to have a more distinct positive impact on the diffusion of EDI in Europe than elsewhere.

4.1.3.3. Hypotheses Relative to Adoption, Implementation, and Diffusion of EDI

Hypothesis C1: The lateness of adoption is negatively related to the size of organizations.

The relative advantage of EDI is dependent on traffic volume. Large organizations with many trading partners and subsequently a large volume of inter-organizational transactions should therefore be more inclined to adopt EDI than SMEs. Moreover, they have superior financial resources at their disposal which makes it more easy for them to experiment with EDI.

Hypothesis C2: SMEs tend to adopt EDI reactively, i.e. as a result of some external stimulus rather than out of internal considerations.

It appears questionable whether the monetary benefits of EDI will exceed the costs of implementation for SMEs that are typically characterized by low transaction volumes. Therefore, SMEs can be expected to need some additional incentive before adoption of EDI is considered.

Hypothesis C3: The majority of SMEs does *not* conduct a benefit analysis before the adoption of EDI.

If such external incentives are being provided, the decision to adopt may be a foregone conclusion, in case of which a benefit analysis becomes more or less superfluous.

Hypothesis C4: The length of the implementation stage is negatively related to the time of adoption.

This hypothesis follows from learning curve effects when information about experiences of early EDI adopters is disseminated.

Hypothesis C5: The length of the implementation stage is negatively related to the perceived degree of responsiveness competition.

Since EDI tends to improve the responsiveness of organizations, implementation should be faster in those circumstances where responsiveness is a critical success factor.

Hypothesis C6: The length of the implementation stage is negatively related to the perceived degree of price competition.

Since EDI tends to reduce transaction costs, it should be more eagerly pursued in industries with commodity-type products where a low cost position is essential to remain competitive.

Hypothesis C7: The use of proprietary syntax standards leads to a shorter implementation stage than the use of public standards.

The implementation of proprietary standards permits organizations to limit development efforts to those elements actually needed in the specific EDI applications pursued. Public standards, by contrast, may require more extensive (i.e. time consuming) systems modification as a result of the need to also support irrelevant applications.

> <u>Hypothesis C8:</u> The perceived utility of EDI is positively related to the degree of integration with the organization's other IS-resources.

The hardware system chosen for EDI can be regarded as a surrogate indicator for the achieved degree of integration. Organizations using stand-alone PCs for EDI will experience less benefits with EDI than those using mainframes or front-end PCs.

> <u>Hypothesis C9:</u> The perceived utility of EDI is positively related to the number of EDI trading partners.

This hypothesis derives directly from the assumption of network externalities.

> <u>Hypothesis C10:</u> The perceived utility of EDI is positively related to the diffusion level reached.

This hypothesis derives directly from the assumption of network externalities.

> <u>Hypothesis C11:</u> Unresolved legal issues of EDI are *not* perceived as important barriers to the diffusion of EDI.

Contrary to claims about impediments to a rapid diffusion of EDI raised by the legal uncertainties associated with electronic contracting, the view projected earlier holds that EDI is only viable in situations characterized by well-established trade relationships between long-term business partners with a large amount of repetitive transactions. The risk of single transactions under those conditions must be considered minor and therefore, legal protection as to the enforceability of contracts seems less important.

> <u>Hypothesis C12:</u> The use of VANS leads to a higher diffusion rate than the use of direct links.

The insulation of systems provided by a VANS intermediary should significantly facilitate the process of establishing new EDI trading relationships.

Hypothesis C13: The use of proprietary standards leads to a lower diffusion rate than the use of public standards.

If public standards are used, expanding the number of EDI trading relationships should succeed almost effortlessly since no major system modifications will be required. By contrast, even in cases where one organization can force trading partners to accommodate its proprietary standards, diffusion will be slow as a result of redundant development efforts.

4.1.4. Research Design

4.1.4.1. Research Methodology

There are generally six empirical research strategies among which to choose when striving to pursue the objectives of this study, and specifically to test the above hypotheses. Ranked in order of their potential to infer causality, those strategies have been referred to as *Laboratory Experiment*, *Simulation*, *Field Experiment*, *Field Study*, *Sample Survey*, and *Case Study*[22]. After ruling out the first three methodologies for obvious reasons, a decision had to be made with respect to the remaining alternatives. The lamentable state of empirical research on EDI, which has been commented on earlier, led to the exclusion of the *case study* approach from further consideration due to the low (non-existent) external validity of this strategy, leaving only *field study* and *sample survey* as viable options.

Given the *desideratum* of generalizability on the one hand, and the typically "listless" way by which respondents fill out mail questionnaires on the other[23], a sample survey based on personal interviews appeared to be the most promising research approach[24]. Unfortunately, the small number and geographical dispersion of EDI user organizations,

---

22) Cf. here and in the following: Stone (1978) p. 116 *et seqq.*

23) Cf. e.g. Selig (1986) p. 14.

24) Advantages and disadvantages of the various research and data collection methodologies have themselves been the subject of intensive examination for more than three decades by now; see e.g. Kahn/Cannell (1957). It is neither possible nor necessary to provide an exhaustive or even superficial literature review of this topic here. Suffice it to say that the bulk of the arguments put forth in this section relies heavily on the comparison of empirical research strategies in chapter 7 of Stone (1978), and there particularly on Table 7-1.

especially in Europe[25)], in conjunction with the project's resource constraints prevented implementation of this strategy. As a consequence, a combination between a preliminary, interview-based field study and a large-sample mail survey was considered the most appropriate among the feasible alternatives to reduce some of the many threats to the internal and external validity of the conclusions derived from analyzing the empirical data[26)]. The entire research process is summarized in Exhibit 4-1.

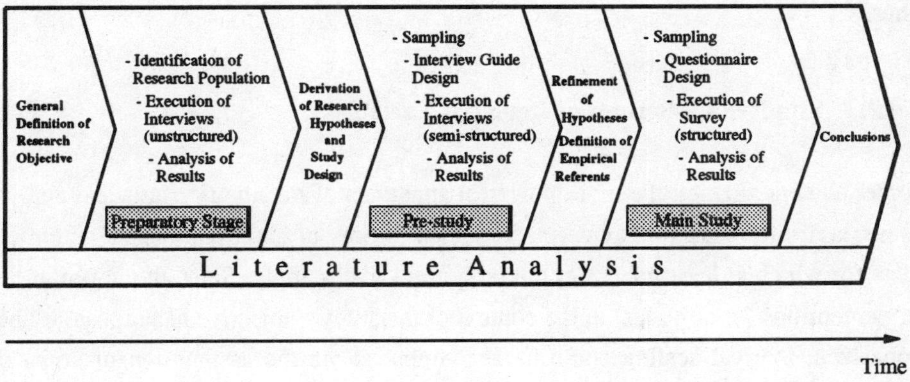

Exhibit 4-1 Stage-Model of the Research Process

As can be seen, the process is separated into three main stages and entails a continuous narrowing of the investigation's focus. After digesting available literature on EDI, a proposal for research outlining the main research objectives and the overall research strategy was prepared and submitted to various institutions in order to obtain the necessary funding. In the preparatory stage of the research, the sampling population (i.e. current EDI user organizations) was determined, addresses were obtained, contacts with personnel responsible for EDI established, and a first round of unstructured user interviews was conducted in order to gain a more profound practical familiarity with the subject matter. The information gathered during this initial investigation allowed to finalize the study design and derive a number of tentative research hypotheses.

The second phase of the project is comprised of the preliminary field study in the course of which some 30 user organizations and EDI service suppliers were personally visited

25) Refer to section 2.5.2.

26) A thorough treatment of the various threats to external and internal validity can be found in Cook/Campbell (1979) p. 37 *et seqq.*

and interviewed. The main objective of the semi-structured interviews was to prepare the sample survey in the next stage by assessing the quality of the working hypotheses and developing empirical referents for the research variables. An interview guide was used as the main data gathering device during the pre-study.

Finally, after designing and pre-testing the questionnaire, the mail survey was administered. Responses received were visually inspected for useability and entered into a database for the purpose of descriptive statistical analysis and evaluation of the research hypotheses.

4.1.4.2. Empirical Referents of Research Variables

In order to capitalize on the more powerful apparatus of parametric statistical analysis, it is necessary to operationally define variables by way of empirical measurement constructs for which at least interval, preferably ratio scales apply. Since the importance of user perceptions (or attitudes) in the context of the study's objective has repeatedly been emphasized, interval scaling could be accomplished via the assumption of equal distances between adjacent points along a semantic scale or by means of 7-point Likert-type scales which measure the respondent's degree of accord/discord with an *a priori* defined attitude[27]. The questionnaire that was used as the sole measurement instrument during the sample survey heavily relies on such scales.

It was occasionally possible to obtain ratio-scale data, e.g. when determining the respondent organizations' annual turnover, the size of the EDI-staff within IS-departments, etc. However, constructing interval or ratio scales was not feasible in all cases. For instance, respondents were asked to provide information concerning the type of EDI syntax standards employed, which only yields nominal data.

Many of the research variables mentioned in the hypotheses formulated above are directly measurable and therefore need no further explanation; those which must be measured indirectly via empirical referents are discussed below. Additional information about variables used to classify participating organizations may be found in section 4.3.2.

---

27) An introduction to measurement and scaling for the purpose of empirical data collection is provided e.g. by Hammann/Erichson (1978) p. 135 *et seqq.*, Stone (1978) p. 35 *et seqq.*

a) 'Perceived Utility of EDI' (Hypotheses A2, C8, C9, C10)

It was already shown in section 2.4. that the benefits of EDI can be roughly classified according to the dichotomous categories *tangible* and *intangible*, each of which having its own sub-structure. Because the benefits and costs associated with an EDI implementation can be expected to vary considerably across organizations as a result of differences in scale, it was deemed necessary to develop a scale-independent measure as an indicator of the overall advantageousness of EDI, which lends itself as a basis of comparison for different adopters. A potential candidate measure would be the internal rate of return (IRR) of the EDI investment. Due to the quantification difficulties alluded to earlier, however, such data would neither be easy to come by nor be very reliable. In addition, respondents would not necessarily be willing to share that information even if anonymity of responses was guaranteed. For these reasons, a much cruder measurement device was defined:

> *The perceived utility of EDI is measured as the degree to which respondents believe that the tangible benefits of EDI outweigh the costs of implementation and use.*

Despite its lack of precision, the measure fulfills the aforementioned criterion of comparability across organizations and appears to have a reasonable amount of face validity as it leaves little room for misconception. Furthermore, reliability should be enhanced because of the deliberate restriction to *tangible* benefits which was intended to eliminate purely speculative considerations[28].

b) 'Perceived Utility of VANS' (Hypothesis B1)

The site-specific utility derived from VANS intermediaries intuitively depends on the extent to which the services provided are regarded as useful by subscribers. Various common services of VANS were described in detail in section 2.3.3.2. In order to illuminate their relative importance from a practical rather than theoretical perspective, respondents were asked in the questionnaire to evaluate each one of 16 such services individually on a Likert-scale. The utility provided overall may thus be defined as a composite index, i.e. for each observation a utility vector is derived which consists of the 16 measurements allowing multivariate comparisons. Alternatively, an aggregate utility

---

28) For the practical relevance of the chosen indicator, see also Litecky (1981).

index may be established which, according to some *a priori* defined rule, combines the 16 measurements into a single aggregate number which can subsequently serve as a basis for univariate comparison. In light of the specific hypothesis to be tested, choosing the second approach seemed more appropriate. Consequentially:

> *The perceived utility of VANS is measured as the unweighted sum of the 16 individual attitude scores obtained regarding the relevance of services provided by VANS.*

For lack of any compelling rationale to use a more complex formula, each measurement arbitrarily receives a weight of 1 which leads to a zero-centered utility index ranging from a minimum of -48 through a maximum of +48.

c) 'Length of Implementation Stage' (Hypotheses C4, C5, C6, C7)

The introduction of EDI is usually conceived of as a step-by-step process that begins with an initial contemplation in the form of a cost/benefit analysis or a feasibility study and concludes with the gradual expansion of usage towards new trading partners and applications[29]. While this process can be described with much finer granularity[30], it suffices here to distinguish between four major stages[31].

After the feasibility of EDI was established in the *evaluation stage* and a decision to proceed with the implementation has been taken, the next phase, *development and installation*, begins in which the basic project organization is established, hard- and software are being evaluated and procured, interfaces to internal application systems are programmed, interchange agreements are worked out, etc. If all preparations have been successfully completed, EDI is tested with a select number of trading partners in trial mode, i.e. in tandem with conventional (paper-based) procedures, in order to demonstrate the feasibility of EDI and discover and rectify malfunctioning system components. At the end of the *pilot stage*, and after a status of sufficient stability has been reached, parallel paper procedures are gradually phased out and the EDI systems become fully operational.

---

29) Cf. e.g. Metcalf (1988), Gebker (1989).

30) See e.g. the sequence of implementation steps shown in Emmelhainz (1990) p. 127.

31) For coinciding views, see e.g. Monczka/Carter (1988) p. 3, Payne (1989) p. 16 *et seq.*

Since 'implementation' in the context of the above mentioned hypotheses refers to the period during which systems and procedures are established or undergo major revision prior to the beginning of the operational phase, it is meant here to consist only of development and installation stage as well as trial stage:

> *The length of the implementation stage is measured as the time lapse between the beginning of the development and installation stage and the end of the pilot stage.*

d) '(Micro-level) EDI Diffusion Rate' (Hypotheses C12, C13)

In order to draw meaningful conclusions from empirical data regarding the micro-level diffusion of EDI it is mandatory to devise a measurement construct that reasonably well summarizes the expansion of EDI utilization from the perspective of a single adopter. According to the conventional interpretation of diffusion[32)], the rate of the adoption process is an indicator of the speed by which an innovation spreads among the members of a social community. When applied to EDI, this rate concept would entail determining the growth in the number of EDI trading partners over time. However, this is only one of several (complementary) alternatives to describe the expansion of EDI. As was mentioned before, implementation, i.e. the extent and type of usage, is particular important in the context of tool-technologies such as EDI. Since it has been recognized in the literature that implementation measures "are likely to be idiosyncratic to the innovation(s) in question"[33)], the measure to be used should reflect the characteristic properties of EDI. EDI implementations may evolve over time not only in the number of communciation partners but also with respect to the transaction sets used, and the fraction of conventional transactions replaced by EDI. Thus, when taking implementation into account, four different alternative diffusion measures can be distinguished:

- Adoption of EDI by trading partners
- Number of different transaction sets used
- Proportion of transactions conducted via EDI
- Any combination of the above

---

32) See section 3.2.1.1.

33) Tornatzky/Klein (1982) p. 42. Cf. further the discussion in section 3.2.1.4.

After carefully examining the various choices, the decision was made to proceed with a derivative of the last option which measures the rate of diffusion in terms of the growth in the number of transactions exchanged via EDI per month *relative to an estimated saturation point.* Although respondents were asked in the questionnaire to provide detailed information about the number of EDI trading partners and monthly EDI transactions separated by message type, aggregating those data into a single univariate statistic rather than operating with several independent categories was regarded essential for analyzing the general impact of using standard interfaces on the rate of diffusion[34]. Given the historical data on the number of monthly transactions and estimates as to the respective figure in 1995, it is possible to calculate the relative usage in each year as a percentage of the saturation level[35]. This yields a set of data points which can be used to estimate the parameters of a diffusion function by applying a curve fitting procedure.

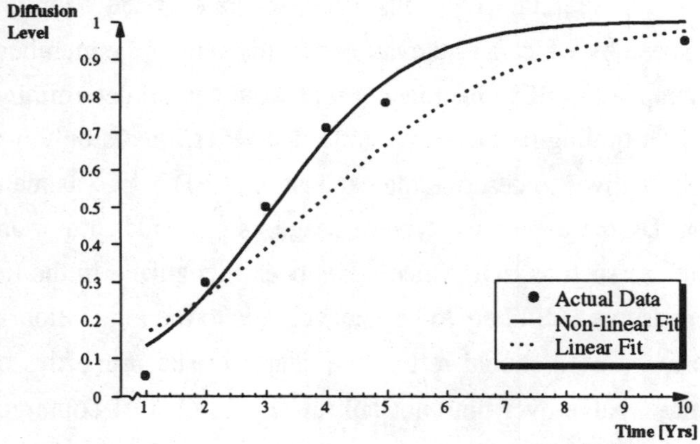

[Linear curve fitting was conducted after logarithmic transformation of the data.]

Fit Statistics:

Logistic Function: $F = \frac{1}{1 + ae^{-ßt}}$

	Linear	Non-linear
$\hat{a}$	8.85	16.20
$\hat{ß}$	.58	.89
R^2	.83	.99

Exhibit 4-2	Comparison of Linear and Non-linear Curve Fitting

34) Individual categories together constitute a profile whose evolution over time may be analyzed by multivariate statistical procedures. Besides such a longitudinal evaluation, the profiles obtained would also lend themselves to cross-sectional analysis. However, for testing the rather simplistic hypotheses C12 and C13, the use of multivariate statistics was considered unnecessary and less discriminative than the univariate approach. The superiority of document volume over the number of EDI trading partners is also suggested in Hansen/Hill (1989) p. 405.

35) One result of the interviews conducted in the course of the preliminary field study was that interviewees generally concurred in their assessment of approaching the point of saturation regarding EDI usage by the end of 1995. This information was assumed to be valid also for the respondents of the mail survey with the consequence that the 1995 transaction volume estimates were interpreted as representing a 95% usage level.

For reasons outlined in section 3.2.2., the diffusion process is assumed to follow a sigmoidal pattern modeled by a logistic function[36]. Exhibit 4-2 shows an example of such a curve fitting exercise with actual data obtained from one of the survey respondents.

Despite the popularity of the conventional two-step procedure of logarithmic transformation and linear regression[37], the example clearly demonstrates the superiority of a non-linear estimation technique[38]. In many cases, the coefficient of determination improves significantly when a non-linear estimation procedure is applied[39]. Since the β-parameter of the logistic function is responsible for the steepness of the diffusion curve, its estimate is being used as a surrogate indicator for the speed of the diffusion process[40]:

> *The micro-level diffusion rate is measured as the β-estimate of the logistic function obtained by means of a non-linear curve fitting procedure applied on the actual (past) and predicted (future) usage levels of EDI.*

4.1.4.3. Data Analysis Methods

The distribution parameters (e.g. mean, variance, standard deviation) used for presenting the empirical data were calculated on an IBM-PC with spreadsheet software such as LOTUS 1-2-3 and Microsoft EXCEL. Due to its large size of more than 25'000

---

36) Admittedly, the assumption of an underlying logistic model is rather arbitray and based on no specific *a priori* knowledge of the actual situation. While this approach may be criticized, the question remains whether other S-curve functions such as the Gompertz would improve the analysis significantly.

37) Cf. e.g. Sahal (1981); see further *formulae* (3.4) and (3.5).

38) As was pointed out in section 3.2.1.3., the linear regression in logarithmics yields only approximate parameter estimates which may differ considerably from the optimal values.

39) To be sure, either procedure can only be used when a minimum number of data points are available. Therefore, diffusion rates could only be determined for organizations that have been using EDI for several years. Two computational methods were applied when calculating the diffusion parameters of the sample organizations by the non-linear procedure: The multivariate secant method and, alternatively, the Marquardt formula when the secant failed to converge; for further details, see SAS Institute Inc. (1985b) p. 586.

40) *Nota bene*, the presumption of a 95% usage level in 1995 (see *supra* note 36) is critical for the outcome of the regression analysis since the value of the β-estimate *may* be sensitive to changes in this forecast. Sensitivity analyses with the empirical data revealed that in one case, the estimate varied from 0.572 when assuming a usage level of 90% over 0.646 at a level of 95% to 0.687 in case the diffusion niveau was actually 98%. To restate a previously advanced argument, consistent application of the most plausible assumption may mitigate some problems arising from the potential unreliability of individual observations; nonetheless, the results of the statistical analyses presented in section 4. and the conclusions drawn in section 5. should always be interpreted in appreciation of the measurement methods' inherent weaknesses.

entries, the data matrix had to be transferred from the PC to a DEC VAX 6420 minicomputer for all inferential data analyses; those were conducted using the Statistical Analysis System SAS[41], Version 6.06.

In order to test the above mentioned hypotheses, the following tests/analysis procedures were applied[42]:

- One-tailed t-tests of parameter-estimates against $H_{[0]}$ and for mean-differences between groups
- F-tests for evaluating variance ratios (primarily within the context of linear regression analysis)
- Linear regression to analyze the linear relationship between at least interval-scaled variables
- Factor analysis to group (merge) variables according to their degree of covariation

Table 4-1 contains information about the significance levels α and their symbolic indicators as used in the various tables and exhibits of section 4.3.

Significance Level	$\alpha > .1$	$.1 \geq \alpha > .05$	$.05 \geq \alpha > .01$	$.01 \geq \alpha$
Interpretation	not significant	weakly significant	significant	highly significant
Symbol		+	*	**

Table 4-1 Significance Levels and their Symbolic Indicators

The quality of the conclusions drawn from applying those test procedures *inter alia* rests on the assumption that parameter-estimates come from a normal distribution. Therefore, evaluating the data for normality is imperative before any of the tests can be administered. A particularly advantageous consequence of the Central Limit Theorem in this respect is that the mean of a sufficiently large number of independent, equally distributed random variables (the observations) is *approximately* normal. As a result,

41) Cf. SAS Institute Inc. (1985a,b).

42) Mean difference tests were conducted assuming unequal population variances and independent sampling. SAS provides for such tests within the Analysis of Variance (ANOVA) procedures for unbalanced designs; yet the output generated only contains significance indicators for mean differences rather than the actual t-values. Since those were considered more informative, test-statistics were computed instead on a PC. Although not completely free of errors, a comprehensive listing of test procedures for various population parameters may be found in Albright (1987) pp. 429 - 432.

normality of the mean was considered as given for all group sizes greater than or equal to 20. Unfortunately, not all groups defined in the hypotheses contained more than 20 observations and checking those for normality, can become a non-trivial task.

One possible solution would be to show that the independent random variables are drawn from an underlying (parent) normal distribution; while the Central Limit Theorem applies to all types of parent distributions for sufficiently large sample sizes, the sample mean is *exactly* normal if the parent distribution itself is normal, regardless of sample size. In order to decide whether the empirical data approximate the normal form reasonably well, the immediate impulse was to conduct a simple χ^2 goodness-of-fit test; unfortunately, this frequently used technique has some major drawbacks in this instance. Firstly, the χ^2 test lacks statistical power and is thus susceptible to type II errors[43)]. Secondly, and even more important, its application generally requires observation counts in excess of 20 which effectively renders the method useless for the given purpose[44)].

The approach taken here is to construct Q-Q plots[45)]. According to this technique, quantiles of the empirical observations are plotted against theoretical quantiles of the hypothesized distribution. If the points in the resulting scatter diagram do not deviate very much from a straight line, as can be verified e.g. by visual inspection, the empirical data appear to be consistent with the distribution assumption[46)]. Not surprisingly, Q-Q plots are no panacea for small sample sizes. Analogous to the χ^2 procedure, the informativeness of Q-Q plots and pertinent test procedures positively correlates with sample size and it is not considered advisable to base decisions about the assumption of normality on Q-Q plots for samples with fewer than ten or so observations.

---

43) Cf. e.g. Albright (1987) p. 660 *et seq.*

44) The requirement of a minimum sample size of 20 can be found in many standard textbooks on statistics. Wetzel (1973) p. 233 e.g. calls attention to the heuristic that the sample observations should be divided into categories such that each category contains at least ten observations, otherwise they have to be merged.

45) See e.g. Johnson/Wichern (1982) p. 151 *et seqq.*

46) Evidently, the straightness of the scatter plot can also be evaluated by calculating the Pearson product-moment correlation coefficient *r*. Normality of the observations can then be tested by comparing the *r*-value with certain critical points that depend on the significance level desired and the sample size. For further information see Filliben (1975).

4.2. Preliminary Field Study

4.2.1. Study Objectives

As pointed out in the discussion of the research process, the basic purpose of the preliminary field study was to prepare the main data collection effort of this project, i.e. the questionnaire-based mail survey[47]. To that end, three specific objectives were defined at the outset which were to be pursued by means of conducting open-ended interviews with technical and managerial representatives of EDI user organizations:

(1) Systematically explore and gather data about EDI applications with maximally different purpose in a variety of industries and locations in order to develop a broader perspective about the diversity of EDI utilization in practice.

(2) Evaluate the practical relevance (focus) and conducive wording of the *a priori* defined research hypotheses.

(3) Develop questionnaire items and possible empirical referents for the variables referred to in the hypotheses.

A subsequent interview analysis was to generate additional information that could be used in refining, eliminating, and supplementing the tentative hypotheses as well as play a major role in the design of the survey questionnaire.

4.2.2. Administration of Field Study

After developing the interview guide and obtaining address information about EDI user organizations that were reported to have advanced at least into the pilot stage of the implementation process, interviewees were selected according to a two-stage sampling effort that might be called *stratified-convenience sampling* because after stratification some randomly picked enterprises refused to participate when initially contacted by telephone. Eventually, interviews were scheduled and conducted with approximately 30 organizations in various European countries during the 6-month period from September 1989 through March 1990. The listing below provides an overview of the sample.

---

47) This approach is rather typical for investigations with similar types of objectives; see e.g. Kaplan/Duchon (1988), p. 571.

Automotive Industry: Six manufacturers or suppliers in Scandinavia, Germany, and the U.K.

Banking: Three financial institutions in Switzerland and France.

Chemical Industry: Four organizations belonging to the European Association of Chemical Manufacturers CEFIC from Switzerland, The Netherlands, France, and the U.K[48].

Electronics Industry: Six organizations from The Netherlands, Germany, and the U.K.

Raw Materials/Utilities: Four organizations in France and the U.K.

Transportation: Four organizations in Sweden, Germany, France, and The Netherlands.

Miscellaneous: Five further organizations including businesses in textiles, home appliances, health care, a customs agent, as well as one conglomerate from Sweden, Norway, and the U.K.

EDI Service Supplier: Three VANS and two EDI software distributors in Scandinavia, Germany, France, and The Netherlands.

While refusals and drop-outs prevented drawing a true random sample from the research population, the composition of the set of organizations visited for approximately 2-hour discussions about their respective experiences and intentions with EDI can at least be characterized as 'varied' because a number of important industries[49] and major European countries are represented, which was one of the previously stated objectives.

4.2.3. Findings of Field Study

The interviews conducted with user organizations listed in the preceding section generated a wealth of specific information about individual experiences and efforts to implement and utilize EDI or to provide EDI services. Detailed accounts of the interviews were provided in three (unpublished) intermediate project reports. A brief summary of major findings is given below, yet due to the disparity of EDI applications, drawing generally applicable conclusions is no easy task and can only be accomplished at the cost of sacrificing detail.

Except perhaps for the automotive industry, EDI applications in Continental Europe do not seem to have advanced significantly beyond pilot stage which manifests itself in the fact that technical communciation problems rather than management issues dominate

48) CEFIC is the acronym of Conseil Européen des Fédérations de l'Industrie Chimique.

49) The relevance of the chosen industries is emphasized e.g. in Müller-Berg (1991).

the discussions[50]. Even the most advanced organizations concede a severe lack of experience with the utilization of EDI, which nevertheless did not prevent them from predicting strong growth rates in the number of their EDI communciation partners. The situation in the U.K. is generally characterized as more mature. Interviewees ascribed this fact to two advantageous circumstances: (1) The existence of cross-industry EDI syntax standards (TRADACOMS) prior to the introduction of EDIFACT, and (2) the early commercial availability of private VANS. Both factors are seen as having contributed significantly to the initial spread of EDI usage in the U.K. The large installed base of TRADACOMS applications may, however, become a long-term liability when the diffusion of EDIFACT elsewhere gathers enough momentum to impose migration upon TRADACOMS users with potentially disruptive ripple effects during the transition.

According to the respondents, two main reasons for pro-adoption decisions can be distinguished: On the one hand, organizations implement EDI systems in response to some external stimulus, usually taking the form of coercion by influential trading partners or government institutions such as customs authorities[51]. On the other hand, motivation may stem from some internal efficiency enhancement program which included EDI as but one element of the entire catalogue of organizational measures; most sources specifically cited the pursuit of JIT materials management concepts in this connection. While SMEs generally admit that without the necessary outside pressure from their customers they would not have contemplated EDI, the JIT argument applies specifically to large manufacturing organization. A good example is the automotive industry where EDI is mostly used for electronically transmitting delivery instructions (call-offs) to suppliers, with CAD-drawings as well as shipment advices gradually gaining prominence. Therefore, besides the exchange of EDI messages in a customer-supplier relationship, transportation intermediaries, who play a pivotal role within the logistical supply chain, are potential early adopters of EDI. A growing tendency towards international sourcing provides new opportunities for members of this industry to distinguish themselves from the competition by supporting their clients' JIT strategies with EDI, which allows one to quickly provide status information about goods in transit. The ability to separate both services, i.e. the physical movement of the goods and the provision of logistics information, may induce some organizations to either spin off telecommunications/IS departments into wholly owned, yet independently managed sub-

---

50) This is contrary to popular wisdom according to which EDI is to 80% a management problem; see e.g. Carlisle (1990), Laidet (1990) p. 70, Müller-Berg (1991).

51) For authority-induced adoption see e.g. Rogers (1983) p. 30 *et seq.*

sidiaries or turn them into profit centers[52]. Due to the importance of the information side of the business, EDI is often regarded as a matter of strategic concern in this industry[53].

The picture regarding the prospects for VANS appears mixed. The viability of VANS-based EDI between large organizations with considerable communication volume is frequently questioned. In those cases, transaction volumes may render the lease of a dedicated telecommunication link economical. Multidivisional firms could then e.g. interconnect their internal networks by means of a central network node (inhouse VAN), which performs all required message formatting and routing functions, rather than having each division hire the services of a (separate) VANS supplier. EDI in batch mode will be primarily applicable to transactions between low volume trading partners, which underscores the need for a large geographical reach of VANS. Furthermore, the complexity arising from the proliferation of EDI standards and VAN operators occasionally instigates SMEs to outsource their EDI telecommunications activities or search for a professional EDI-provider who assumes exclusive management and operational responsibility for all facets of the external message exchange.

Some industries (automotive) are adamantly opposed to any type of VAN-involvement and promote the use of international packet-switched transmission services based on X.25 standards as the superior alternative. VANS are perceived as expensive and posing security risks since clearing-house mailboxes may be fraudulently accessed to retrieve confidential information. This negative view, however, is not shared by all user organizations. While it is generally recognized that the clearing-center function may be less important in the future when X.400 services become available on a wide scale, some observers are convinced that the capability gap between PTTs and private VANS to quickly respond to a demand for innovative communication services and to provide custom-tailored solutions is sufficiently large to offer the latter a quite profitable market niche for the foreseeable future. VANS not only appear to have a *raison d' être* as facilitators during the early stages of EDI implementation (when special expertise about how to establish EDI trading relationships is needed) but also the ability for subscribers to track the status of messages sent through the VAN, i.e. determining whether those mes-

52) Analogous examples can be found in the airline industry in connection with the development of computerized reservation systems such as SABRE and APOLLO; cf. e.g. Griese (1990) p. 11. For the profit center potential of the information services function, cf. e.g. Allen (1987).

53) See e.g. Barret/Konsynski (1982) p. 103, McFarlan (1984), Porter/Millar (1985).

sages have been deposited in the recipient's mailbox, or retrieved, was considered valuable by respondents.

Interviewees also commented on a number of obstacles to a more rapid diffusion of EDI. Dominant among the more frequently mentioned barriers was the *limited systems development capacity* which effectively constrains the speed of adapting internal application systems to EDI. Although the availability of turnkey EDI workstations represents a quick solution to meeting an urgent customer demand for EDI communication, it provides little operational efficiencies due to the lack of integration with internal application systems, which is why a pro-active stance towards EDI is recommended. Furthermore, some IS-managers lamented about the difficulty to demonstrate or determine the benefits of EDI, which was portrayed as a serious hindrance to obtain commitment by high-level executives. The development of EDIFACT-subsets is hailed as a promising means to (a) permit syntax extensions to take industry-specific requirements into account and (b) to overcome the inherent redundancy and ambiguity problems of a universal standard while preserving most of its advantages. None of the respondents expressed much concern about the unresolved legal questions associated with EDI. However, most organizations were trying to mitigate any real or imagined risk by negotiating bilateral interchange agreements with their EDI trading partners. Specific contractual arrangements are considered the appropriate vehicle to reduce the uncertainties created by the lack of established business practice and legal precedence cases.

4.3. Sample Survey[54)]

4.3.1. Identification of Research Population

The problem of identifying and locating experienced EDI-user organizations proved much more difficult than anticipated. Based on the literature review and the observations made during the field study, the conclusion seemed warranted that despite often similar circumstances, the specific approach to EDI differed significantly with respect to geographical area, time of EDI's introduction into the organization, size of the company, as well as industrial sector. It was therefore necessary to pursue a stratified sampling approach and seek address information simultaneously from several sources. In Canada, the EDI Council of Canada kindly provided a member listing for the purpose of this research project. Whereas the EDI-Yellow Pages proved to be a promising starting

54) Cf. also Pfeiffer (1990b).

point in the U.S., its European *pendant*[55] was not nearly as helpful since by the end of 1988, the directory mainly contained addresses of individual EDI-experts and consultancy organizations rather than actual EDI users[56]. In order to obtain addresses in the U.K., two providers of Value-Added Network Services (VANS) were contacted which kindly returned publicly available client listings that could be screened for potential study participants. In Continental Europe, EDI-user groups, which had been established in many countries to coordinate the activities of their constituents, were likewise often able and willing to provide a short list of their members.

Having identified a total of about 1500 organizations in Europe and North America that were supposedly active users of Electronic Data Interchange, the aforementioned stratified sampling procedure was applied to determine the precise subset of the population that was to be included in the research. 719 organizations were eventually chosen which received the survey questionnaire between March and April of 1990. 139 questionnaires were returned over a period of five months ranging from April through August, for an overall response rate of slightly above 19%. 128 of those questionnaires turned out to be usable for analysis. Table 4-2 shows a breakdown of responding organizations by industry and country.

For reasons of external validity, taking a random sample from the stratified research population would have been desirable, which guarantees that each member of the population has exactly the same probability to be included in the sample. As stated before, the boundary conditions subject to empirical research in the social sciences do rarely, if ever, allow such random sampling. Since participation is voluntary, even if the identification problem was solved adequately, it must be considered virtually impossible to persuade all selected members to take part in the research study. Given the only alternative of conducting no research at all, the inherent limitations of convenience sampling had to be accepted. However, the degree of external validity may be assessed by classifying respondents according to *a priori* defined categories and determining to what extent each class is represented in the research sample, which is the topic of the following section.

---

55) Cf. Euromatica (1988).

56) Since then, the situation has improved considerably with the more recent publication of the EDI Yellow Pages International; see EDI, spread the word! (1989).

Industries \ Countries	USA	CND	UK	FRG	CH	NL	FRA	NOR	SWE	BEL	ITA	TOTAL
Banking		2	1		1	1				2		7
Electrical, Electronics*	2		5	4								11
Automotive*			3	1					1			5
Engineering & Manuf.*	1		6	2	1				1			11
Utilities*	1											1
Chemicals/Plastics*	1	1	3	1			1				1	8
Distribution**	9	2	1	2								14
Healthcare*	1	1	2									4
Food/Grocery*	7	7	3	1								18
Government					1							1
Household Goods*	3		2	2								7
Insurance					1	1						2
Computers*	1											1
Aerospace*	1											1
Retail**	4	2	1	1								8
Transportation**	8	4		3	2			2				19
Apparel*	1		1									2
Services		1			1		1					3
Consumer Durables*						1						1
Broker	1	1										2
Other	1			1								2
TOTAL	42	21	28	18	7	3	2	2	2	2	1	128

[*Manufacturing, **Logistics]

Table 4-2 Survey-Organizations by Industry and Country

4.3.2. Classification of Survey Participants

4.3.2.1. Industry Sector and Geographical Area

Table 4-2 shows that participating organizations cover a wide range of industrial sectors and countries. While it would have been preferable to examine the situation for each industrial sector in each geographical area on its own, the sample studied here does not contain a sufficient number of entities in any cell to enable meaningful generalizations. Therefore, by exploiting certain similarities between countries and industrial sectors, it was decided to group the organizations into aggregate categories. While aggregation yields larger clusters, the trade-off is a deterioration of the accuracy with which conclusions can be drawn because the intra-group homogenity of subjects decreases, a consequence which can be readily observed by a higher variance of responses.

When considering the various syntactical standards that have emerged and which allegedly play "pivotal" roles[57)] in determining the evolution of EDI, establishing three geographical clusters seems reasonable:

57) Cf. e.g. McGuffog (1988), Walker (1988).

- North America (N. America): Refers to the U.S. and Canada. Both countries are using the ANSI X12 framework of EDI standards.

- U.K.: The TRADACOMS standards are predominant in this region.

- Continental Europe (Cont. Europe): Organizations there have been frequently adopting the EDIFACT syntax.

As utilization of EDI is also (to some extent) contingent upon the type of economic activity pursued by an organization, a distinction was made between four different industrial sectors:

- Manufacturing: Industries that are primarily concerned with producing goods.

- Logistics: Industries that are concerned with the distribution of goods to the consumer such as transport agencies, shippers, warehousing enterprises, and retailers.

- Banking: Those types of organizations that comprise the banking system.

- Services: Industries such as brokers, insurance companies etc. with auxiliary functions.

Classifying the research sample on both dimensions yields the following distribution:

Sector \ Area	North America	U.K.	Cont. Europe	Total
Banking	2	1	4	7
Manufacturing	**28**	**25**	**17**	**70**
Logistics	**29**	2	10	**41**
Services	4		6	10
Total	**63**	**28**	**37**	**128**

Table 4-3 Survey-Organizations by Industry Sector and Area

Figures in boldface type indicate those cells which contain a sufficient number of entities to permit generalizations. As neither Services nor Banking are adequately represented, the subsequent discussion of research findings was deliberately restricted to Manufacturing and Logistics organizations. As a result, the net sample size for the investigation is a total of 111 entities whose answers to the questionnaire items provide the basis for the descriptive and inferential statistical analyses.

4.3.2.2. Functional Area and Hierarchical Position of Respondents

The survey results should also be interpreted in light of the particular respondents' business functions. Table 4-4 categorizes respondents by functional area and hierarchy.

Function \ Hierarchy	CEO	Director	V.P.	Manager	Staff	Consultant	NA	**Total**
Information Systems		12	6	30		2		**50**
EDI-Group				16		2		**18**
Data Processing				13	1			**14**
Logistics				6	1			**7**
Operations				5				**5**
Marketing		2	1	1				**4**
Finance		1	2	1				**4**
Administration	3			1				**4**
Accounting				2				**2**
NA			1				2	**3**
Total	**3**	**15**	**10**	**75**	**2**	**4**	2	**111**

Table 4-4 Survey-Respondents by Business Function and Organizational Hierarchy

Most individuals (59) belong to the information systems branch and describe themselves as managers. This result reinforces findings of the field study that, in contrast to the popular wisdom of EDI being primarily an organizational problem rather than a technical one, the concept is still at such an early stage in most organizations that technical issues take precedence. Otherwise, one would expect administration officials to account for a larger proportion of the respondents.

4.3.2.3. Organizational Size

The importance of organizational size was already emphasized in Hypotheses C1-C3. In order to examine whether size can actually serve as a meaningful differentiation criterion, an attempt was made to classify sample entities accordingly. The difficulty encountered with this task is to find a "correct" class separation criterion. For lack of a sound theoretical basis with respect to the particular population given, a pragmatic approach was chosen. According to Council Directive 78/660/EEC of the European

Community concerning the statutory annual reporting requirements of enterprises in the European Community, the size of organizations is to be determined by a combination of three criteria: Total assets, net annual turnover, and average employment during the reporting period. Based on those variables, three sizes of organizations can be distinguished:

- Small Enterprises (Article 11): Organizations with
  - total assets of less than or equal to 1 million European Currency Units (ECU),
  - annual turnover of up to 2 million ECU,
  - maximum average employment of 50 people.

- Medium-Sized Enterprises (Article 27): Organizations with
  - total assets of less than or equal to 4 million ECU,
  - annual turnover of up to 8 million ECU,
  - maximum average employment of 250 people.

- Large Enterprises: Organizations which excede at least two of the criteria pertaining to Medium-Sized Enterprises.

If the sample of this survey is measured against those criteria, the distribution displayed in Exhibit 4-3 is obtained:

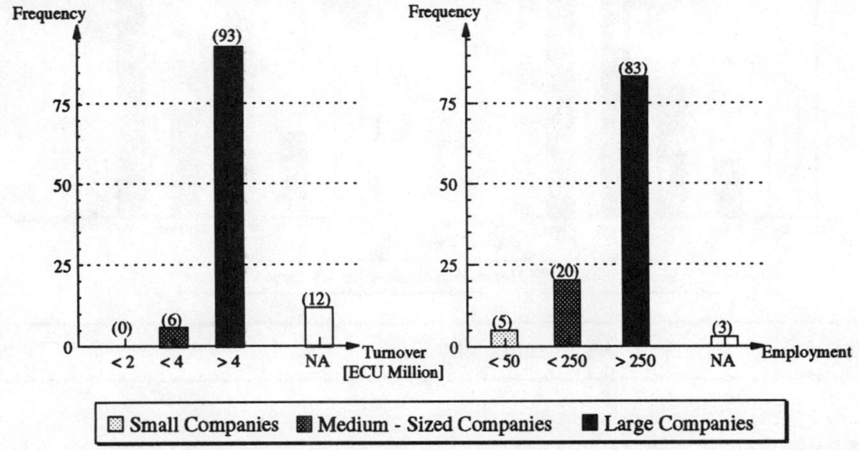

Exhibit 4-3	Survey-Organizations by Size (EC-Criteria)

Under these circumstances, the majority of organizations included in the sample would have to be rated "large"[58]. The directive does not contain a compelling rationale for this classification scheme dating back to 1978, and because (due to inflation) it must be regarded unsound to set absolute values, upwardly adjusted criteria will be employed here. EDI usage is unlikely to differ significantly between companies with 50 employees and those with 100. Differences may be due rather to questions of organizational structure such as whether the enterprise is organized into more or less independently operating profit centers or whether staff is unambiguously assigned to self-contained functional areas. Since such structural variances are likely to occur only at organizations with much higher employment and turnover figures, the EC-criteria have been raised considerably:

1. Discriminant point: Average employment: 200; annual turnover: 20 million ECU

2. Discriminant point: Average employment: 2000; annual turnover: 200 million ECU

Under those assumptions, the sample distribution shown in Exhibit 4-4 is obtained. Again, categories are differentiated by shading:

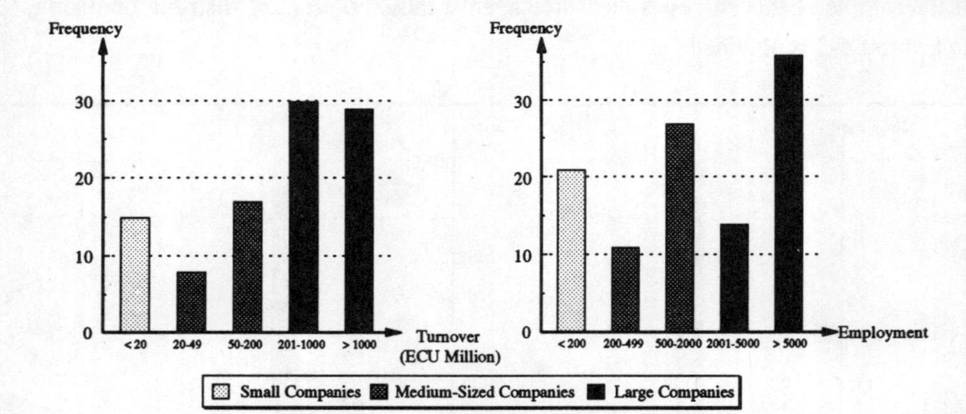

Exhibit 4-4	Survey-Organizations by Size

As can be seen, both criteria lead to fairly different distributions and therefore, a combination of both was decided to serve as the discriminant function. Thus, for the purposes of this analysis, organizations are categorized according to the following system:

58) All financial data have been transformed into ECU by applying the London and Zurich exchange rate closings of July 26, 1990.

- Small Companies: Those with average employment of less than 200 and/or an annual turnover of less than 20 million ECU.
- Medium-Sized Companies: Those with an average employment of no more than 2000 or annual turnover of no more than 200 million ECU.
- Large Companies: Those exceding both limits mentioned for Medium-Sized Organizations.

Exhibit 4-5 shows a breakdown of study participants by size and other categories introduced previously:

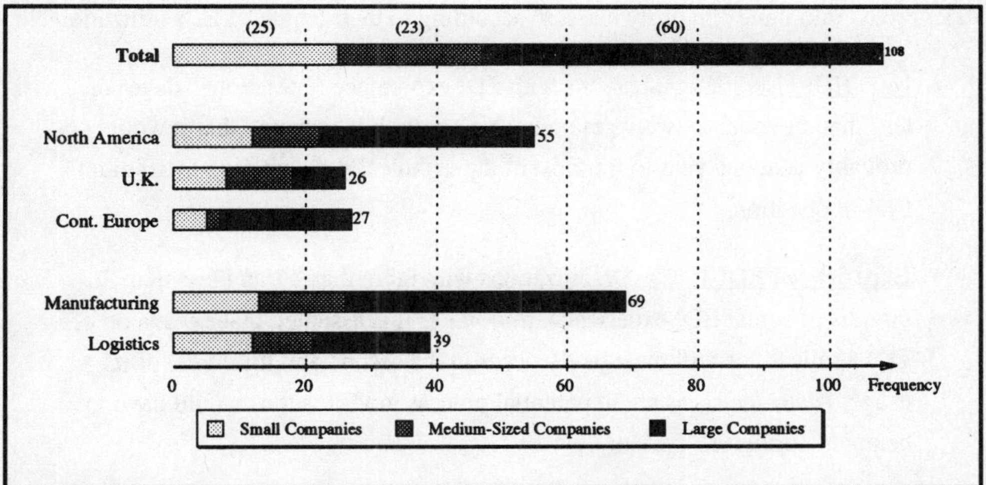

Exhibit 4-5	Survey-Organizations by Size, Industry Sector, and Area[59)]

Even though the discrimination points have been raised substantially, it must be conceded that the sample is slightly biased towards larger organizations; in general, however, there are at least several entities in each category allowing cautious generalizations.

59) The empirical data shown in various exhibits throughout section 4.3. do not always correspond with those displayed in Table 4-3 since not all respondents provided data to all items in the questionnaire. This holds true especially for the distinction made later between different EDI-usage rates. Thus, the data of Table 4-3 merely determine upper bounds.

4.3.2.4. Length of EDI Utilization

While size, location, and industry sector can be important determinants of an organization's attitude towards EDI, the utility users derive may - according to a learning curve effect - also depend on the amount of experience gathered with this technology, i.e. the length of time EDI has been employed. Even after reaching the operational stage, systems complexity will necessitate ongoing maintenance work. Moreover, the system will need to be gradually extended in terms of additional transaction sets as well as additional communication partners. These processes take time, especially when they are accompanied by adjusting internal operating procedures to EDI. Therefore, taking the time requirements for systems development and implementation into account, users are categorized into three "maturity classes" according to their length of EDI utilization[60]:

- New EDI-Users: Organizations with EDI experience (operational stage) of less than or equal to twelve months. *Rationale:* It is assumed that it would probably take one year to fix most of the technical deficiencies of the initial EDI-application.

- Experienced EDI-Users: Organizations with more than 12 and less than 36 months of actual EDI experience. *Rationale:* It is assumed that expansion of EDI applications will most likely occur in the second and third year of its usage. Also, decisions about potential process modifications would have to be made during this period.

- Long-Term EDI-Users: Organizations with more than three years of EDI experience. *Rationale:* After a long period of EDI utilization systems and procedures should have reached a state of equilibrium where the entire concept has become an integral part of the business.

When the sample organizations are classified according to those maturity criteria, only 18 entities fall into the group of New EDI-Users, 40 entities qualify as Experienced EDI-Users and 37 organizations must be regarded as Long-Term EDI-Users. Hence, it can be concluded that the companies in the sample draw upon a considerable body of EDI-experience, which is yet another indication of the survey findings' reliability.

---

60) A similar approach to classify EDI user organizations was taken by Bakkenist (1990).

4.3.2.5. Volume of EDI Communication

As was mentioned before, the volume of EDI-traffic, i.e. the number of messages exchanged per period, can be expected to strongly influence the perception of EDI's effectiveness as a business tool. For this reason, organizations were also classified according to their level of EDI utilization. Lacking any theoretical model on which to base separation points, groups are arbitrarily distinguished as follows:

- Low-Volume EDI-Users: Organizations with less than 240 EDI-transactions per month or, on average, less than 10 per day; 22 companies in the sample represent this group.

- Medium-Volume EDI-Users: Organizations with more than 240 but less than 2400 transactions per month or, on average, between 10 and 100 per business day; the sample contains 27 of such organizations.

- High-Volume EDI-Users: Organizations with EDI-transactions in excess of 2400 per month or 100 per business day; 24 companies of the sample fall into this category.

Adding up those numbers reveals that 38 of the 111 organizations included in the sample did not provide sufficient information about their volume of EDI-traffic. As a consequence, the data analysis is occasionally restricted to that subset of the sample where those 38 subjects have been removed.

4.3.2.6. Other Classification Criteria

Besides the dimensions outlined in the preceding paragraphs, additional classification criteria that may influence an organization's assessment of EDI need to be considered on a contingent basis. For instance, the chosen hardware system would certainly be an important determinant of the costs incurred. Those and other criteria, such as syntax standards used, etc., are occasionally employed in order to complement and enrich the discussion wherever deemed appropriate.

4.3.3. Assessment of Sample Representativeness

Before presenting selected results of the empirical investigation, a brief appraisal of the overall representativeness of the survey sample may be in order. Again, any method to select a research sample other than random sampling will introduce an unestimable sampling error which tends to distort data analysis by an unknown extent in an unknown direction, and which inhibits the use of (sophisticated) statistical techniques to draw general inferences about the research population as a whole, regardless of sample size.

The investigation conducted here suffers from the same consequential defects of a non-random sampling procedure. However, this deficiency does not imply the total futility of the subsequent analysis. The previous classification of EDI user organizations shows: (1) Generalizations seem to be possible for at least some EDI user categories; (2) tentative conclusions about aspects of EDI can be drawn with respect to certain for intuitive and theoretical reasons interesting variables such as e.g. the amount of a subject's EDI communication volume. In that sense, the contribution of this research is to provide a component of the overall picture and thereby complement the endeavors of other researchers in the same field.

4.3.4. Survey Findings and Hypotheses Testing

It is customary for empirical investigations to present selected excerpts from the large volume of data gathered and the statistical output generated in graphical form, due to the behavioral advantages associated with a pictorial design[61]. However, in many instances this is accomplished in a rather unsatisfactory way. For example, graphical renditions simply showing mean values convey messages which can lead to premature conclusions. In order to protect the data against misinterpretation it would be desirable to show the entire distribution of responses which unfortunately has a detrimental effect upon the legibility of the graphics. Therefore, a compromise solution is being employed in this text wherever suitable:

61) Cf. e.g. Kroeber-Riel (1986).

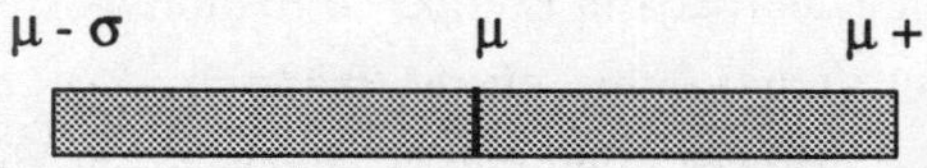

Exhibit 4-6 μ/σ Box-Plot Graph[62]

Exhibit 4-6 shows such a box-plot which characterizes the distribution of the data by three points: Mean minus one standard deviation ($\mu - \sigma$), mean (μ), and mean plus one standard deviation ($\mu + \sigma$). The display of minimum and maximum scores, usually depicted by pointed arrows, was suppressed in most cases either because their respective position follows immediately from the measurement scale (mostly semantic scales, cf. questionnaire), or because extreme outliers would lead to a blurred picture. The advantage of this method relates to the fact that the symbol provides some idea of the variable distribution without necessarily cluttering the graphic[63].

Responses to most questionnaire items are characterized by a rather large variance which underscores the inherent dangers associated with drawing general conclusions from a few case studies on EDI and thus vindicates the soundness of the broader research approach taken here. Irrespective of the considerable distribution of responses, the graphics reveal underlying patterns, and as many hypothesis tests are based on a comparison of category means, differences are often significant because group mean errors are evidently much smaller (depending upon the size of the group). The main results of the hypothesis tests are reported in narrative form throughout this section.

4.3.4.1. EDI-Decision Stage

According to the stated research objective of determining factors that affect the technology's rate of adoption it was deemed appropriate to investigate the decision-stage of EDI, i.e. the time period just preceding the start of an EDI-project. Hence, respondents were asked at the outset at what time the initial idea for EDI emerged. It is often stated

---

62) μ and σ usually refer to the unknown *population mean* and *population standard deviation*. What is shown in the following exhibits actually is the *sample mean* and the *sample standard deviation*.

63) In general, the subsequent analysis tries to comply with some guiding principles of statistical graphics design as discussed in Tufte (1983). In order to enhance data density and support exploration of associations between variables, most exhibits depict summary statistics of several variables simultaneously. Thus, pie-charts, which by definition show only a single dimension and tend to only inflate a handful of numbers to page-size rather than summarize information, have been deliberately avoided.

in the pertinent literature that organizations in North America have been using EDI earlier than their counterparts in Europe[64]. Exhibit 4-7 reveals, however, that while there may be some truth to this claim (the difference between group means is some 18 months), the likewise often mentioned statement, that U.K.-companies are far more experienced than those on the Continent[65], is not supported by the data.

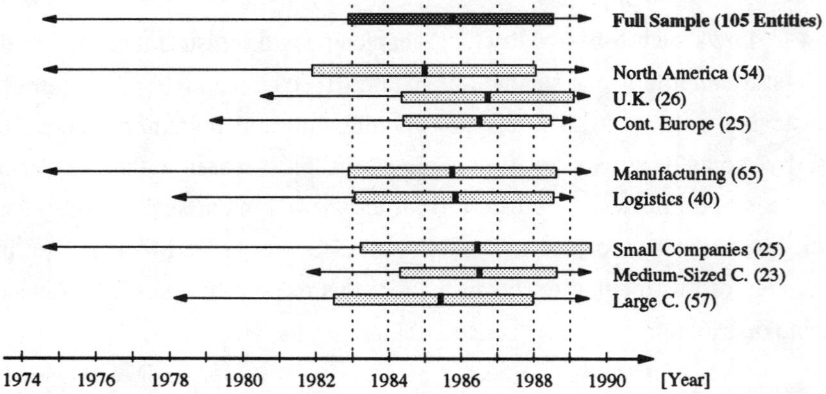

Exhibit 4-7	Time of Initial Idea for EDI

Whereas no distinction can be made between manufacturing and logistics companies in this regard, there is, on average, a small but significant time-lag of about eleven months between large and small organizations in terms of contemplating EDI, which is consistent with the presumption that large organizations, due to their much higher trade volume and number of transactions per period, should have started earlier with EDI than small enterprises who may lack sufficient business incentive to start an EDI program on their own, i.e. without some external "encouragement". The difference is even more distinct when the time of adoption is considered:

> Hypothesis C1: The time of adoption is negatively related to the size of organizations.
>
> *Finding: Hypothesis is consistent*[66] *with the data (mean difference*

---

64) Cf. e.g. Meier (1989) p. 60.

65) Cf. e.g. Gregg (1988), Stanton (1989).

66) In appreciation of the chosen measurement instrument's typical deficiencies and the sampling-procedure-dependent unresolvable question of generalizability, a rather cautious interpretation of research findings with respect to the hypotheses was deemed appropriate. Hence, only 'consistency' between data and hypothesis is determined rather than using stronger yet unjustified terms such as 'confirmation' or even 'falsification' in the Popperian sense. However, consistency always implies rejection of the respective Null Hypothesis; cf. e.g. Cook/Campbell (1979) p. 20 *et seqq*.

Δ = 17.15 [months] between large and small organizations, and*
Δ = 11.94 [months] between large and medium-sized organizations).*

To further analyze the various elements contributing to the EDI-adoption decision, Exhibit 4-8 indicates the relative importance of factors frequently cited as circumstances or events that led organizations to pursue EDI. The figures, ranked in descending order of importance (manufacturing organizations), are broken down by industrial sector and size of the entities, and are given in percent of their respective categories.

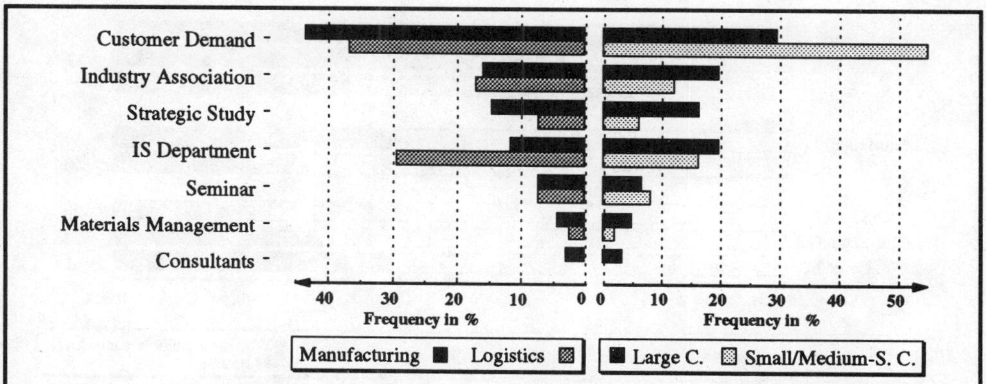

Exhibit 4-8	Events/Circumstances leading to EDI

The reason to introduce EDI mentioned most often is *customer demand*, a fact which surprisingly also applies to large organizations that would theoretically be more inclined to develop an internal rationale for EDI, e.g. to support the implementation of Just-in-Time concepts or to streamline administrative overhead activities. For those organizations which did not cite customer demand as primary motivator for pursuing EDI, the impetus is almost evenly distributed between *internal projects of IS-departments* - which is essentially a 'technology push' argument - and participation in *programs of industry associations*. Strategic arguments seem to play a far less important role. Overall, most organizations (65%) apparently adopt EDI reactively, i.e. as a result of customer pressure or external events and not because of some expected superior return on investment or a carefully plotted strategy to realize competitive advantage.

> Hypothesis C2: SMEs tend to adopt EDI reactively, i.e. as a result of some external stimulus rather than out of internal considerations.
> *Finding: Hypothesis is consistent with the data (proportion of SMEs adopting EDI because of external stimulus $\pi = 0.67 > 0.5^{**}$).*

In the sense that a capital outlay not justifiable on financial grounds is often called a 'strategic investment', EDI may well fall into this category. Support for this interpretation can be found in Exhibit 4-9 which illustrates that almost two thirds of the respondents either did not conduct any type of cost benefit analysis at all or performed only a token examination to obtain a crude estimate about the costs incurred when investing in EDI.

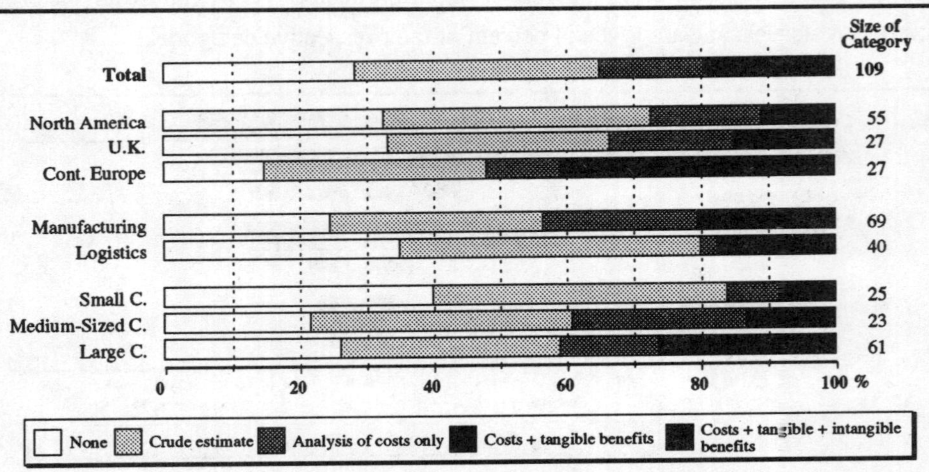

Exhibit 4-9	EDI Cost/Benefit Analyses

Especially small organizations and those active in the logistics area seem to introduce EDI without much concern for financial consequences; apparently more hesitant to press forward without at least some kind of *ex ante* economic assessment are organizations located in Continental Europe, albeit the proportion of large companies in this sample subset is above average as was emphasized before. In general, the decision to adopt EDI appears to have been mainly viewed as a forgone conclusion by the majority of sample organizations and therefore did not require a capital budgeting analysis.

> Hypothesis C3: The majority of SMEs does not conduct a benefit analysis before the adoption of EDI.
> *Finding: Hypothesis is consistent with the data (proportion of SMEs adopting EDI without benefit analysis $\pi = 0.9 > 0.5^{**}$).*

The importance which companies assign to EDI may be illuminated by identifying the hierarchical level and functional area where the adoption decision was made. The following Exhibit 4-10 provides information with respect to the former question:

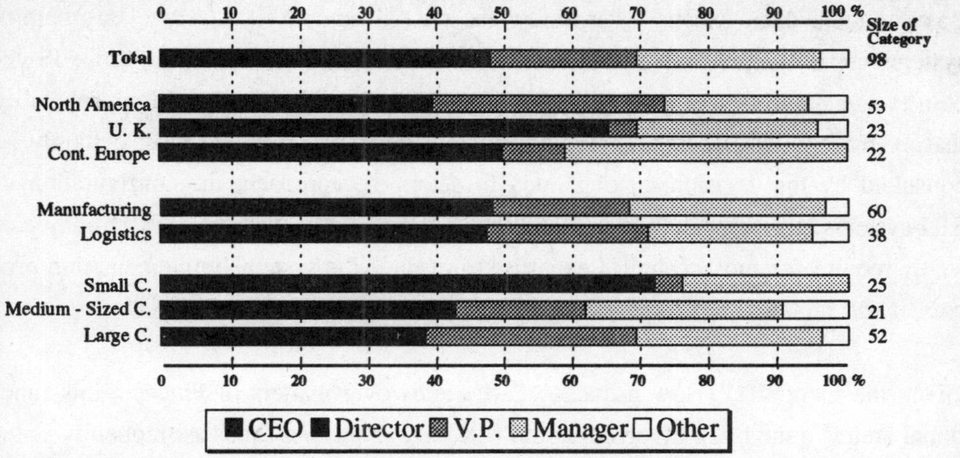

Exhibit 4-10 EDI Adoption Decision: Decision Maker

If one disregards the (artificial) distinction between board members referred to as "Director" and "(Executive) Vice President" (V.P.), it is found that in about 70% of all instances EDI-adoption seems to have been a top-management decision. Given the fact that funding requirements for EDI are quite low in comparison with other capital investments, such as in new production facilities, this high level of attention can only be attributed to the potential influence of EDI on customer relationships. This view is further vindicated by Table 4-5 which shows that - except for those organizations whose primary function is to provide logistics services - in only about one third of all instances was the decision to adopt EDI made in the information systems department.

\ Bus. Function Segmentation \	Adm. %	IS %	Fin. %	Mkt. %	Log. %	Other %	Total #
U.K.	36	23	**18**	14	5	5	**22**
North America	35	31	8	12	10	6	**52**
Cont. Europe	33	33	10	**5**	**19**	0	**21**
Manufacturing	34	21	12	12	16	5	**58**
Logistics	35	**43**	8	8	3	3	**37**
Small C.	**54**	33	8	**4**	0	0	**24**
Medium - Sized C.	32	32	11	16	5	5	**19**
Large C.	27	27	12	12	17	6	**52**
Total #	**33**	**28**	**10**	**10**	**10**	**4**	**95**

Table 4-5 EDI Adoption Decision: Functional Area[67)]

67) The numbers inside the table are row percentages.

Based on the data, exactly determining the overall amount of leverage information systems departments had over the outcome of this decision is impossible. Since IS-departments have to take responsibility for implementing EDI, there is a high probability that even when the department was not directly in charge, it would most certainly be consulted by the decision making body to determine approach, the configuration of EDI-systems, project management details, etc. Nonetheless, even though EDI may presently require foremost technical expertise to manage the systems implementation process, it still remains an organizational decision.

Given the theoretically low influence EDI wields over matters of Finance, this functional area is quite often involved; in the U.K. e.g. about four times as frequently as logistics departments. This result may be partly explained by reference to organizational architecture. According to Nolan's well-known stage-models of EDP-growth[68)], it is not unusual that (especially during the early phases of IS-utilization) heads of IS-departments report to Finance which is generally responsible for all IS-decisions. Viewed from this angle, the columns for IS and Finance in Table 4-5 could perhaps be aggregated; thus, differences between groups shrink significantly. Quite interestingly, logistics departments in Continental Europe are more frequently in charge of EDI than elsewhere, which may be a direct consequence of the greater fragmentation of markets in this area.

4.3.4.2. Costs of EDI

4.3.4.2.1. Tangible Costs

The various cost categories of EDI were discussed in section 2.4.2.1. Respondents were asked to rate their particular EDI-systems according to the significance of each category. As manpower-requirements are to some extent hidden in systems development costs, the decision was taken to investigate operational demands individually; those findings are presented later.

As Exhibit 4-11 shows, irrespective of organizational size or choice of the hardware system, only systems development costs and, to a lesser extent, software costs are generally perceived as significant by the sample organizations. Mainframe users consider communication costs relevant and only frontend-PC users rate hardware-costs highly.

---

68) See e.g. Gibson/Nolan (1974).

This may be attributed to the fact that EDI will hardly require companies to purchase a new mainframe, and standalone-PCs have become inexpensive commodity items. However, connecting a PC via LAN to a mainframe port may be somewhat more costly.

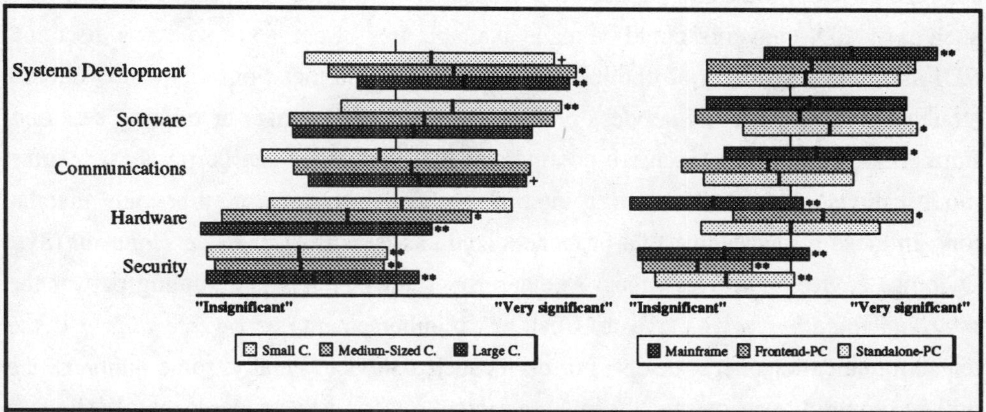

Exhibit 4-11	Costs Incurred for EDI by Category

These findings offer some insight as to what type of subsidies for EDI are needed most. Giving incentives to tradings partners in order to entice them to begin using EDI has been widely advocated, especially during the early stages of the diffusion process [69]. As Exhibit 4-12 clearly demonstrates, however, this advice is not heeded very frequently. With the possible exception of education and training, parties claim to have rarely if ever received any support from their trading partners, nor are they similarly very keen on providing any help.

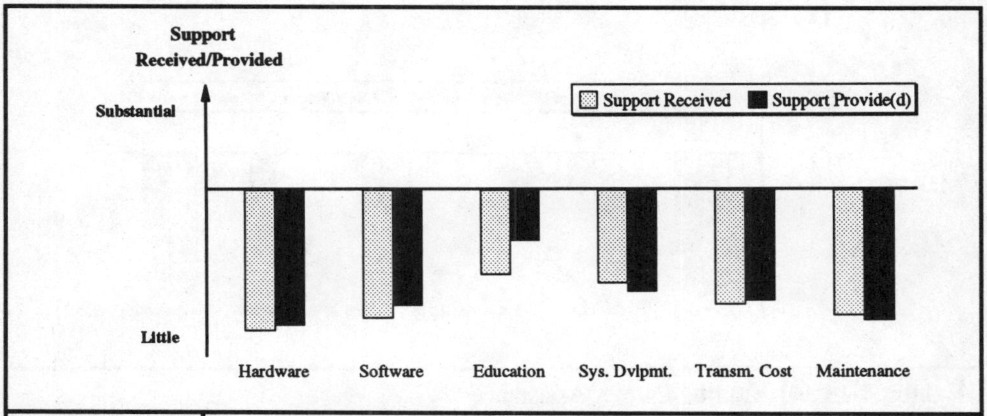

Exhibit 4-12	EDI Support between Trading Partners

69) Cf. e.g. Carter et al. (1987).

According to the manifold requirements of implementing and operating EDI-systems, six leverage points may be distinguished where support can be received or provided. Since EDI necessitates some computing equipment, the first alternative consists of providing *hardware* to trading partners, e.g. a specially configured PC. Likewise, *software* such as an EDI-converter could be made available free of charge or sold at a discount. EDI users have a variety of options to *educate* trading partners; one frequently chosen strategy is to hire a VAN services provider to organize seminars or training sessions. Furthermore, even if inexpensive commercial EDI-converters can be purchased, some modifications/adaptions to existing internal application systems may become mandatory. In those instances, the EDI proponent could assist with *systems development* (Sys. Dvlpmt.) advice and/or resources. Another opportunity relates to assuming part of the *telecommunication costs* (Transm. Cost) via reimbursements or *reverse billing* if the telecommunications network operator offers such a service. Finally, some *maintenance* will be required to accommodate new transaction sets, update standards, etc. While it is hardly conceivable that maintenance support will be provided alone, such assistance may nonetheless be offered in conjunction with hard- and/or software.

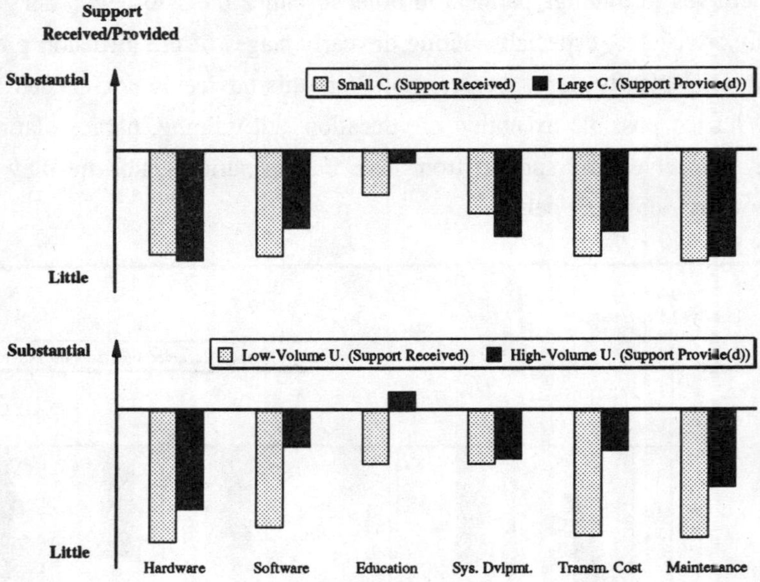

Exhibit 4-13	Trading Partner Assistance

In contrast to Exhibit 4-12, this exhibit compares the support received/provided for different categories of organizations. The empirical data negate any presupposition that large companies or high-volume users regularly grant support to their smaller (or low-volume) trading partners. Only training and systems development assistance have occasionally been extended. When consideration is given to the cost categories evaluated previously, software seems to have been largely neglected so far although it represents one of the two most urgent areas for assistance.

4.3.4.2.2. Overview of Actual Costs Incurred

After identifying relevant cost categories and measuring costs on ordinal scales for the purpose of comparison, obtaining more precise figures about actual expenditures was deemed desirable. Given such information, prospective EDI users would be better able to estimate the capital requirements of EDI under various scenarios.

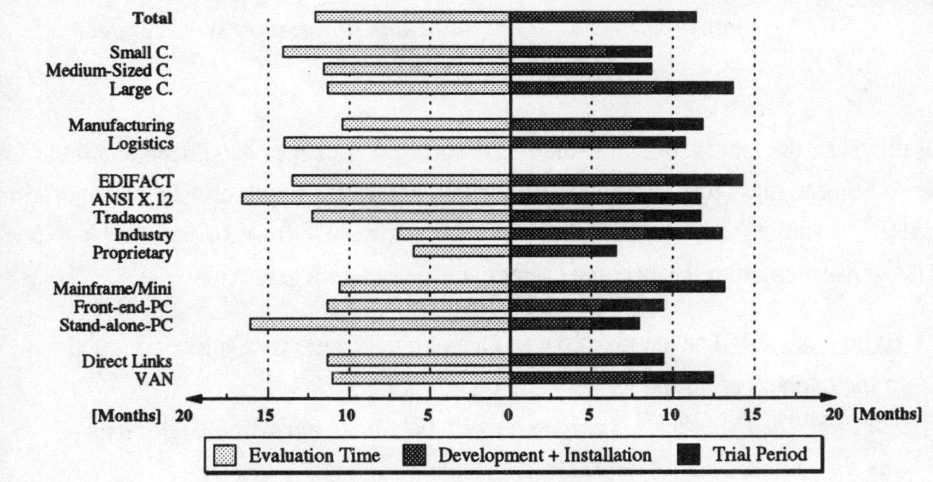

Exhibit 4-14	EDI Project Times

The first important determinant of actual costs incurred relates to the duration of an EDI-development project. Exhibit 4-14 illustrates the average length of time required to evaluate, implement, and test EDI until the system became operational. *Evaluation Time* was calculated as the period between the initial idea and the decision to start a trial project. *Development and Installation* refers to the time between starting the EDI project and the date when the first message was being exchanged with an external communication partner. The length of the *Trial Period* was determined as the time between exchange of the first message and official completion of the trial[70].

According to the data given in Exhibit 4-14, the most rapid approach to get started in EDI would be to select a proprietary message syntax and implement the system on a standalone-PC using direct communication links with trading partners as opposed to going through a Value-Added Network. Whereas this may actually represent the quickest solution, nothing can be said about the speed and ease of modification with which such a system can be adapted towards additional communication partners and new message types.

> Hypothesis C7: The use of proprietary syntax standards leads to a shorter implementation stage than the use of public standards.
> *Finding: The hypothesis is consistent with the data (mean difference $\Delta = 5.77^{**}$ [months] between users of public and proprietary syntax standards)*[71].

Overall, given the fact that off-the-shelf EDI-software packages have been available for quite some time now, it is startling to notice that regardless of which EDI configuration is chosen, installing and testing takes from approximately 6 to 14 months[72]. Nonetheless, implementation has become easier over time as anticipated.

> Hypothesis C4: The length of the implementation stage is negatively related to the lateness of adoption.
> *Finding: The hypothesis is consistent with the data (regression coefficient has the required sign $\beta_1 = -0.19^{**}$)*[73].

---

70) This procedure registers the amount of time required to turn the original prototype into a fully operational product. If one were to interpret the term 'trial period' only in the narrow sense of using EDI in parallel with paper-based methods with at least one external communciations partner, obviously, the time intervals would be shorter. The former question was considered to be more relevant for the purposes of this study.

71) It should be noted that the group of organizations in the sample using proprietary standards has only 14 members. Therefore, the Pearson product-moment correlation coefficient *r* of the respective Q-Q plot had to be calculated to assess the validity of the normality assumption before conducting the mean difference test. With r = 0.9402 and a critical point of approximately 0.938 at the 5% significance level, the hypothesis of normality could not be rejected. For the critical points of Q-Q plot correlation coefficients see Johnson/Wichern (1982) p. 156.

72) These findings are in accordance with many case study reports; see e.g. Gebker (1989).

73) *Nota bene*, 'lateness of adoption' is here and elsewhere measured indirectly via the length of EDI utilization. Because of the negative relationship between both variables, the sign of the regression parameter must in all such cases be reversed prior to hypothesis testing.
General regression equation: $VAR_1 = \beta_0 + \beta_1 VAR_2 + \varepsilon$

The costs of EDI-systems may conceptually be divided into an *initial investment* that represents the fixed upfront expenditures for development and installation as well as *recurring costs* for transmission and systems maintenance, the latter of which comprises such items as back-up and recovery, standards upgrades etc. Exhibit 4-15 depicts ranges for initial EDI-investments.

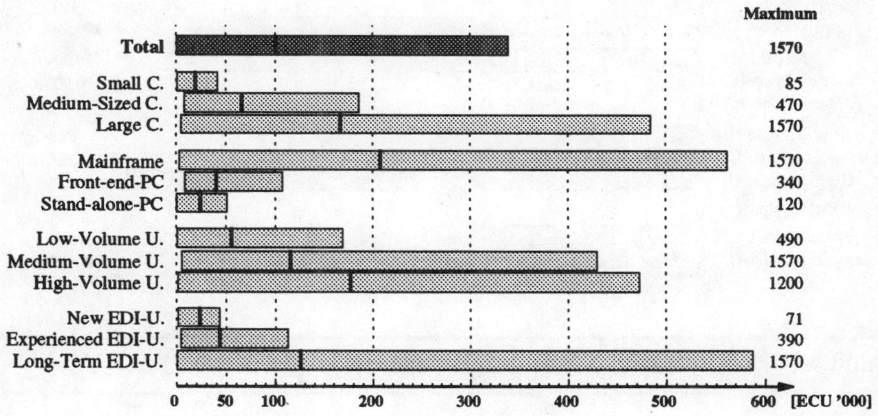

Exhibit 4-15	Initial Investment in EDI-Systems

Evidently, the data distributions shown in Exhibit 4-15 (as well as those in Exhibit 4-14) are heavily skewed to the lower end of the scale. As was to be expected, the standalone-PC solution is the most inexpensive setup with 60% of the implementations costing less than 50'000.- ECU and is therefore favored by the majority of small organizations. By contrast, mainframe systems on average required an initial investment of appr. 200'000.- ECU with a maximum of almost 1.6 Million ECU. Enterprises contemplating EDI mainframe systems should nonetheless take solace in the fact that recent EDI-implementations appear to be far more cost effective than earlier systems, which may be due to the increasing availability of standard EDI-software. Cost-estimates should not be based on transaction volume which is a poor predictor of the capital needed to implement systems of required functionality and capacity.

> Hypothesis A1: The cost of systems implementation is negatively related to the lateness of adoption.
> *Finding: The hypothesis is consistent with the data (regression coefficient has the required sign β_1 = -3061.83**)*

Besides the initial investment in systems, outlays also comprise recurring expenses e.g. for message transmission and maintenance. The pattern for those variable costs is slightly different as can be seen in Exhibit 4-16.

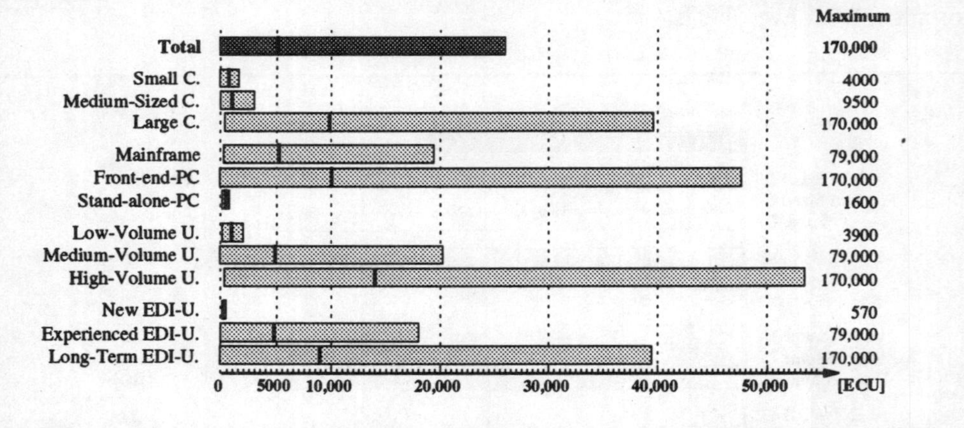

Exhibit 4-16	Recurring Monthly EDI Expenses

Monthly costs are obviously dependent on communications volume. More intriguing, however, is the correlation between EDI-experience and monthly expenditures. Apparently, it takes about a year of operation before the system is sufficiently stable to allow expansion beyond the initial partners and transaction sets. Then, usage quickly surges in both dimensions until a saturation point is reached where all major business partners are connected and all applicable message types are implemented. Further growth will closely follow the overall expansion of the business. The empirical data are consistent with the hypothesis of an epidemic (logistic) diffusion pattern.

The average variable costs for organizations in all categories is about 5000.- ECU per month, with low-volume users and those with standalone-PCs paying much less. Moreover, the considerably larger amounts shown in other subgroups are partly due to the single outlier who claimed monthly costs of 170'000.- ECU.

To reiterate, the uncertainty about the true requirements of EDI provided the impetus to gather data concerning the financial consequences associated with EDI. Therefore, respondents were not only asked about capital investments and operating costs of their respective EDI systems, but an attempt was made to determine the staffing requirements of EDI. Before requesting exact figures, information was obtained about the establishment of formal EDI groups. This turned out to be the case for a surprisingly large number of enterprises.

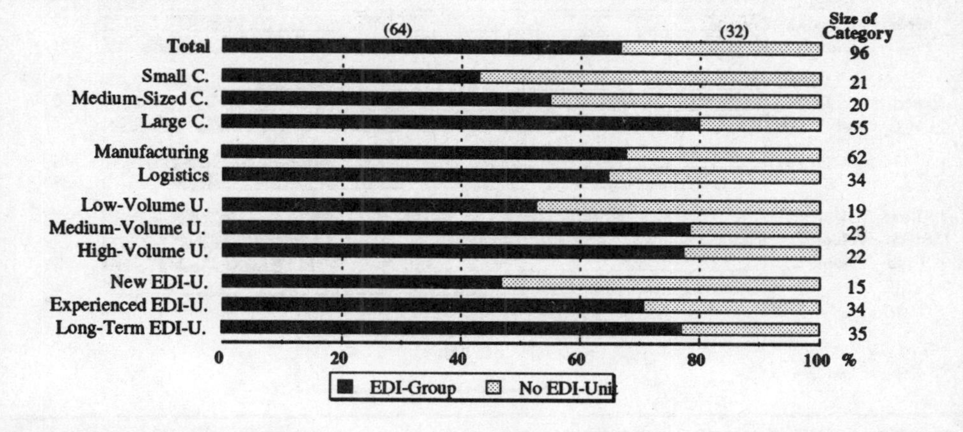

Exhibit 4-17	Existence of Organizational EDI Units

Exhibit 4-17 reveals that even for small companies every second entity claims to have established an organizational group with particular responsibility for EDI. However, as will become evident later, most such groups consist of only a single individual. Equally surprising may be the fact that despite their size and degree of EDI-utilization, neither large companies nor those with a high-volume of EDI-transactions have established special EDI-units without exception; nonetheless, they tend to have a higher proclivity to form some kind of EDI-group.

Since job advertisements occasionally underscore the need for EDI-knowledge, staff with special expertise may have to be made available for those EDI-units which could theoretically be either hired externally or transferred from a different position. Exhibits 4-18 and 4-19 display to what extent both options applied to the sample organizations.

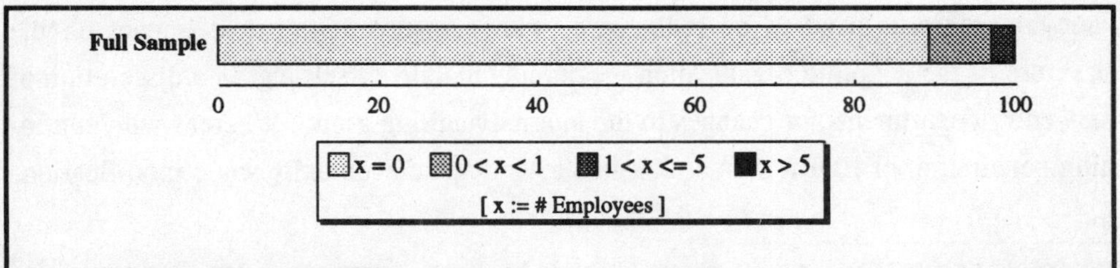

Exhibit 4-18	Additional EDI Staff: External Recruiting

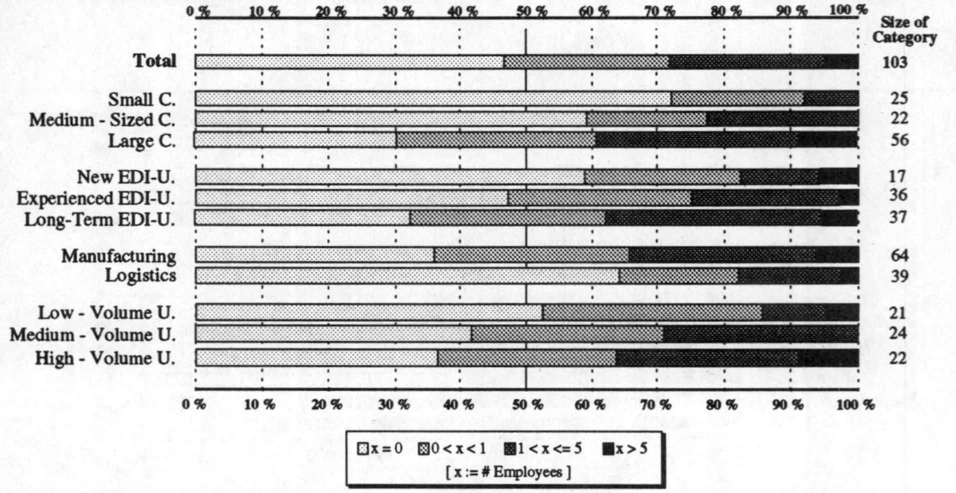

Exhibit 4-19	Additional EDI Staff: Internal Transfer

As it turns out, close to 90% of all organizations said that they did not hire any person with particular responsibility for EDI, and even though internal reassignments have occurred more frequently, approximately 50% of all respondents claim to have no full-time EDI position at all. With the exception of large organizations and high-volume EDI users, personnel commonly performing EDI related tasks also has other responsibilities.

4.3.4.2.3. Intangible Costs

In addition to readily identifiable expenditures for implementing and operating EDI systems, indirect cost effects are also often presumed to emanate from EDI. The most dramatic contention in this regard is the claim that EDI will "fundamentally alter the way business is being conducted"[74]. This suggests that at least administrative organizational processes need to be redesigned, with a potential transitive impact on the structure of the adopting organization which may manifest itself e.g. in a dissolution of data entry departments, or changes to the internal auditing group. Whereas with continuing penetration of EDI it seems plausible to anticipate eventually some modifications

74) Such and similar statements can be found in numerous articles on EDI; cf. e.g. Horan (1989) p. 35, Emmelhainz (1990) p. 3.

with respect to internal processes[75], how the organizational structure may be affected, however, remains fairly elusive. Even process modifications are likely to be introduced only after the majority of transactions are executed via EDI as corporate systems and infrastructure must continue to cope with those communication partners that do not have EDI capability. As Exhibit 4-20 shows, this view is apparently being shared by survey respondents.

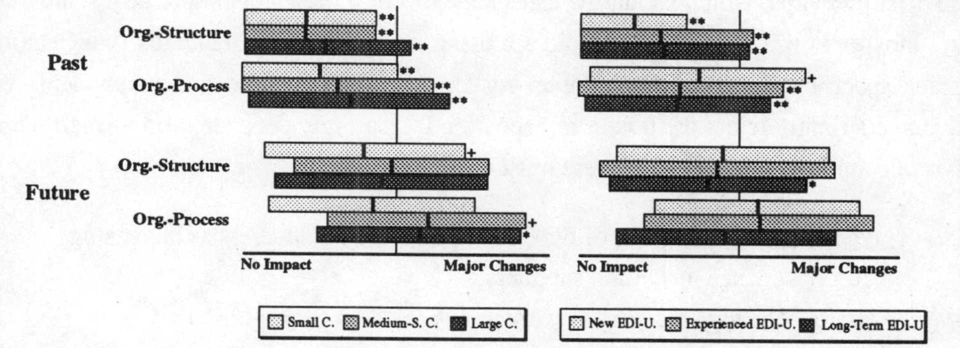

Exhibit 4-20	Past and Future Organizational Changes due to EDI

Without specifying further which type of changes respondents have experienced or foresee with the continuing proliferation of EDI, neither organizational structure nor processes have thus far been affected to any significant extent. And even in the future about 40% of the organizations included in the sample do not expect major process changes, let alone any impact on corporate structure. It is interesting to note that these findings do neither depend at all on the length of time EDI is being used nor on the volume of EDI messages being exchanged. Contrary to expectations, users who have been involved in EDI for a longer period of time are, on average, even more critical towards such statements.

> <u>Hypothesis A12:</u> The adoption of EDI is expected to induce modifications of organizational processes.
> *Finding: Inconclusive evidence. The Null Hypothesis can only be rejected for some subgroups such as medium-sized ($\mu = 0.61^{+}$) and large organizations ($\mu = 0.45^{*}$)*[76].

75) See e.g. Scheer (1987b).

76) Unless stated otherwise, measurement is always based on 7-point Likert scales (-3 through +3).

Hypothesis A13: The adoption of EDI is not expected to induce modifications of organizational structures.
Finding: Inconclusive evidence. Mean values have the required negative signs, yet the Null Hypothesis cannot be rejected.

Another indirect (strategic) form of costs may arise from a reduction in "bargaining power"[77] vis-à-vis suppliers as a result of higher switching costs due to established EDI partnerships, which should be especially severe in cases of proprietary standards. As most organizations in the sample are using non-proprietary standards (which mitigates specificity induced transactions costs), it seems plausible that respondents on average strongly reject the notion of becoming increasingly dependent on a small number of suppliers, at least not because of EDI.

Hypothesis A11: The use of EDI is not perceived by adopters as increasing their dependence on certain suppliers.
Finding: The hypothesis is consistent with the data ($\mu = -1.27^{**}$).

4.3.4.3. Benefits of EDI

As the perception of EDI's inevitability may not be shared by all organizations, being able to identify and estimate the benefits offered could become an important element of a persuasion strategy. Yet due to the mostly indirect, intangible effects of EDI that are inextricably intertwined with other organizational decisions, measurement is difficult if not impossible to accomplish. Fortunately, user perceptions of benefits are more relevant in the context of adoption decisions than concrete but unreliable estimates. Therefore, users' subjective assessments were chosen as the focus of the investigation which has the side benefit of circumventing potential disagreements on terms and definitions, measurement variables, etc. and thus allows to make meaningful comparisons. The trade-off, however, is that no precise quantification of benefits can be given.

4.3.4.3.1. Tangible Benefits

The first question aimed at the significance of the direct monetary benefits due to EDI as examined in section 2.4.2.2. According to the sample subjects, EDI provides little if any direct financial benefits for users let alone a "substantial" advantage. Even high-

77) Porter (1980) p. 27.

volume users paint a sobering picture with respect to the monetary rewards EDI has to offer. Only in terms of transaction costs (and displacement of clerical staff) did high-volume users indicate some returns due to EDI; on all other counts EDI does not seem to make a difference. Particularly striking is the lack of impact on inventory savings which is supposedly one of the prime motivators for external systems integration.

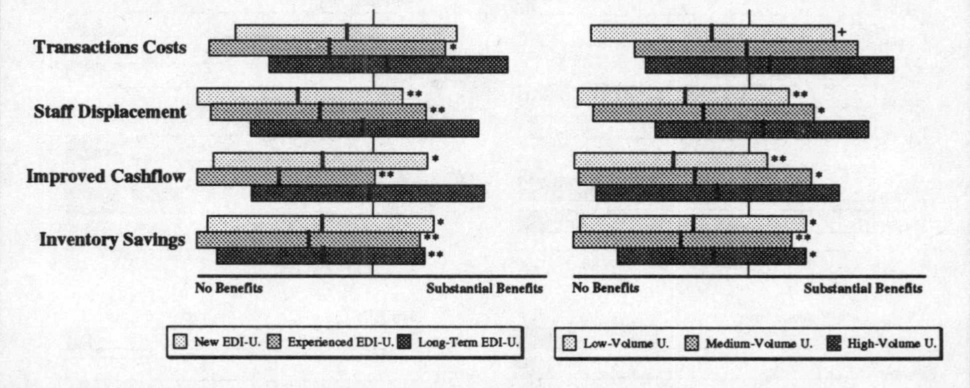

Exhibit 4-21	Monetary Benefits due to EDI

Hypothesis A3: The use of EDI is perceived to have a significant positive impact on transaction costs.
Finding: The hypothesis is inconsistent with the data (with few exceptions $\mu < 0$*) and the Null Hypothesis cannot be rejected.*

Hypothesis A4: The use of EDI is not perceived to have a significant impact on lowering inventory levels.
Finding: The hypothesis is consistent with the data ($\mu < 0$**).*

If in fact EDI were generally perceived as a tool to achieve major cost savings, one would expect that organizations facing a business environment characterized by intensive price competition would vigorously pursue EDI in order to increase profitability or simply to remain viable. Given such a strategic incentive, the time to implement EDI should *ceteris paribus* be comparatively small. This proposition, however, does not hold.

Hypothesis C6: The length of the implementation stage is negatively related to the perceived degree of price competition.
Finding: Hypothesis is inconsistent with the data (regression coefficient has the wrong sign $\beta_1 = 0.09$*)*

As it is the only benefit category that can be measured with some degree of accuracy, respondents were requested to specify to what extent EDI contributed to the displacement of clerical staff in the past and would likely be able to do so in the future. Exhibit 4-22 summarizes the data.

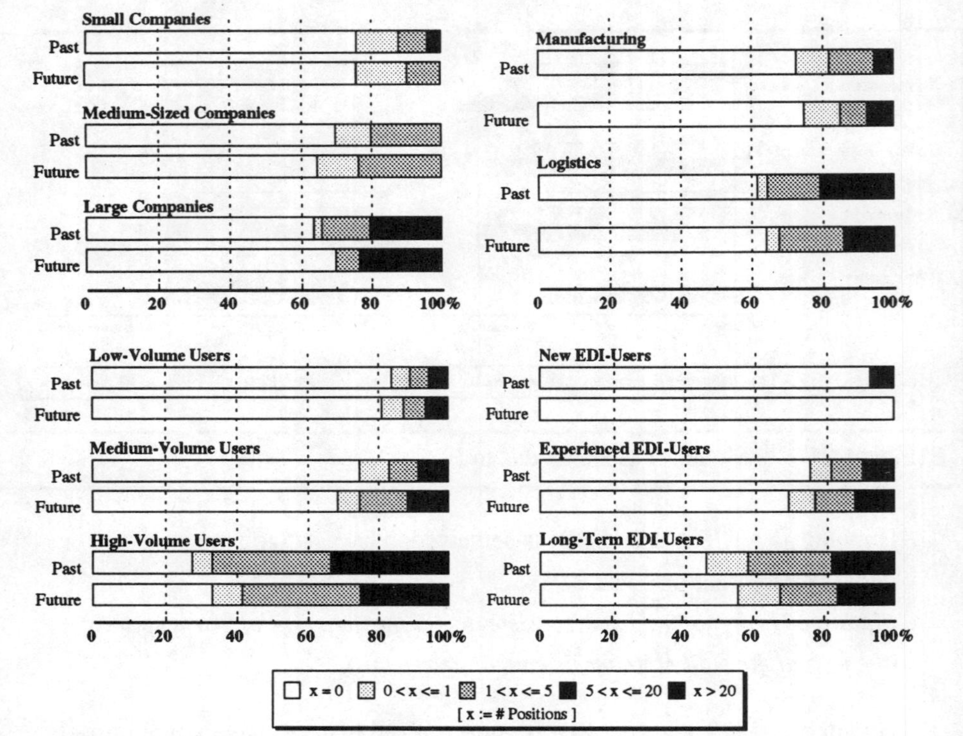

Exhibit 4-22	Displacement of Clerical Staff due to EDI

Almost 70% of the respondents declared that EDI did not have and will not have any effect on clerical staffing levels. Especially new EDI-users consider the potential for staff-savings to be negligible, a phenomenon that supports the hypothesis that organizations gradually learn how to capitalize on their EDI-investments. Particularly intriguing is the consistency of answers between past experience and future expectations. Neither organizational size nor the distinction between logistics and manufacturing type companies yields a clear indication for opportunities to streamline administrative overhead. The ability to displace staff seems to be directly proportionate to trading volume. In contrast to the other organizations, more than 2/3 of high-volume users claim to have saved at least one clerical position and 1/3 of those have been able to displace five or more.

The preceding analysis suggests that, evaluated from a purely financial perspective, EDI is hardly perceived as a profitable investment. This interpretation is reinforced by replies to the question whether EDI has produced sufficient tangible benefits to outweigh the costs incurred.

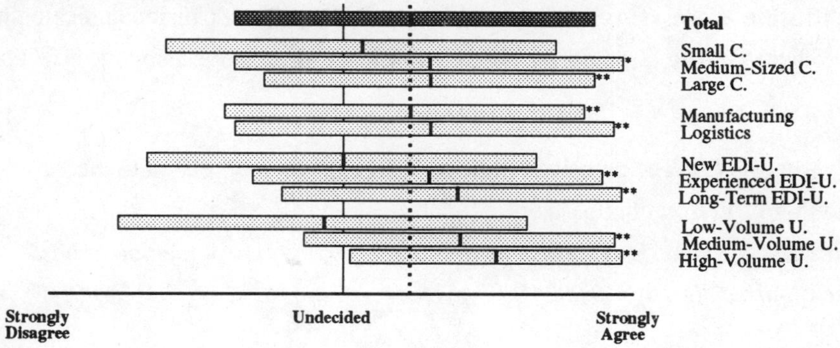

Exhibit 4-23	"EDI's Tangible Benefits Outweigh Costs."

As Exhibit 4-23 shows, only high-volume users generally seem to agree that EDI makes sense from a financial perspective. By contrast, even long-time EDI advocates are not fully convinced that EDI has been a positive-net-present-value investment.

> <u>Hypothesis A2:</u> The perceived utility of EDI is positively related to transaction volume.
> *Finding: Hypothesis is consistent with the data (regression coefficient has the required sign β_1 = 0.00001*).*

Another question of interest not answered by Exhibit 4-23 relates to the influence of integrating EDI systems with other IS on the user perception of EDI. Theoretically, a high degree of integration should provide more benefits in terms of transaction cost savings than stand-alone systems. This proposition is supported by the data when the utility assessments of mainframe and stand-alone PC users are compared.

> <u>Hypothesis C8:</u> The perceived utility of EDI is positively related to the degree of integration with the organization's other IS-resources.
> *Finding: Hypothesis is consistent with the data (mean difference Δ = 1.15* between mainframe-based EDI and organizations using stand-alone PCs).*

Furthermore, it was for conceptual reasons argued repeatedly in section 3. that EDI is subject to network externality effects. Given the user assessments about the advantageousness of EDI, it becomes feasible to test this contention against the collected data. If the hypothesized proposition was true, users having reached a high micro-level state of diffusion should on average appreciate EDI more highly than those at the early stages of the diffusion process. As it turns out, irrespective of the diffusion indicator being used, the data seem to strongly support the existence of positive network effects with EDI.

> Hypothesis C9: The perceived utility of EDI is positively related to the number of EDI trading partners.
> *Finding: Hypothesis is consistent with the data (regression coefficient has the required sign $\beta_1 = 0.0024^*$).*

> Hypothesis C10: The perceived utility of EDI is positively related to the diffusion level reached.
> *Finding: Hypothesis is consistent with the data (regression coefficient has the required sign $\beta_1 = 1.85^{**}$).*

4.3.4.3.2. Intangible Benefits

The characteristics of EDI as a technology with positive network externalities are inconsistent with the notion of a lasting competitive advantage due to EDI. Thus, EDI, and this holds true particularly for recent users, should merely help organizations to avoid being at a service disadvantage vis-à-vis the competition.

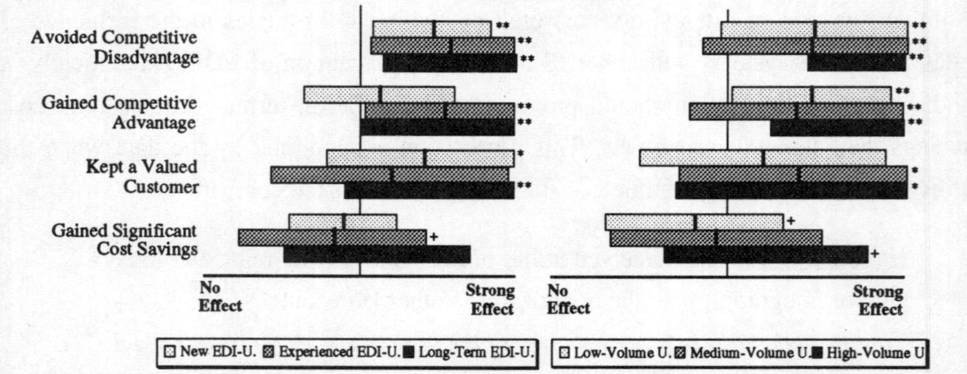

Exhibit 4-24	Competitive Effects of EDI

The survey findings generally vindicate this interpretation although the results are again ambiguous as the wide distribution of responses illustrates. Companies that only recently began to use EDI rate the competitive advantage achievable through EDI unmistakeably lower than those which have been sending and receiving EDI messages for quite some time. Nonetheless, the idea of competitive advantage still permeates the thinking of respondents.

> Hypothesis A8: The use of EDI is perceived as allowing organizations to avoid competitive disadvantage, irrespective of the lateness of adoption.
> *Finding: Hypothesis is consistent with the data (mean values for all adopter groups are significantly greater than zero:* $\mu = 1.89^{**}$ *for long-term EDI users,* $\mu = 1.76^{**}$ *for experienced EDI users, and* $\mu = 1.5^{**}$ *for new EDI users).*

> Hypothesis A9: The use of EDI is perceived by early adopters as providing competitive advantage.
> *Finding: Hypothesis is consistent with the data (mean value* $\mu = 1.51^{**}$ *for long-term EDI users).*

> Hypothesis A10: The use of EDI is not perceived by late adopters as providing competitive advantage.
> *Finding: Inconclusive evidence. The mean value* ($\mu = 0.41$) *is positive yet not significantly so which would allow to reverse the hypothesis*[78]*.*

To further analyze the perceived strategic impact of EDI, respondents were asked first to what extent they felt a positive contribution could be attributed to EDI with respect to four criteria alluded to in section 2.4.3.: Improved Service, Improved Responsiveness, Improved Control, and Increased Flexibility.

Exhibit 4-25 provides an overview of the responses. With the noticeable exception of more recent EDI adopters, it is the service advantage that is most palatable to EDI-user organizations regardless of their size, volume of EDI-traffic or length of EDI-experience.

---

78) Since the group of late EDI adopters in the sample consists of only 17, respectively 18 organizations, Q-Q plots were used to test for normality. With correlation coefficients $r = 0.99$ for both questions, normality was assumed.

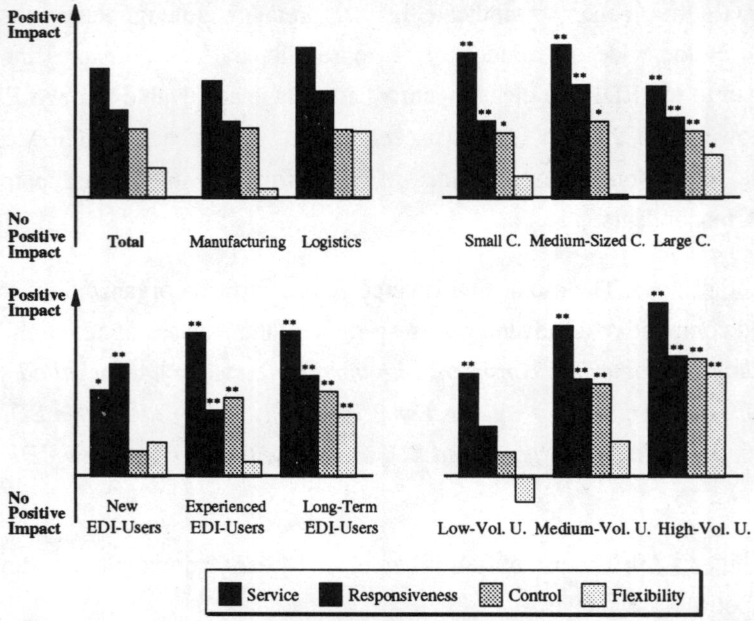

Exhibit 4-25	Strategic Impacts of EDI Applications

Flexibility generally receives low marks but, similar to the control benefits, soars in relevance with the number of messages exchanged per period. For organizations primarily involved in logistics, the flexibility advantage due to EDI is more important than for manufacturing companies. Strikingly, only more recent EDI-users found the responsiveness-effect of EDI more significant than service aspects which may be due to a growing sophistication in employing EDI for marketing purposes. However, the results, particularly the low score with respect to control, are not inconsistent with the hypothesis that many organizations still conceive of EDI primarily as a marketing gadget to please customers rather than as a tool to more efficiently conduct business transactions. At any rate, the strategic benefits perceived appear to be highly correlated with the extent of EDI-usage as opposed to other variables such as the length of EDI experience.

> Hypothesis A5: The use of EDI is perceived to have a positive impact on customer service.
>
> *Finding: Hypothesis is consistent with the data (mean values of responses are significantly greater than zero, ranging from 0.94* to 2.25**, depending upon the subgroup).*

Hypothesis A6: The use of EDI is perceived to have a positive impact on customer responsiveness.
Finding: Hypothesis is consistent with the data (mean values of responses are significantly greater than zero, ranging from 0.61^{+} to 1.56^{**}, depending upon the subgroup).

The degree to which EDI is believed to improve the responsiveness of organizations may also be deduced indirectly by analyzing the time it took to implement EDI systems and correlate this measure with the perceived intensity of responsiveness competition. The rationale behind this hypothesis is that (*ceteris paribus*) EDI should be pursued with greater vigor by organizations who depend on the technology for competitive reasons. However, the data collected provide no indication in support of this argument.

Hypothesis C5: The length of the implementation stage is negatively related to the perceived degree of responsiveness competition.
Finding: Hypothesis is inconsistent with the data (the regression coefficient has the wrong sign $\beta_1 = 0.09$).

Hypothesis A7: The use of EDI is perceived to have a positive impact on internal control.
Finding: Inconclusive evidence. Mean values have the required sign but the Null Hypothesis cannot be rejected for late adopters or organizations with only a low volume of EDI traffic.

4.3.4.4. Role of Value-Added Networks and Services

The role of VANS in the context of EDI was analyzed from three different angles[79]: Firstly, some perceptions about the general merits of VANS are being evaluated. Secondly, respondents were asked to assess the relevance of common VAN services/functions. Thirdly, an attempt was made to identify criteria that EDI users applied to select a VANS provider.

Exhibit 4-26 shows that VANS are deemed important contributors to establishing and operating EDI trading clusters. Regardless of trading volume or size of the organization, respondents generally agree that VANS play an important role during the implementation stage of EDI-systems. Quite interestingly, their service charges are generally re-

79) 85 organizations in the sample allegedly use VANs.

garded as fair, with the noticeable exception of high-volume users who seem to advocate a steeper volume-based discount-system for tariffs. However, since high-volume users generally derive the largest amount of benefits from EDI, tariff structures seem to be more or less commensurate with economic returns.

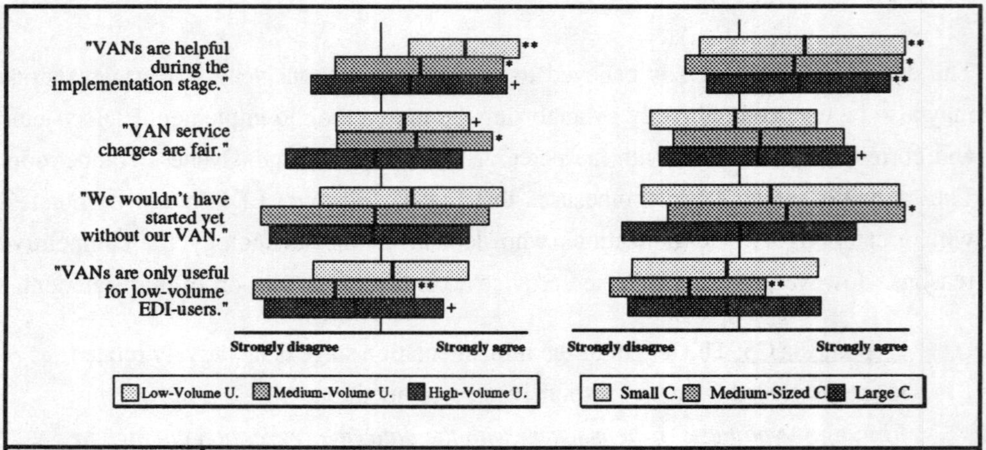

Exhibit 4-26 Perception of VAN Services

More than 50% of the organizations frankly admit that they probably would not have started EDI without the existence of VANs, and the argument that VANs, by virtue of their store-and-forward messaging systems, are only viable for low-volume users whereas others integrate their DP systems directly, is rejected by most sample organizations.

While the market for VAN services is well-established in the U.S., it is only emerging in Europe where comparatively high growth rates are predicted for the next few years[80]. As a consequence, some uncertainty exists about which types of services are needed most against those which are either irrelevant or the large-scale deployment of which can be postponed until the use of EDI has become more sophisticated. In light of these circumstances, EDI users where asked how VAN services fit their particular requirements. Exhibit 4-27 provides an overview of how clients value common VAN functions/services.

80) According to a recent report by Frost and Sullivan, the European VAN market is predicted to expand by some 250% between 1988 and 1994. See also Mulder (1989).

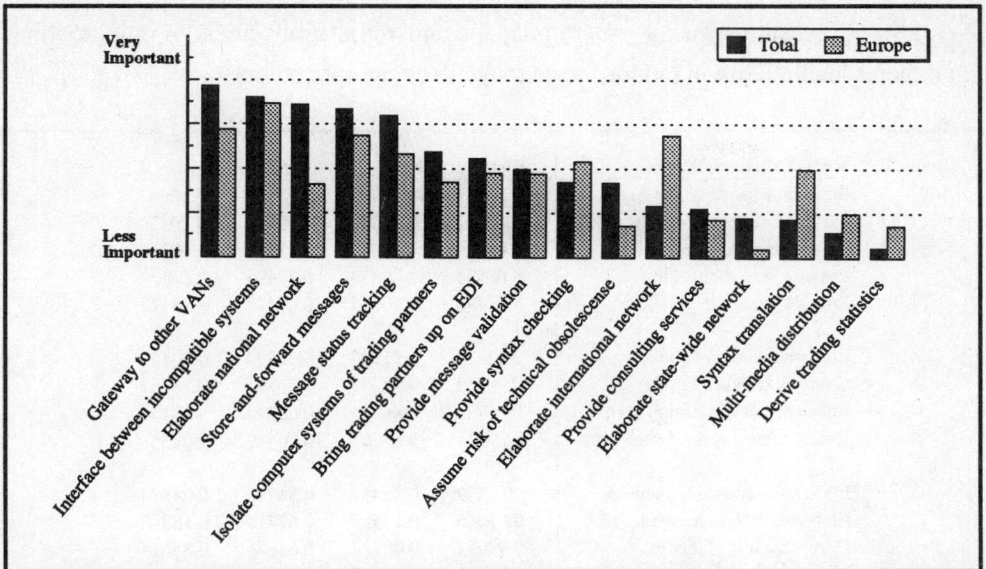

Exhibit 4-27	Evaluation of VAN Functions/Services

From a European perspective, VANS are needed most to (1) interface between incompatible systems and to provide a wide reach by means of (2) an elaborate international network as well as (3) gateways to other VANs. Of secondary importance are functions such as message status tracking, store-and-forwarding, and checking messages for correct syntax. Presently more or less irrelevant, on the other hand, are such widely discussed services as multi-media capability, consulting, and the derivation of trading-statistics. The data are consistent with the interpretation that EDI is still very much in its infancy because the most urgent problems are primarily of technical nature. Users seem to be highly concerned about the inability to reach their trading partners via EDI as a result of insufficient regional network expansion rather than lack of technical sophistication of their communication services provider. Consequentially, VANs and public telecommunication operators should strive to quickly spread their networks in order to provide adequate geographical coverage.

> Hypothesis B1: The perceived utility of VANS is positively related to the number of EDI communication partners.
> *Finding: The hypothesis is consistent with the data (regression coefficient has the required sign $\beta_1 = 0.1^{**}$).*

In order to see whether the functions/services listed in Exhibit 4-27 could be aggregated into fewer, more generic categories, the data were subjected to a factor analysis. Table

4-6 shows the resulting factor pattern after rotation and rearrangement of the variables; high factor loadings are in boldface type to facilitate interpretation[81]:

VAN-Functions/Services	Factor 1	Factor 2	Factor 3	Factor 4
Store-and-forward messages	**0.66959**	0.32901	0.12838	0.26967
Message status tracking	**0.64411**	0.41298	0.09952	0.20324
Provide message validation	**0.88769**	0.19189	0.17902	0.10716
Provide syntax checking	**0.88984**	0.0839	0.27405	0.13139
Provide syntax translation	**0.61495**	0.00614	0.45725	0.33427
Elaborate national network	0.12731	**0.71587**	0.38274	-0.00154
Gateway to other VANs	0.00739	**0.72393**	0.33861	0.18159
Interface betw. incomp. syst.	0.26789	**0.6724**	-0.08928	0.3133
Isolate comp. syst. of trad. prtn.	0.27457	**0.69501**	0.04442	0.08563
Elaborate state-wide network	0.0839	0.35487	**0.54726**	-0.04824
Elaborate intern. network	0.11066	0.17555	**0.67715**	0.13362
Derive trading statistics	0.38971	0.08727	**0.63675**	0.35014
Multi-media distribution	0.39748	0.0086	**0.72549**	0.33161
Bring trad. partners up on EDI	0.18788	0.2218	0.17224	**0.83642**
Provide consulting services	0.2471	0.12907	0.20161	**0.80929**

Table 4-6 Factor Analysis of VAN Functions/Services

Interpretation of factor loadings may well be more of an art than a science. Nonetheless, it appears as if four broad categories of functions/services can be identified. The first category (Factor 1) consists of services directly related to the messaging task. It may therefore be called "Message Services". The second group (Factor 2) contains what may be considered as "Basic Services", i.e. those functions/services which from the perspective of subscribers constitute the *raison d' être* of VANS: Providing a communications infrastructure and establishing compatibility between the communicating IS. The next group of services (Factor 3) could be called "Special Services" that are only required in certain applications. In contrast to the classification of VANS functions/services developed in section 2.3.3.2., consulting and training are sufficiently different from the viewpoint of users to merit a separate group (Factor 4).

> Hypothesis B2: According to the perceptions of EDI user organizations, the services provided by VANS can be grouped into the three categories "Transmission Services", "Message Services", and "Auxiliary Services".

81) The specific factor estimates were obtained by applying the principal components method while observing the eigenvalue criterion. The grouping of variables did not change when maximum likelihood estimation was used for verification purposes. The factors were subsequently rotated according to the familiar varimax method; cf. e.g. Johnson/Wichern (1982) p. 426..

Finding: The hypothesis is inconsistent with the data. While "Transmission Services" could possibly be equated with the group of basic services pertaining to Factor 2, it is necessary to further differentiate the class of auxiliary functions into the two subclasses of special and consulting services (67% of the total variance in the original 16 variables is explained by the four factors).

Since Hypothesis B3 depends on B2, it becomes necessary to slightly adjust the formulation in order to accommodate the results just obtained. *Mutatis mutandis*:

> Hypothesis B3': VANS basic (transmission) services are considered more valuable by EDI user organizations than message, special or consulting services.
> *Finding: Inconclusive evidence. The Null Hypothesis cannot be rejected for the mean difference between basic and message services (Δ = 1.01); it can, however, for the differences between basic and special services (Δ = 5.69**) and between basic and consulting services (Δ = 4.96**).*

The importance of network expansion is further emphasized by the answers obtained with respect to VAN selection criteria. As Exhibit 4-28 shows, VANs are most frequently chosen as a result of their established relationship with an organization's trading partners rather than a thorough cost/benefit analysis.

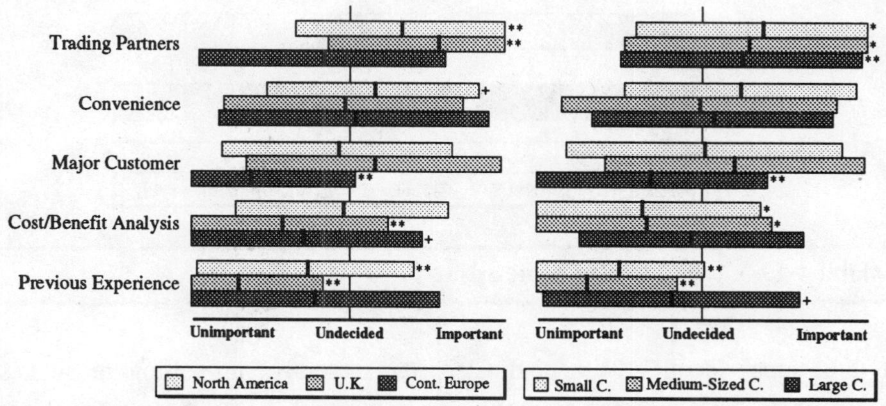

Exhibit 4-28	VAN Selection Criteria

The predictive power of responses is, again, somewhat limited due to the large variance. However, the data suggest that financial aspects are mostly irrelevant, especially in Continental Europe. Convenience or lack of viable alternatives often dictate the outcome of the selection decision. Interestingly, the impact of a major customer is often greatly exaggerated. The particularly in the U.K. highly successful "hub-and-spoke" marketing approach of VANs to solicit new business may, according to the data, not be the most effective strategy in Continental Europe.

4.3.4.5. Diffusion and Future Evolution of EDI

The final section of the questionnaire was devoted to gathering information about the respondents' general attitude towards EDI. Special emphasis was given to planned future activities as well as near-term anxieties. Moreover, the objective was to determine which barriers to EDI are relevant from the viewpoint of practicioners and which measures should be taken to overcome those obstacles.

At the outset of section 4.3.2. it was argued that distinguishing between geographical areas would be sensible because they correspond to certain EDI-syntax standards. As Exhibit 4-29 illustrates, the findings of the survey are consistent with this proposition:

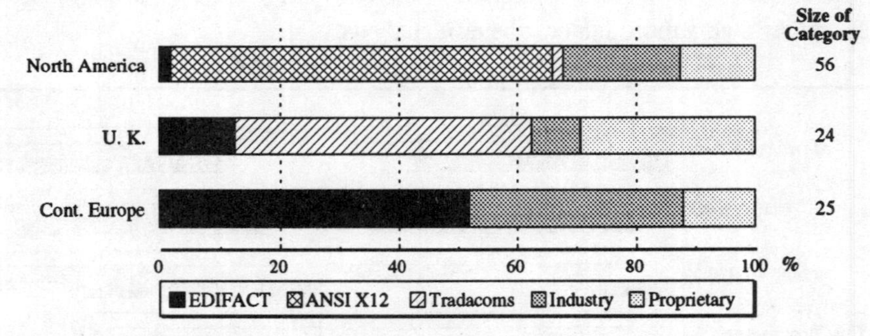

Exhibit 4-29	EDI Syntax Standards by Area

All three areas identified are dominated (the respective proportion in all cases is approximately 50%) by a single EDI message standard. In North America most companies rely on the ANSI X12 syntax. By contrast, no British entity in the sample was using the American standard; whereas a few organizations were leaning towards the international EDIFACT syntax, most of them were either employing TRADACOMS or some kind of proprietary standard. Companies in Continental Europe are either striving to implement EDIFACT-based EDI-systems or pursue industry-specific standards such as ODETTE.

In combination with Exhibit 4-30, the findings do lend support to the notion that Continental Europe is firmly behind EDIFACT which will continue to grow in importance and gradually replace other standards. The picture in the U.K. is different in that national standards are deeply entrenched giving rise to the expectation that migration to EDIFACT will take more time. In North America, however, it is doubtful that EDIFACT will gain acceptance let alone ubiquity any time soon. 30% of the respondents completely rule out the possibility of switching to EDIFACT or X.400 standards; scarcely 20% express their definite intention to do so, which underscores the importance of established market standards[82]. As soon as a standard has gained adherents, those organizations may lack sufficient incentive to switch even though new standards may be slightly superior. Not surprisingly therefore, more than one third of the sample organizations explicitly confirmed that they would become actively involved in the standards debate and vowed to support several standards if necessary. Hence, it seems much more likely that for the foreseeable future EDI-user organizations in North America will either stick to or adopt ANSI X12 standards; the only exception may be those users with a comparatively large proportion of their business attached to international trade[83].

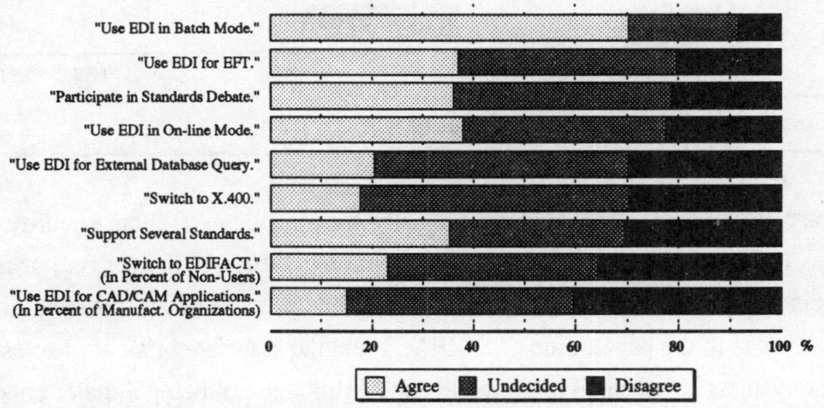

Exhibit 4-30	Future EDI Application Domains

82) This problem has been labeled "excess inertia"; cf. Farrell/Saloner (1986) and section 3. of this thesis.

83) See e.g. Warner (1989) p. 131.

According to the data presented in Exhibit 4-30, some uncertainty prevails regarding the domains to which EDI will be applied in the future. With the exception of sending EDI messages via batch-mode, in each prospective area of EDI utilization about 40% of the respondents remain undecided as to whether they will become involved at some later stage. Whereas most users intend to (continue to) use EDI in batch-mode, almost 40% have already decided to run EDI on-line, i.e. interactively, as well. This poses special problems for VANs because it requires installation of some kind of direct/immediate message delivery mechanism which relays messages received instantaneously to the addressee without his prior request. Since some networks already offer such services, the technical difficulties associated with direct delivery seem to be managable.

The concern about the possible impact EDIFACT might have on existing systems can also be taken from the data shown in Exhibit 4-31.

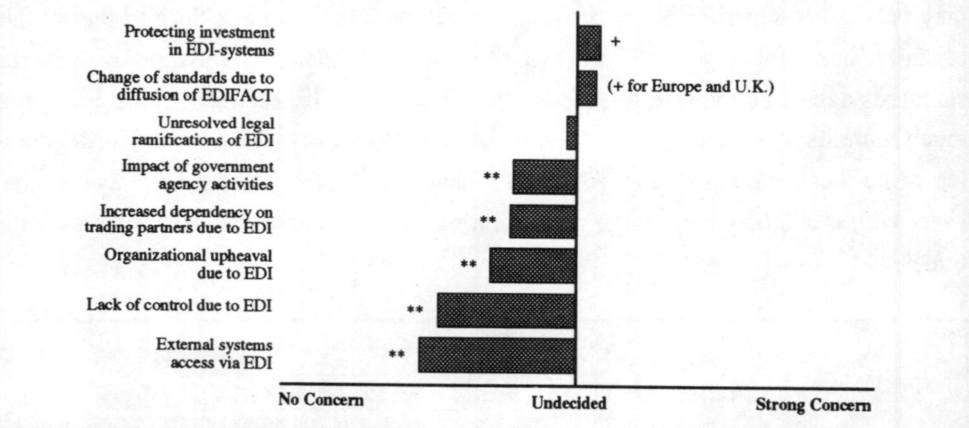

Exhibit 4-31	User Concerns about EDI

Contrary to anxieties expressed occasionally by practicioners about security aspects, such as fraudulent systems access, and contentions portraying the dangers of increased switching costs as potentially harmful consequences of EDI, the possible change of standards due to the penetration of EDIFACT and the associated risk of obsolescence of current systems are deemed more threatening. Although not being a major concern, the unresolved legal ramifications of EDI continue to arouse some uneasiness among EDI-users.

> <u>Hypothesis C11:</u> Unresolved legal issues of EDI are not perceived as important barriers to the diffusion of EDI.

Finding: Inconclusive evidence. The mean value has the required sign (μ = -0.09), yet is not sufficiently deviant from zero to permit rejection of the Null Hypothesis.

As the diffusion of EDI and those factors that influence the rate of adoption are at the center of this investigation, respondents were finally asked to assess the relevance of frequently mentioned barriers to EDI. As can be seen in Exhibit 4-32 below, the most important EDI barrier is the need to change internal application systems when linking applications directly rather than sending and receiving messages in door-to-door mode. Practicioners still deplore a general lack of know-how which is insofar important as that this problem can be mitigated by means of intensified awareness and education campaigns. In other words, whereas only user organizations themselves are able to deal with such issues as e.g. a lack of systems integration, external institutions can foster the diffusion of EDI by providing expertise and offering advice, e.g. as to which EDI-configuration to choose, how implementation should be managed, or how to evaluate EDI financially.

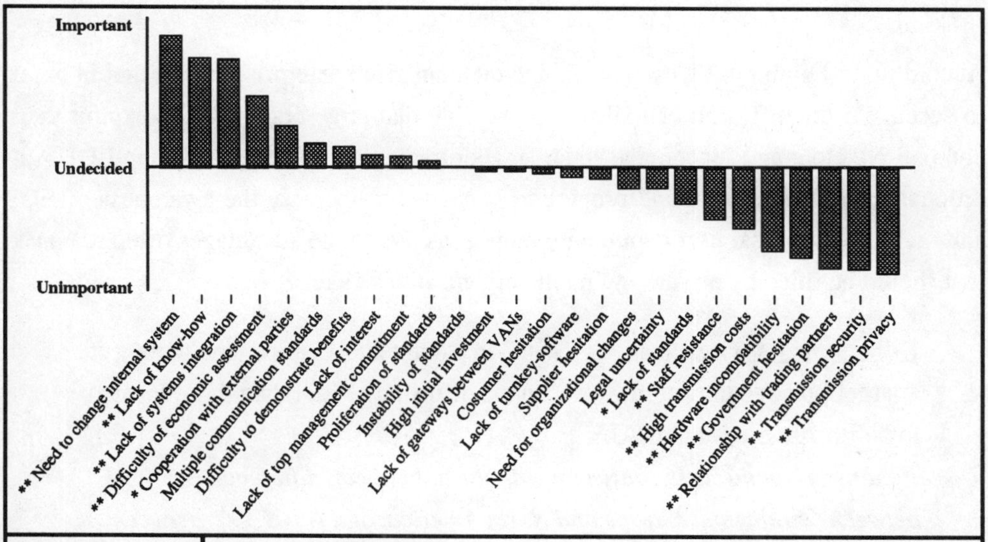

Exhibit 4-32	Perceived EDI Barriers

Irrelevant, at least from the perspective of organizations in the sample, are those concerns that relate to the security and privacy of EDI transmissions. Apparently, users have great confidence in the ability of telecommunication networks and systems to protect the integrity and privacy of messages. Likewise, adverse relationships with trading partners or the lack of government involvement do not tend to delay the introduction of EDI systems. Even the uncertain legal situation mentioned before may be of some concern to organizations but in general does not raise insurmountable barriers.

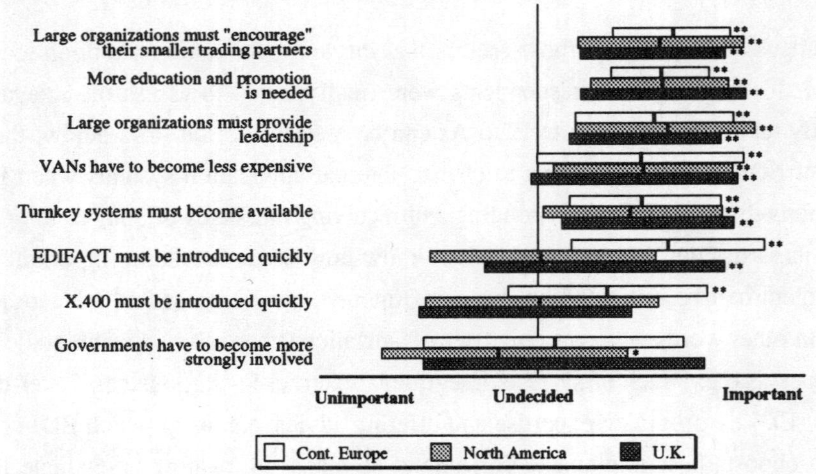

Exhibit 4-33 | Strategies for Accelerated EDI-Diffusion

According to Exhibit 4-33, even small and medium-sized enterprises agree that in order to accelerate the diffusion of EDI it is inexorable that large organizations exploit their competitive clout and "encourage" their smaller trading partners to start using EDI. Additionally, more education and promotion is needed to increase the awareness of EDI and make the potential user community more sensitive to the advantages offered, a task that should be filled by private and public organizations alike.

> Hypothesis B4: Organizations located in Continental Europe tend to expect a larger positive impact of X.400 on the diffusion of EDI than those located in North America and the U.K.
> *Finding: Hypothesis is consistent with the data (mean difference $\Delta = 0.98^{**}$ between Continental Europe and North America, and $\Delta = 1.19^{**}$ between Continental Europe and the U.K.).*

> Hypothesis B5: Organizations located in Continental Europe tend to expect a larger positive impact of EDIFACT on the diffusion of EDI than those located in North America and the U.K.

*Finding: Hypothesis is consistent with the data (mean difference Δ = 1.75** between Continental Europe and North America, and Δ = 0.89* between Continental Europe and the U.K.).*

Finally, the data offer the opportunity to analyze to what extent the use of VANS on the one hand and the use of public EDI standards on the other exert a positive influence on the diffusion rate. Whereas contrary to expectations, no association between a subscription to VANS and micro-level diffusion could be detected, organizations who are willing to absorb higher initial set-up costs by adopting non-proprietary standards, later reap the benefits in terms of a higher diffusion rate, which may be one of the most important results of this investigation.

Hypothesis C12: The use of VANS leads to a higher diffusion rate than the use of direct links.
Finding: Inconclusive evidence. The mean difference between VANS users and those with direct communciation links to their trading partners has the wrong sign (Δ = -0.04) but is not sufficiently negative to allow reversing the hypothesis[84].

Hypothesis C13: The use of proprietary standards leads to a lower diffusion rate than the use of public standards.
Finding: Hypothesis appears consistent with the data (mean difference in the diffusion rate Δ = 0.23+ between users of public and proprietary syntax standards)[85].

In fact, when entering the β-estimates into the logistic function, formula (3.3), it turns out that users of public standards reach a 90% diffusion level more than two years earlier than their counterparts[86].

84) Moreover, diffusion rate data were only available for nine organizations advocating direct communication linkages, which renders the assumption of normality questionnable. No Q-Q plot test can be performed with such a small number of entities.

85) Some caution however needs to be exercised since the number of organizations using proprietary standards for which diffusion data are available is only ten. Thus, the assumption of normality, a critical prerequisite for testing the hypothesis, could not be evaluated.

86) As can be easily verified with $\beta_{proprietary} = 0.747$, $\beta_{non\text{-}proprietary} = 0.984$, and assuming $a = 100$.

5. Summary and Conclusions

5.1. Research Summary

The empirical investigation conducted within the framework of this research project was driven by the objective to account for the apparent discrepancy between the substantial operational and strategic benefits frequently attributed to EDI and the comparatively low level of adoption among the potential user community. The existence of positive network externalities was postulated at the outset as a tentative explanation that was to be evaluated by means of a conceptual analysis as well as an empirical research study based on a large sample of EDI user organizations.

In order to confirm the proposition of network effects and rule out alternative explanations, commencing the analysis with an effort to determine the defining characteristics of EDI was deemed necessary, in order to unambiguously distinguish it from related concepts. Having accomplished this task, the various technical and operational prerequisites of EDI were examined to (a) verify that the diffusion of EDI was not impaired simply due to the non-availability of essential requirements, and (b) to explore the range of basic EDI implementation options. Subsequently, direct and indirect business implications of EDI as reported in the contemporary business press and management literature were discussed. A plausibility analysis revealed that the suggested causality between organizational efficiency improvements and the introduction of EDI systems is often unjustified.

Examination of the literature on positive network externalities provided further support to the notion that the benefits individual users are able to derive from EDI are, analogous to other telecommunications technologies, dependent on the diffusion level reached. Consequentially, the focus of attention shifted to determinants of the diffusion process as taken from innovation diffusion research, properly adapted for network effects. According to the analysis presented, network externalities are primarily relevant with respect to the adopter's restricted set of major communications partners, which led to the emphasis on micro-level diffusion as opposed to the overall diffusion of EDI.

Given the presumption that the benefits of EDI depend to some extent on the level of adoption within distinct communities of interest, the empirical investigation was deliberately geared towards the question of why organizations adopt EDI early, i.e. before the postulated critical mass effects precipitate the diffusion process. Another factor believed to retard the proliferation of EDI in practice relates to the uncertainty confronted by potential users regarding the economic consequences associated with EDI and the long-term viability of different system configuration alternatives with respect to the choice of communications standards, including protocols and message syntax. Hence, the envisaged contribution of this research was twofold: One, to reduce this uncertainty by means of systematically gathering and analyzing the collective experiences of a sufficiently large number of EDI users in various industries and geographical areas; two, to provide some hints for institutional intervention efforts aimed at accelerating the pace of EDI diffusion.

The empirical research was conducted through a first round of interviews with some 30 carefully selected EDI user organizations and services suppliers in Europe, representing a cross-section of important industries and countries, followed by a mail survey in the course of which a 14-page questionnaire was sent to several hundred enterprises located in Europe and North America that had been identified as active in EDI; more than 100 of those organizations participated in the survey. The information obtained was then subjected to statistical analysis in order to determine patterns that could be generalized to certain subsets of the overall population of EDI users, and to test the more than 30 hypotheses derived from the conceptual evaluation.

5.2. Research Conclusions

5.2.1. Conclusions Relative to Business Implications of EDI

According to the findings of this research, the organizational implications of EDI are far less revolutionary than often claimed. Aside from the customary establishment of EDI subunits or groups, which in most cases are staffed with only a single individual who was internally transferred rather than hired in the labor market, the survey failed to produce any evidence that EDI will seriously affect organizational structures, at least not until its use has become pervasive. Even with respect to administrative processes, only users with a comparatively high volume of EDI transactions predict some changes in the future, yet no radical overhaul is foreseen any time soon.

The economic advantages that can be derived from the use of EDI are positively related to the degree of integration between EDI systems and other organizational IS as well as to the volume of the message exchange. Respondents generally concur in the assessment that, with the possible exception of a transaction cost reduction for high-volume users, EDI provides little if any immediate, pecuniary benefits, neither, coinciding with expectations, in terms of a reduction in capital holding costs due to lower inventories, nor with respect to diminished clerical staffing requirements. This conclusion must be qualified, however, in that the data suggest the existence of a gradual learning process, i.e. the familiarization with EDI and the necessary organizational adjustments that ultimately may affect employment take years rather than months to materialize. Therefore, no firm conclusions about the eventual employment effect can be offered, except for the trivial proposition that it can be expected to vary considerably across organizations.

With average investment requirements in the vicinity of a few ten thousand ECU and recurring monthly operating expenditures of just a few hundred ECU, the costs of implementing and operating EDI systems are neither negligible nor prohibitive for most organizations. In general, only systems development and software costs are perceived as significant. Furthermore, costs have declined substantially over time, due in part to the emergence of commercially available EDI converter software.

In light of the uncertainty about the amount of tangible benefits it provides, the impetus for EDI is frequently attributed to strategic considerations, and here above all the desire to avoid a competitive disadvantage in not being able to meet a specific customer demand. Thus, early adopters of EDI can expect to temporarily achieve a marketing advantage over competitors which, however, tends to quickly vanish when the growing diffusion of EDI turns the competitive advantage into a cost of the business, forcing adopters to find more indirect ways to harness the opportunities offered by EDI. For example, a low cost business strategy may be supported with EDI through operational savings achieved by means of a higher integration of EDI systems into the corporate IS-architecture. In conjunction with the adoption of public communications standards, the ongoing diffusion will eliminate strategic opportunities existing in the past to create switching cost barriers for customers arising from the specificity of the technical communications solution implemented. Besides the service advantage, EDI is appreciated mostly for its positive impact on responsiveness, i.e. the ability to more quickly take notice of changing environmental conditions and react accordingly.

5.2.2. Conclusions Relative to Communication Aspects of EDI

Of the two main alternatives to private communication linkages between trading partners, where any mutually agreeable protocols could be used, the services of VANS intermediaries are considered superior to X.25 packet-switched connections when the use of EDI expands beyond the limited initial set of trading partners. By virtue of providing a flexible communications interface, VANS are able to effectively shield subscribers from the various technical and procedural incompatibilities impairing a multilateral message exchange. This buffer function reduces the level of complexity that must be managed by individual EDI users and thus facilitates the micro-level diffusion process.

The services provided by VANS can broadly be divided into four categories: *Basic services*, related to the compatibility function of VANS and the infrastructure component; *messaging services*, related to the operational requirements of the message exchange process; *special services* and *consulting services*. Commensurate with the early stage of the EDI diffusion process, basic transmission and messaging functions are rated most important by subscriber organizations which seem to be foremost concerned about the ability to communicate with the desired trading partners through the VAN rather than being overly interested in the technical gimmickry of ever more sophisticated telecommunication services. It is therefore imperative that VANS strive to improve their network reach either by geographical expansion through establishing new network nodes or by inter-networking with other VANS. Moreover, the general insecurity of users, resulting from a lack of experience with the electronic mode of message exchange, demands that VANS offer message tracking facilities for subscribers to verify the status of the messages submitted to the network.

While specialized services, such as the generation of marketing research information or multi-media message distribution, are least important of all according to the current assessment of user organizations, VANS consulting services are considered a valuable contribution, especially during the implementation stage of EDI systems where VANS are frequently hired by major organizations to provide the necessary technical and administrative expertise to their smaller and less sophisticated trading partners. Given the influence that those large organizations wield with respect to the choice of the communications intermediary, the conventional hub-and-spoke marketing strategy pursued by most VANS must be deemed appropriate.

The medium- to long-term prospects for VANS in EDI appear unclear at this time for several reasons. On the one hand, it might well be more economical for communciation partners with a comparatively large amount of data exchange to lease a fixed communications line from a common carrier in lieu of using VANS for their EDI and other communication purposes; on the other hand, the emergence of EDI store-and-forward X.400 services by PTOs may lessen the extent to which EDI users with low message volumes need to rely on VANS. Moreover, parallel to the growing standardization of IT equipment, the need for special intermediaries to bridge technical system incompatibilities can be expected to decline, leaving only the currently less sought after consulting and specialized services as the not necessarily exclusive province of VANS in EDI. However, one further conceivable domain for VANS that seems to be of growing importance is the ability to accommodate interactive EDI. This is not feasible with the current version of X.400 but would require that VANS suppliers extend the functionality of their systems with a *direct* or *forced delivery* messaging service.

5.2.3. Conclusions Relative to Adoption, Implementation, and Diffusion of EDI

In general, EDI appears to be at a very early stage of diffusion with only a few thousand adopters out of a total of several million organizations. Even adopters have in many cases not progressed considerably beyond pilot phase. With the exception of a few large organizations which develop an internal impetus for EDI, either as a result of technology push or in connection with a JIT materials management strategy, most organizations adopt EDI only in response to some external stimulus. The empirical investigation revealed that two main sources of such a stimulus can be distinguished: One, an explicit customer demand, and two, to a much lesser degree, EDI activities of respective industry associations. As the postulated existence of network effects was supported by the empirical evidence, it seems plausible that especially smaller organizations appear to lack sufficient intrinsic motivation to start EDI on their own. Thus, without some 'encouragement' by their trading partners, the characteristic start-up problem of the diffusion process would be difficult if not impossible to overcome. Besides thinly veiled coercion, in order to promote the use of EDI, major organizations could facilitate adoption by providing some implementation help, yet, except for marginal contributions in terms of education and training, EDI user organizations rarely if ever grant any support to their trading partners.

Besides a still deplorable level of ignorance about EDI among the community of potential adopters, the most important impediment to the diffusion of EDI is the need to modify internal IS which is exacerbated by the limited systems development capacity available for this task in most organizations. Generally, EDI is not retarded by such frequently cited barriers as staff resistance, fraudulent systems access, or a hypothetical increase in switching costs. Neither do the uncertainties surrounding the enforceability of contracts closed with EDI pose serious difficulties to user organizations which ordinarily enter into bilateral interchange agreements to mitigate the associated legal risks.

The time required to implement EDI systems, while gradually declining, is dependent on the type of standards chosen and ranges from anywhere between 6 and 14 months. Whereas the use of proprietary standards leads to a significantly shorter implementation stage, adopters of public standards have been found to obtain a return for their more expensive up-front investment in a higher diffusion rate. Each of the three major areas covered in this investigation, North America, the U.K., and Continental Europe is currently dominated by a single cross-industry EDI syntax standard. Although domestic standards in North America and the U.K. are deeply entrenched, it can be expected that EDIFACT (or EDIFACT subsets for that matter), due to its universality and the international commitment, will prevail over the long-run. The proliferation of EDIFACT has already become the cause of increasing anxiety among non-EDIFACT users. Given the dependence on functioning EDI systems, those users explicitly articulate their intention to protect currently installed EDI systems from obsolescence.

A considerable degree of uncertainty exists regarding prospective future EDI applications. The data gathered in the course of the investigation reveal only one pattern, namely, that many organizations seem to contemplate the use of EDI in interactive mode which would either require them to resort to direct communication links or necessitate a forced message delivery capability by their VANS provider. If this mode of EDI communication was to become prominent in the future, X.400 would lose much of its current appeal as the envisaged universal EDI messaging service.

5.3. Research Implications

The research findings presented in the previous sections have several implications for institutional intervention that more or less all derive from the basic premise of this research, i.e. the assumption that EDI is subject to network externalities, which has been vindicated by the empirical evidence gathered.

First, given the very low overall diffusion level of EDI at present, combined with rather uncertain tangible benefits for early adopters, it was shown that the majority of organizations will only adopt EDI because of some external stimulus. Therefore, in order to surmount the start-up problems in the various EDI trading clusters it is imperative that large organizations show leadership in implementing EDI systems and exert pressure on their trading partners to follow suit. This holds especially true for major government institutions such as customs authorities and departments of defense, to name only two, which by virtue of their institutional role or their purchasing volumes wield substantial influence over the behavior of their business partners.

Second, as a result of the empirical data analysis concerning micro-level diffusion rates, a powerful argument can be made in favor of using public rather than proprietary standards. While the implementation of proprietary systems requires less initial effort in terms of development time and costs, organizations should nonetheless be exhorted to pursue the more difficult route of implementing public standards because they will eventually be rewarded with a significantly higher diffusion rate. For existing user communities with proprietary or industry-specific EDI standards, migration must be carefully prepared. Industry associations would seem to be the most natural institution to manage the collective transition.

Third, according to the findings of the field study, there seems to be a growing need to develop industry-specific subsets of public standards, the use of which should be mandatory for all industry members. Again, industry associations would be the most effective starting point for establishing a project organization to develop such standards. Those efforts should, however, be coordinated by the respective standards bodies who would be responsible for ensuring the overall compatibility between the various standard subsets.

5.4. Suggestions for Future Research

Based on the the experiences of this study, some suggestions for promising research topics within the general framework of EDI research can be made. To begin with, a potentially fruitful area of research would be an in-depth study of the organizational implications of EDI. While it must be regarded a futile endeavour to attempt a more precise quantification of the mostly intangible benefits of EDI, a longitudinal study should be able to illuminate in greater detail in which way EDI affects organizational procedures over time. As the use of EDI expands, even some typical patterns of structural reorganization may be determined with a concomitant impact on staffing requirements.

The second topic that may justify the attention of researchers relates to the problem of standards migration. The question to investigate would be in which specific cases EDI user communities should be able to benefit from switching standards and how the problem of excess inertia could be overcome. Equally interesting would be the project managment aspects of the transition including technical details such as, for instance, whether the use of versatile EDI converters, capable of supporting several standards, during the transition phase should be contemplated or perhaps special VANS syntax translation services.

Finally, research should be conducted with respect to the telecommunications services required for EDI in the future. Respective studies should not only investigate those services from a communications technology perspective, but also point to the particular business applications supported and further examine to what extent PTOs and VANS are likely to compete in those markets.

Bibliography

Abend, J., UPC + QR = JIT Inventory, in: Stores (May 1987), pp. 44 - 54.

Adams, D.A., Lacity, M.C., Mullins, J.R., Telecommunication Research in Information Systems: An Investigation of the Literature, in: Data Base 21 (1990), No. 2 and 3, pp. 21 - 26.

ADL, Electronic Data Interchange for the Grocery Industry - Feasibility Report, Cambridge: Arthur D. Little, Inc. 1980.

ADL, Direct Store Delivery Store-Level Study, Cambridge: Arthur D. Little, Inc. 1987.

Akerman, G.C., Introduction to Electronic Data Interchange - A Primer, s.l.: General Electric Information Services Company 1985.

Akerman, G.C., Introduction to Electronic Data Interchange - The First Steps, s.l.: General Electric Information Services Company 1987.

Akmajian, A., Demers, R.A., Harnish, R.M., Linguistics: An Introduction to Language and Communication, Cambridge-London: MIT Press 1979.

Albach, H., Innovationsstrategien zur Verbesserung der Wettbewerbsfähigkeit, in: Zeitschrift für Betriebswirtschaft 59 (1989), Nr. 12, pp. 1338 - 1352.

Albright, S.C., Statistics for Business and Economics, New York-London: Macmillan 1987.

Allen, B., Make Information Services Pay its Way, in: Harvard Business Review 65 (1987), No. 1, pp. 57 - 63.

Allen, D., New Telecommunications Services, in: Telecommunications Policy 12 (1988), No. 3, pp. 257 - 271.

Alonso, R., Barbará, D., Negotiating Data Access in Federated Database Systems, in: IEEE Computer Society (ed.), Proceedings of the Fifth International Conference on Data Engineering (Los Angeles), Washington: IEEE Computer Society Press 1989, pp. 56 - 65.

Amory, B.E., EDI and the Conclusion of Contract, in: The TEDIS - EDI Legal Workshop (Brussels), Brussels: Commission of the European Communities 1989, pp. 10 - 47.

Anderson, D.L., Bovet, D.M., Going Paperless Isn't just for Suppliers or OEMs, in: Actionline 7 (1988), No. 5, pp. 25 - 29.

Anner, R., Kommunikation mit EDI-Partnern: Nutzung Öffentlicher Netze und Mehrwertdienste, in: EWI (Hrsg.), Electronic Data Interchange EDI 90, Elektronischer Geschäftsverkehr mit EDIFACT: Perspektiven, Anwendungspraxis, Erfahrungen, Starnberg: EWI 1990, pp. 115 - 126.

Annis, T., JiT via EDI, in: Manufacturing Systems 4 (1986), No. 11, pp. 62 - 63.

ANSI ASC-X12, An Introduction to Electronic Data Interchange, New York: ANSI 1987.

Arnold, U., Wann ist JIT vorteilhaft?, in: Beschaffung aktuell (1989), Nr. 4, pp. 58 - 63.

Artle, R., Averous, C., The Telephone System as a Public Good: Static and Dynamic Aspects, in: Bell Journal of Economics and Management Science 4 (1973), No. 1, pp. 89 - 100.

Atkinson, M., Kilby, D., Roca, I., Foundations of General Linguistics, 2nd ed., London et al.: Unwin Hyman 1988.

AWV, Telekommunikation in Handel, Transport und Verwaltung nach Internationalem Standard, AWV s.l.e.a.

Bairstow, J., EDI May Force E-Mail Standards, in: PC Week (October 20, 1987), p. 3.

Bakkenist, EDI Software Products and User Requirements, Report to the Commission of the European Communities, Eindhoven: Bakkenist 1990.

Bakos, J.Y., Treacy, M.E., Information Technology and Corporate Strategy: A Research Perspective, in: MIS Quarterly 10 (1986), No. 2, pp. 106 - 119.

Banville, C., Landry, M., Can the Field of MIS be Disciplined?, in: Communications of the ACM 32 (1989), No. 1, pp. 48 - 60.

Bariff, M.L., Ginzberg, M.J., MIS and the Behavioral Sciences: Research Patterns and Prescriptions, in: Data Base 14 (1982), No. 1, pp. 19 - 26.

Barrett, S., Konsynski, B., Inter-Organization Information Sharing Systems, in: MIS Quarterly 6 (1982), Special Issue, pp. 93 - 105.

Bass, E.J., The Language of EDI, in: N.C.Hill/J.V.Hansen (eds.), EDI Forum, Founding Issue, Oak Park: EDI Publications 1989, pp. 114 - 119.

Batini, C., Lenzerini, M., Navathe, S.B., A Comparative Analysis of Methodologies for Database Schema Integration, in: ACM Computing Surveys 18 (1986), No. 4, pp. 323 - 364.

BCS, The British Computer Society Data Dictionary Systems Working Party Report, in: Data Base 9 (1977), No. 2, pp. 2 - 24.

Belitsos, B., EDI Becomes a Necessity, in: Computer Decisions 20 (1988), No. 10, pp. 38 - 40.

Benbasat, I., Dexter, A.S., Drury, D.H., A Critique of the Stage Hypothesis: Theory and Empirical Evidence, in: Communications of the ACM 27 (1984), No. 5, pp. 476 - 485.

Benini, P., Erfahrung mit Austausch und Verwaltung von CAD-Daten, in: CIM Management 2 (1986), Nr. 1, pp. 36 - 41.

Benjamin, R.I., Dickenson, C., Rockart, J.F., Changing Role of the Corporate Information Systems Officer, in: MIS Quarterly 9 (1985), No. 3, pp. 177 - 188.

Benjamin, R.I., De Long, D.W., Scott Morton, M.S., The Realities of Electronic Data Interchange: How Much Competitive Advantage?, in: Long Range Planning 23 (1990), No. 1, pp. 29 - 40. Also: Center For Information Systems Research, Working Paper No. 166, Management in the 1990s Working Paper No. 88-042, Cambridge: MIT 1988.

Bergsten, E., Goode, R.M., Legal Questions and Problems to be Overcome, in: H.B.Thomsen/B.S.Wheble (eds.), Trading with EDI - The Legal Issues, London: IBC Financial Books 1989, pp. 127 - 150.

Bernard, P., The Carrying Cost Paradox: How Do You Manage It?, in: Industrial Engineering 21 (1989), No. 11, pp. 40 - 46.

Bidgood, A., VADS Interworking: A Cloud on the EDI Horizon, in: M.Gifkins/D.Hitchcock (eds.), The EDI Handbook - Trading in the 1990s, London: Blenheim 1988, pp. 211 - 216.

Bierschenk, M., EDI-Anwendungspraxis: VDA - ODETTE - EDIFACT, in: EWI (Hrsg.), Electronic Data Interchange EDI 90, Elektronischer Geschäftsverkehr mit EDIFACT: Perspektiven, Anwendungspraxis, Erfahrungen, Starnberg: EWI 1990, pp. 221 - 248.

Biller, H., Neuhold, E.J., Semantics of Data Bases: The Semantics of Data Models, in: Information Systems 3 (1978), No. 1, pp. 11 - 30.

Blackburn, J.D., Time-Based Competition: The Next Battle Ground in American Manufacturing, Homewood: Business One Irwin (1991).

Blacker, K., CAD/CAM Data Interchange in Europe, in: Actionline 7 (1988), No. 5, pp. 21 - 23.

Blacker, K., Using EDI across Industry Sectors, in: J.Sanders/P.Coathup (eds.), EDI'88, Conference Proceedings (London), London: Blenheim 1988, pp. 60 - 66.

Boland, A.S., Justifying an EDI Implementation, in: N.C.Hill/J.V.Hansen (eds.), EDI Forum, Founding Issue, Oak Park: EDI Publications 1989, pp. 138 - 143.

Bomers, G.B.J., Ontwikkelingen in de Bedrijfskunde, in: Bedrijfskunde 55 (1983), Nr. 1, pp. 84 - 94.

Bone, R.W., Electronic Communications at Bergen Brunswig: Past, Present and Future, in: N.C.Hill/J.V.Hansen (eds.), EDI Forum, Founding Issue, Oak Park: EDI Publications 1989, pp. 41 - 43.

Bonoma, T.V., Case Research in Marketing: Opportunities, Problems, and a Process, in: Journal of Marketing Research 22 (May 1985), pp. 199 - 208.

Bostrom, R.P., Heinen, J.S., MIS Problems and Failures: A Socio-Technical Perspective; Part I: The Causes, in: MIS Quarterly 1 (1977a), No. 3, pp. 17 - 32.

Bostrom, R.P., Heinen, J.S., MIS Problems and Failures: A Socio-Technical Perspective; Part II: The Application of Socio-Technical Theory, in: MIS Quarterly 1 (1977b), No. 4, pp. 11 - 28.

Bowers, D.S., From Database to Information Base: Some Questions of Semantics and Constraints, in: Information and Software Technology 31 (1989), No. 8, pp. 402 - 410.

Brabner, S., X.500: A Global Directory Standard, in: Telecommunications 23 (1989), No. 2, pp. 71 - 74.

Brändli, N., Standardisierung von Datenaustauschformaten, in: CIM Management 7 (1991), Nr. 1, pp. 9 - 16.

Brealey, R., Myers, S., Principles of Corporate Finance, 2nd ed., New York et al.: McGraw-Hill 1984.

Bright, R., From POTS to VANS, in: C.Chang/D.Hitchcock (eds.), The VANS Handbook, 2nd ed., London: Blenheim 1989, pp. 3 - 20.

Bromwhich, M., Bhimani, A., Management Accounting: Evolution not Revolution, London: CIMA 1989.

Brown, B., EDI-Dienste über ISDN-Linien übertragen, in: Computerworld Schweiz (16. Mai 1989), Nr. 20, p. 11.

Brown, L.A., Innovation Diffusion - A New Perspective, London-New York: Methuen 1981.

Bruns Jr., W.J., McFarlan, F.W., Information Technology puts Power in Control Systems, in: Harvard Business Review 65 (1987), No. 5, pp. 89 - 94.

Buchanan, J.M., Stubblebine, W.C., Externality, in: Economica 29 (1962), No. 116, pp. 371 - 384.

Buckley, C., Tariffs Get Tougher, in: Datamation 33 (1987), No. 3, pp. 56-11 - 56-16.

Bullinger, H.-J., Wasserloos, G., Reduzieren der Produktentwicklungszeiten durch Simultaneous Engineering, in: CIM Management 6 (1990), Nr. 6, pp. 4 - 12.

Burch, J., The Case of the Reluctant EDIer, in: Journal of Systems Management 40 (1989), No. 3, pp. 8 - 13.

Burns, A., Software Architecture of EDI, in: Blenheim Queensdale (ed.), EDI '89, Conference Proceedings (London), London: Blenheim 1989, pp. 145 - 147.

Butler Cox, Electronic Data Interchange, Research Report 59, London et al.: Butler Cox 1987.

Cabral, L.M.B., On the Adoption of Innovations with 'Network' Externalities, in: Mathematical Social Sciences 19 (1990), No. 3, pp. 299 - 308.

Campbell, D.T., Stanley, J.C., Experimental and Quasi-Experimental Designs for Research, Dallas et al.: Houghton Mifflin 1963.

Campbell-Grant, I.R., Office Document Architecture, the Standard for Document Interchange and its Future Development, in: Electronic Message Systems 88, Conference Proceedings (London), London: Blenheim 1988, pp. 323 - 332.

Canning, R.G., The "Data Administrator" Function, in: EDP Analyzer 10 (1972), No. 11, pp. 1 - 14.

Canright, C., EDI: The Acronym that Means Business, in: Systems/3X World 15 (1987), No. 1, pp. 40 - 46.

Canright, C., EDI: Business and Standards, in: Datapro Research (ed.), Datapro Report CS93-220, Standards & Protocols, Delran: McGraw-Hill 1988a, pp. 101 - 116.

Canright, C., Seizing the Electronic Information Advantage, in: Business Marketing (January 1988b), pp. 81 - 86.

Cardenas, A., Pirahesh, M., Data Base Communication in a Heterogeneous Data Base Management System Network, in: Information Systems 5 (1980), No. 1, pp. 55 - 79.

Carlisle, B., The Four Keys to Implementing EDI in: Information Center 6 (1990), No. 1, pp. 10 - 11.

Carter, J.R. et al., Education and Training for Successful EDI Implementation, in: Journal of Purchasing and Materials Management 23 (1987), No. 2, pp. 13 - 20.

Cash Jr., J.I., Interorganizational Systems: An Information Society Opportunity or Threat?, Reprint Series, Division of Research, Graduate School of Business Administration, Cambridge: Harvard University 1985.

Cash Jr., J.I., Konsynski, B.R., IS Redraws Competitive Boundaries, in: Harvard Business Review 63 (1985), No. 2, pp. 134 - 142.

Caswell, S.A., Planning and Implementing E-Mail, in: Datapro Research (ed.), Datapro Report CS20-260, Delran: McGraw-Hill 1989, pp. 101 - 109.

CCITT, Data Communication Networks - Message Handling Systems, CCITT Recommendations X.400 - X.430, Red Books, 1984.

CCITT, Data Communication Networks - Message Handling Systems, CCITT Recommendations X.400 - X.420, Blue Books, 1988.

Ceri, S., Pelagatti, G., Distributed Databases - Principles and Systems, New York et al.: McGraw-Hill 1984.

Chang, C., Hitchcock, D., (eds.), The VANS Handbook, 2nd ed., London: Blenheim 1989.

Chaplin, J.P., Dictionary of Psychology, New York: Dell Publishing 1975.

Chen, P.P., The Entity-Relationship Model: Toward a Unified View of Data, in: ACM Transactions on Database Systems 1 (1976), No. 3, pp. 9 - 36.

Chmielewicz, K., Forschungskonzeptionen der Wirtschaftswissenschaft, Stuttgart: Poeschel 1970.

Chou, C., Shy, O., Network Effects without Network Externalities, in: International Journal of Industrial Organization 8 (1990), No. 2, pp. 259 - 270.

Clark, E.V., What's in a Word? On the Child's Acquisition of Semantics in his First Language, in: T.E.Moore (ed.), Cognitive Development and the Acquisition of Language, New York: Academic Press 1973, pp. 65 - 111.

Clark, S., How to Recruit Trading Partners, in: Datamation 36 (1990), No. 21, pp. 76 - 76.

Clemons, E.K., McFarlan, F.W., Telecom: Hook up or Lose out, in: Harvard Business Review 64 (1986), No. 4, pp. 91 - 97.

Clemons, E.K., Row, M.C., Information Technology and Economic Reorganization, in: J.I.DeGross et al. (eds.), Proceedings of the Tenth International Conference on Information Systems (Boston), Baltimore: ACM 1989, pp. 341 - 351.

Coathup, P., Jackson, D., Selecting an EDI Supplier, in: C.Chang/D.Hitchcock (eds.), The VANS Handbook, 2nd ed., London: Blenheim 1989, pp. 141 - 147.

Codd, E.F., A Relational Model for Large Shared Data Banks, in: Communications of the ACM 13 (1970), No. 6, pp. 377 - 387.

Codd, E.F., Further Normalization on the Data Base Relational Model, in: Data Base Systems, Courant Computer Science Symposia Series, Vol. 6, Englewood Cliffs: Prentice-Hall 1972.

Codd, E.F., Extending the Database Relational Model to Capture More Meaning, in: ACM Transactions on Database Systems 4 (1979), No. 4, pp. 397 - 434.

Codd, E.F., Mastering the Art of Database Fusion, in: Datamation 36 (1990a), No. 20, pp. 61 - 64.

Codd, E.F., Mastering the Art of Database Fusion Part II, in: Datamation 36 (1990b), No. 21, pp. 81 - 82.

Commission of the European Communities - DG XIII - Telecommunications, Information Industries and Innovation, Trade Electronic Data Interchange Systems TEDIS, in: European Telecoms, Fact Sheet No. 15 (1987), pp. 15UK.Oct.'87.1 - 15UK.Oct.'87.3.

Cook, T.D., Campbell, D.T., Quasi-Experimentation - Design & Analysis Issues for Field Settings, Boston et al.: Houghton Mifflin 1979.

Cooper, J.A., Computer & Communications Security, New York et al.: McGraw-Hill 1989.

Cooper, R., The Rise of Activity-Based Costing - Part One: What Is an Activity-Based Cost System?, in: Journal of Cost Management 2 (1988a), No. 2, pp. 45 - 54.

Cooper, R., The Rise of Activity-Based Costing - Part Three: How Many Cost Drivers Do You Need, and How Do you Select Them?, in: Journal of Cost Management 2 (1988b), No. 4, pp. 34 - 45.

Cooper, R., Kaplan, R.S., Measure Costs Right: Make the Right Decisions, in: Harvard Business Review 66 (1988), No. 5, pp. 96 - 103.

Copeland, T.E., Weston, J.F., Financial Theory and Corporate Policy, 2nd ed., Reading et al.: Addison-Wesley 1983.

Corey, E.R., The Role of Information and Communications Technology in Industrial Distribution, in: R.D.Buzzell (ed.), Marketing in an Electronic Age, Boston: HBS 1985, pp. 29 - 51.

Craigie, J., ISO 10021 - X.400(88): A Tutorial for Those Familiar with X.400(84), in: Computer Networks and ISDN Systems 16 (1988/89), pp. 153 - 160.

Cullen, B., DeFraigne, P., Political and Economic Aspects of Standards, in: S.Schaff (ed.), Legal and Economic Aspects of Telecommunications, Amsterdam et al.: North-Holland 1990, pp. 535 - 545.

Dahl, B., Eversheim, W., Schütze, P., Integrierter Einsatz von CAD/CAM im Werkzeug- und Formenbau der Automobilzulieferindustrie, in: CIM Management 2 (1986), Nr. 3, pp. 21 - 30.

Dale, P., EMS - Mass Market Development or not?, in: Electronic Message Systems 88, Conference Proceedings (London), London: Blenheim 1988, pp. 47 - 62.

Dalton, G., The Relationship between EDI and E-Mail, in: N.C.Hill/J.V.Hansen (eds.), EDI Forum, Founding Issue, Oak Park: EDI Publications 1989, pp. 30 - 33.

Date, C.J., An Introduction to Database Systems, Volume II, Reading et al.: Addison Wesley 1983.

Date, C.J., An Introduction to Database Systems, 4th ed., Reading et al.: Addison-Wesley 1986.

Davenport, R., Design of Distributed Data Base Systems, in: Computer Journal 24 (1981), No. 1, pp. 31 - 41.

Davies, S. The Diffusion of Process Innovations, Cambridge et al.: Cambridge University 1979.

Davis, G.B., Parker, C.A., Writing the Doctoral Dissertation, New York et al.: Barron's Educational Series 1979.

Davis, G.B., Olson, M.H., Management Information Systems - Conceptual Fondations, Structure, and Development, 2nd ed., New York et al.: McGraw-Hill 1985.

Davis, L., Retailers Go Shopping for EDI, in: Datamation 35 (1989), No. 5, pp. 53 - 55.

Dawkins, P., Open Communications Standards: their role in EDI, in: N.C.Hill/J.V.Hansen (eds.), EDI Forum, Founding Issue, Oak Park: EDI Publications 1989, pp. 144 - 152. Also in: M. Gifkins/D.Hitchcock (eds.), The EDI Handbook - Trading in the 1990s, London: Blenheim 1988, pp. 56 - 73.

Dean, R., Setting-up an Electronic Mail Service, in: C.Chang/D.Hitchcock (eds.), The VANS Handbook, 2nd ed., London: Blenheim 1989, pp. 86 - 96.

Dearing, B., The Strategic Benefits of EDI, in: The Journal of Business Strategy 11 (1990), No. 1, pp. 4 - 6.

Donovan, J., Beyond Chief Information Officer to Network Manager, in: Harvard Business Review 66 (1988), No. 5, pp. 134 - 140.

Drake, D.J., Ciucci, J.A., Milbrandt, B., Electronic Data Interchange, Bethesda: Logistics Management Institute 1990.

Dutka, A.F., Hanson, H.H., Fundamentals of Data Normalization, Reading et al.: Addison-Wesley 1989.

Dybvig, P.H., Spatt, C.S., Adoption Externalities as Public Goods, in: Journal of Public Economics 20 (1983), pp. 231 - 247.

Ebers, M., Datenaustausch sichert Vorteile im Wettbewerb, in: Handelsblatt (1./2. März 1991), Nr. 43, p. D6.

ECE, Introduction to the United Nations Rules for Electronic Data Interchange For Administration, Commerce and Transport, TRADE/WP.4/INF.105, Genève: ECE Trade Division 1988.

EDI, spread the word!, EDI Yellow Pages, International, 4th ed., Dallas: EDI, spread the word! 1989.

Eickers, G., Wir stehen heute erst am Anfang, in: Die Computer Zeitung 21 (1990), Nr. 5, p. 8.

Eidenmüller, B., Auftragsabwicklung im Rahmen einer CIM-Strategie, in: VDI Berichte (1988), Nr. 705, pp. 213 - 240.

Ein-Dor, P., Segev, E., Organizational Context and the Success of Management Information Systems, in: Management Science 24 (1978), No. 10, pp. 1064 - 1077.

Emmelhainz, M.A., The Impact of Electronic Data Interchange on the Purchasing Process, unpublished Ph.D. Dissertation, Ohio State University, Ann Arbor: UMI 1986.

Emmelhainz, M.A., Electronic Data Interchange: Does It Change the Purchasing Process?, in: Journal of Purchasing and Materials Management 19 (1987), No. 4, pp. 2 - 8.

Emmelhainz, M.A., Electronic Data Interchange - A Total Management Guide, New York: Van Nostrand Reinhold 1990.

Emmett, A., Braking Barriers to EDI, in: Datamation 37 (1991), No. 7, pp. 64-1 - 64-4.

Encarnação, J.L., Lockemann, P.C., (eds.), Engineering Databases - Conncecting Islands of Automation Through Databases, Berlin et al.: Springer 1987.

Encarnação, J.L., Schlechtendahl, E.G., Computer Aided Design, Berlin et al.: Springer 1983.

Eppen, G.D., Martin, R.K., Determining Safety Stock in the Presence of Stochastic Lead Time and Demand, in: Management Science 34 (1988), No. 11, pp. 1380 - 1390.

Esser, P., Leruth, L., Marketing compatible, yet differentiated Products, in: International Journal of Research in Marketing 5 (1988), No. 4, pp. 251 - 270.

Etheridge, J., EDI in Europe, in: Datamation 34 (1988), No. 19, pp. 44-15 - 44-18.

Euromatica, Who's Who and What's What in Electronic Data Interchange, Brussels: Euromatica SA 1988.

Everest, G.C., Database Management: Objectives, System Functions, and Administration, New York et al.: McGraw-Hill 1986.

Everest, G.C., Requirements for the Next Generation of DBMS, Management Information Systems Research Center Working Paper MISRC-WP 90-02, Minneapolis: University of Minnesota 1989.

Falke, R., Konvertierung von Inhouse-Nachrichten in EDIFACT, in: dc: deutsche congress gesellschaft starnberg mbH (Hrsg.), EDI 89 Report, Starnberg: dc.starnberg 1989, pp. 267 - 278.

Fandel, G., François, P., Just-in-Time-Produktion und -Beschaffung - Funktionsweise, Einsatzvoraussetzungen und Grenzen, in: Zeitschrift für Betriebswirtschaft 59 (1989), Nr. 5, pp. 531 - 544.

Farhoomand, A.F., Scientific Progress of Management Information Systems, in: Data Base 18 (1987), No. 4, pp. 48 - 56.

Farrell, J., Saloner, G., Standardization, Compatibility, and Innovation, in: Rand Journal of Economics 16 (1985), No. 1, pp. 70 - 83.

Farrell, J., Saloner, G., Economic Issues in Standardization, Management in the 1990s Working Paper No. 86-023, Cambridge: MIT 1986.

Favre, M.-C., EDI - A Tool for Interbusiness Communication and a Factor in European Integration, in: Economic and Social Committee of the European Communities (ed.), EDI - 1992 and Beyond, Conference Proceedings (Brussels), Brussels: Economic and Social Committee 1989, pp. 87 - 88.

Fenton, N., A Review of the Relationships and Roles of the Standards Making Bodies, in: M. Gifkins/D.Hitchcock (eds.), The EDI Handbook - Trading in the 1990s, London: Blenheim 1988, pp. 27 - 39.

Ferguson, D.M., Hill, N.C., The State of U.S. EDI in 1988:, in: N.C.Hill/J.V.Hansen (eds.), EDI Forum, Founding Issue, Oak Park: EDI Publications 1989a, pp. 21 - 29.

Ferguson, D.M., Hill, N.C., The State of EDI in Canada: 1988, in: N.C.Hill/J.V.Hansen (eds.), EDI Forum, Founding Issue, Oak Park: EDI Publications 1989b, pp. 161 - 164.

Filliben, J.J., The Probability Plot Correlation Coefficient Test for Normality, in: Technometrics 17 (1975), No. 1, pp. 111 - 117.

Finch, I., EDI - What is it and What's the Point, in: J.Sanders/P.Coathup (eds.), EDI'88, Conference Proceedings (London), London: Blenheim 1988, pp. 33 - 38.

Finkelstein, C., An Introduction to Information Engineering, Sydney et al.: Addison-Wesley 1989.

FitzGerald, J., Business Data Communications, 2nd ed., New York et al.: Wiley 1988.

Förster, F. et al., Der LISREL-Ansatz der Kausalanalyse und seine Bedeutung für die Marktforschung, in: Zeitschrift für Betriebswirtschaft 54 (1984), Nr. 4, pp. 346 - 367.

Forge, S., Siting the technology of EDI, in: N.C.Hill/J.V.Hansen (eds.), EDI Forum, Founding Issue, Oak Park: EDI Publications 1989, pp. 13 - 20.

Forrester, J.W., Industrial Dynamics, New York-London: Wiley 1961.

Frank, R., Taylor, R., CODASYL Data Base Management Systems, in: ACM Computing Survey 8 (1976), No. 1, pp. 209 - 215.

Furtado, A.L., Neuhold, E.J., Formal Techniques for Data Base Design, Berlin et al.: Springer 1986.

Galbraith, J.R., Organization Design: An Information Processing View, in: J.W.Lorsch/P.R.Lawrence (eds.), Organization Planning - Cases and Concepts, Homewood: Irwin, Dorsey 1972, pp. 49 - 74.

Galbraith, J.R., Designing Complex Organizations, Reading: Addison-Wesley 1973.

Gardener Jr., E.S., Inventory Theory and the Gods of Olympus, in: Interfaces 10 (1980), No. 4, pp. 42 - 45.

Gatignon, H., Robertson, T.S., A Propositional Inventory for New Diffusion Research, in: Journal of Consumer Research 11 (1985), pp. 849 - 867.

Gebker, J., Stufenweise Einführung des elektronischen Datenaustausches: Phasen der Integration, in: dc: deutsche congress gesellschaft starnberg mbH (Hrsg.), EDI 89 Report, Starnberg: dc.starnberg 1989, pp. 279 - 293.

GEIS, The EDI*Express System - An Electronic Data Interchange System, General Electric Information Services Company s.l.e.a.

Genilloud, G., X.400 for EDI communications, Laboratoire d'Informatique Technique, Lausanne: Swiss Federal Institute of Technology 1988a.

Genilloud, G., Proposal for Interim Guidelines for the Use of X.400 for EDI, Laboratoire d'Informatique Technique, Lausanne: Swiss Federal Instititue of Technology 1988b.

Gerus, M., Differences between national and international EDI standards, in: Actionline 8 (1988), No. 5, pp. 16 - 17.

Gibson, C.F., Nolan, R.L., Managing the Four Stages of EDP Growth, in: Harvard Business Review 52 (1974), No. 1, pp. 76 - 88.

Gibson Jr., G.E., Bell, L.C., Electronic Data Interchange in Construction, in: Journal of Construction, Engineering and Management 116 (1990), No. 4, pp. 727 - 737.

Glatzer, H., When Delivering EDI Mail Postman Rings Instantly, in: Software News 7 (1987), No. 5, pp. 70 - 75.

Gold, B., Technological Diffusion in Industry: Research Needs and Shortcomings, in: Journal of Industrial Economics 29 (1981), No. 3, pp. 247 - 269.

Goldhar, J.D., Jeline, M., Plan for Economies of Scope, in: Harvard Business Review 61 (1983), No. 6, pp. 141 - 148.

Gora, W., ASN.1 Stand und Trends, in: Datacom 7 (1990), Nr. 2, pp. 114 - 122.

Gräber, H., Echter Mehrwert entsteht weit über der Netzebene, in: Computerwoche (30. November 1990), Nr. 48, p. 40.

Gregg, P., UK Leads Europe in EDI Race, in: Electronics Weekly (December 9, 1987), p. 19.

Griese, J., Vom zwischenbetrieblichen Informationssystem zum elektronischen Markt, in: Logistik Spektrum 1 (1989), Nr. 6, pp. 127 - 128.

Griese, J., Veredlungsprozess, in: Beilage zu Finanz und Wirtschaft (29. 8. 1990), Nr. 66, pp. 9 - 11.

Grimaldi, J., Paying Carriers Electronically: How Shippers Earn Discounts, in: Cashflow 9 (March 1988), pp. 25 - 26.

Grochla, E., Forschung und Entwicklung auf dem Gebiet der Informationssysteme als Aufgabe der Betriebswirtschaftslehre, in: Zeitschrift für Betriebswirtschaft 42 (1971), Nr. 9, pp. 563 - 582.

Grochla, E., Praxeologische Organisationstheorie durch sachliche und methodische Integration, in: Zeitschrift für betriebswirtschaftliche Forschung 28 (1976), Nr, pp. 617 - 637.

Grochla, E., Betriebliche Konsequenzen der informationstechnologischen Entwicklung, in: Angewandte Informatik 24 (1982), Nr. 2, pp. 62 - 71.

Groß, C., Make or Buy? - Standardlösungen ohne individuelle Anpassungen gibt es nicht, in: EWI (Hrsg.), Electronic Data Interchange EDI 90, Elektronischer Geschäftsverkehr mit EDIFACT: Perspektiven, Anwendungspraxis, Erfahrungen, Starnberg: EWI 1990, pp. 75 - 82.

Grupp, G., Optimale Verschlüsselung bei Online-Datenverarbeitung, Köln: TÜV Rheinland 1987.

Gurbaxani, V., Diffusion in Computing Networks: The Case of BITNET, in: Communications of the ACM 33 (1990), No. 12, pp. 65 - 75.

Gurbaxani, V. et al., Institutions and the International Diffusion of Information Technology, in: J.DeGross/M.Alavi/H. Oppelland (eds.) Proceedings of the Eleventh International Conference on Information Systems (Copenhagen), Baltimore: ACM 1990, pp. 87 - 98.

Hagen, K., EAN: Brücke zwischen den Systemen der Handelspartner, in: Blick durch die Wirtschaft (12. Februar 1987), Nr. 30, p. 3.

Hammann, P., Erichson, B., Marktforschung, Stuttgart-New York: Gustav Fischer 1978.

Hammel, R.G., Grundfragen der externen Integration der Datenverarbeitung, Köln: Wison 1975.

Handwerg, H., Übertragung von EDIFACT-Nachrichten über öffentliche Netze, in: dc: deutsche congress gesellschaft starnberg mbH (Hrsg.), EDI 89 Report, Starnberg: dc.starnberg 1989, pp. 231 - 243.

Hanker, J., Die strategische Bedeutung der Informatik für Organisationen, Stuttgart: Teubner 1990.

Hansen, H.R., Wirtschaftsinformatik, 5. Aufl., Stuttgart: Fischer 1986.

Hansen, J.V., Hill, N.C., Control and Audit of Electronic Data Interchange, in: MIS Quarterly 13 (1989), No. 4, pp. 402 - 413.

Harris, F., Operations and Cost (Factory Management Series), Chicago 1915, pp. 48 - 52 [citation after Müller-Merbach, Operations Research, 3. Aufl., München: Vahlen 1973, p. 545].

Hars, A., Scheer, A.-W., Datenstrukturierung - Grundlage der Gestaltung betrieblicher Informationssysteme, in: Information Management 6 (1991), Nr. 1, pp. 38 - 46.

Hartenbach, K., Faller, W., IGES-Filter optimieren den Datenaustausch, in: CAD-CAM Report 10 (1991), Nr. 3, pp. 86 - 97.

Harvey, A., The Econometric Analysis of Times Series, 2nd ed., New York et al.: Philip Allan 1990.

Häßler, U., EDIFACT - DV-gesteuerter Austausch von Geschäftsunterlagen nach internationalen Normen, in: DATACOM 6 (1989), Nr. 10, pp. 98 - 101.

HBS, American Hospital Supply Corporation: The ASAP System (A), Case Study No. 9-186-005, Boston: HBS 1985.

Heist, H.D., Electronic Mail and X.400: A Tutorial, Washington: Electronic Mail Association 1987.

Herbert, D., X.400 and ISDN - the EDI Connection, in: EDI Analysis (March 1990), p. 5.

Hermes, H., Wer braucht 100 Prozent der Standards?, in: EWI (Hrsg.), Electronic Data Interchange EDI 90, Elektronischer Geschäftsverkehr mit EDIFACT: Perspektiven, Anwendungspraxis, Erfahrungen, Starnberg: EWI 1990, pp. 27 - 38.

Herrlitz, W., 1. Einführung in die allgemeinen Grundlagen der Kommunikation, in: K.Baumgärtner/H.Steger (Hrsg.), Sprache 1 - Eine Einführung in die moderne Linguistik, Frankfurt: Fischer 1973, pp. 27 - 37.

Hill, N.C., Ferguson, D.M., EDI and Payment Terms: Negotiating a Positive-Sum Game, in: Journal of Cash Management (September/October 1987a), pp. 21 - 26.

Hill, N.C., Ferguson, D.M., EDI: Time for a Win-Win Change in Credit Terms, in: Cashflow, (October 1987b), pp. 30 - 36.

Hill, N.C., Ferguson, D.M., Electronic Data Interchange: A Definition and Perspective, in: N.C.Hill/J.V.Hansen (eds.), EDI Forum, Founding Issue, Oak Park: EDI Publications 1989, pp. 5 - 12.

Hill, N.C., Hansen, J.V., The Impact of Electronic Data Interchange on Inventory Levels, in: N.C.Hill/J.V.Hansen (eds.), EDI Forum, Founding Issue, Oak Park: EDI Publications 1989, pp. 55 - 60.

Hill, R., EDIFICE/X.400 Experiences, in: Blenheim Queensdale (ed.), EDI '89, Conference Proceedings (London), London: Blenheim 1989, pp. 152 - 157.

Hill, R., Electronic Data Interchange and X.400 Using PEDI, Isleworth: Technology Appraisals 1990.

Hitchcock, D., Review of EDI Developments in Europe, in: M.Gifkins/D.Hitchcock (eds.), The EDI Handbook - Trading in the 1990s, London: Blenheim 1988, pp. 241 - 294.

Hofer, C., EDIFACT-Standardisierung: Status und Ausblick, in: E.Rösch (Hrsg.), EDIFACT as a Strategic Instrument in European Competition, Colloquy Proceedings, Kolloquium D, Thirteenth European Congress Fair for Technical Communications, Velbert: Online 1990, pp. D-3-01 - D-3-16.

Holder, B., Halstead, J., EDI in Customs, in: Blenheim Queensdale (ed.), EDI '89, Conference Proceedings (London), London: Blenheim 1989, pp. 134 - 136.

Homburg, C., Dobratz, A., Iterative Modellselektion in der Kausalanalyse, in: Zeitschrift für betriebswirtschaftliche Forschung 43 (1991), Nr. 3, pp. 213 - 237.

Horan, T., Electronic Data Interchange: Outlook and Opportunities in: N.C.Hill/J.V.Hansen (eds.), EDI Forum, Founding Issue, Oak Park: EDI Publications 1989, pp. 35 - 40.

Horvath, P., Mayer, R., Prozeßkostenrechnung - Der neue Weg zu mehr Kostentransparenz und wirkungsvolleren Unternehmensstrategien, in: Controlling 1 (1989), Nr. 4, pp. 214 - 219.

Hull, R., King, R., Semantic Database Modeling: Survey, Applications, and Research Issues, in: ACM Computing Survey 19 (1987), pp. 201 - 260.

Hunt, R., X.400 Message Handling System: An Analysis of the Architecture, in: Electronic Message Systems 88, Conference Proceedings (London), London: Blenheim 1988, pp. 113 - 139.

IBM, Business Systems Planning, Handbuch zur Planung von Informationssystemen, IBM-Form GE 20-1400-1, s.l.: IBM 1980.

INPUT, EDI and X.400, Mountain View: Input 1988.

ISO, Information Processing Systems - Open Systems Interconnections - Basic Reference Model, in: Computer Networks (1981), No. 5.

Ioannou, L., EDI: Sharpening the Competitive Edge, in: Euromoney (March 1990) pp. 59 - 62.

Ives, B., Hamilton, S., Davis, G.B., A Framework for Research in Computer-based Management Information Systems, in: Management Science 26 (1980), No. 9, pp. 910 - 934.

Jakobs, K., Addressierung in offenen Systemen, in: CIM Management 2 (1986), Nr. 3, pp. 60 - 65.

Jasany, L.C., Are You Ready for EDI?, in: Automation 37 (1990), No. 3, pp. 24 - 27.

Jenkins, L., EDI Comes of Age, in: Systems/3X World 16 (1988), No. 1, pp. 66 - 72.

Jensen, M.C., Meckling, W.H., Theory of the Firm: Managerial Behavior, Agency Costs and Ownership Structure, in: Journal of Financial Economics 3 (October 1976), pp. 305 - 360.

Jick, T.D., Mixing Qualitative and Quantitative Methods: Triangulation in Action, in: Administrative Science Quarterly 24 (December 1979), pp. 602 - 611.

Jöreskog, K.G., Structural Analysis of Covariance and Correlation Matrices, in: Psychometrika 43 (1978), No. 4, pp. 443 - 477.

Jöreskog, K.G., The LISREL Approach to Causal Model-Building in the Social Sciences, in: K.G.Jöreskog/H.Wold (eds.), Systems under Indirect Observation, Causality * Structure * Prediction, Part I, Amsterdam-New York-Oxford: North-Holland 1982, pp. 81 - 99.

Johnson, J., The Changing DP Organization, in: Datamation 21 (1975), No. 1, pp. 81 - 83.

Johnson, R.A., Wichern D.W., Applied Multivariate Statistical Analysis, Englewood Cliffs: Prentice-Hall 1982.

Jones, T.C., Paving the Way for Universal Document Interchange, in: Data Communications 11 (1982), No. 7, pp. 123 - 131.

Joyce, E.J., Tales of EDI Trailblazers, in: Computer Decisions 21 (1989), No. 2, pp. 62 - 65.

Justenhoven, G., EDI rationalisiert die Datenkommunikation, in: Logistik-Spektrum 2 (1990), Nr. 6, pp. 114 - 115.

Kahn, R.L., Cannell, C.F., Dynamics of Interviewing, New York: Wiley 1957.

Kaplan, B., Duchon D., Combining Qualitative and Quantitative Methods in Information Systems Research: A Case Study, in: MIS Quarterly 12 (December 1988), No. 4, pp. 571 - 586.

Karszt, J., Datenbank-Pascal: Ein ausbaubares Datenbanksystem nach einem Entity-Relationship-Modell für Personal-Computer-Anwendungen, unveröffentlichte Dissertation, Karlsruhe: Universität Karlsruhe 1984.

Katz, M.L., Shapiro, C., Network Externalities, Competition, and Compatibility, in: American Economic Review 75 (1985), No. 3, pp. 424 - 440.

Katz, M.L., Shapiro, C., Technology Adoption in the Presence of Network Externalities, in: Journal of Political Economy 94 (1986), No. 4, pp. 822 - 841.

Katz, R.L., Business/Enterprise Modeling, in: IBM Systems Journal 29 (1990), No. 4, pp. 509 - 525.

Keefe, P., Study shows EDI is on the Fly, in: Computerworld 22 (1988), No. 7, p. 50.

Keen, P.G.W., Competing in Time - Using Telecommunications for Competitive Advantage, Cambridge: Ballinger 1988.

Kemezis, P., EDI being Translated into Money by more Corporations, in: Data Communications (October 1987), pp. 64 - 68.

Kemezis, P., The Manufacturing Beat - Manufacturers Log On to EDI, in: BusinessWeek Newsletter for Information Executives (February 17, 1989), p. 5.

Kemmler, K., Die Positionierung von EDI im Umfeld neuer Informations- und Kommunikationstechniken, in: dc: deutsche congress gesellschaft starnberg mbH (Hrsg.), EDI 89 Report, Starnberg: dc.starnberg 1989, pp. 157 - 190.

Kenny, P., EDI and X.400 - Implementation Issues, in: Electronic Message Systems 88, Conference Proceedings (London), London: Blenheim 1988, pp. 231 - 240.

Kent, W., Data and Reality, Amsterdam-New York-Oxford: North Holland 1978.

Kerr, S., On the Folly of Rewarding A, While Hoping for B, in: Academy of Management Journal 18 (1975), No. 4, pp. 769 - 783.

Kindleberger, C.P., Standards as Public, Collective and Private Goods, in: KYklos 36 (11983), Fasc. 3, pp. 377 - 396.

King, J.L., Kraemer, K.L., Evolution and Organizational Information Systems: An Assessment of Nolan's Stage Model, in: C.A.Ross/E.B.Swansons (eds.), Proceedings of the Fourth International Conference on Information Systems (Houston) 1983, pp. 129 - 131.

Klein, G., X.400 - Basis für die offene Kommunikation, in: Technische Rundschau (1988), Nr. 27, pp. 52 - 58.

Klein, H.K., Hirschheim, R.A., A Comparative Framework of Data Modelling Paradigms and Approaches, in: Computer Journal 30 (1987), No. 1, pp. 8 - 15.

Knolmayer, G., Programmierungsmodelle für die Produktionsprogrammplanung, Basel-Boston-Stuttgart: Birkhäuser 1980.

Knolmayer, G., Die Auslagerung von Service-Funktionen als Strategie des IS-Managements, to be published in: L.J.Heinrich/G.Pomberger (Hrsg.), Die Informationswirtschaft im Unternehmen, Linz et al.: Trauner 1991.

Knolmayer, G., Lemke, F., Auswirkungen von Losgrössenreduktionen auf die Erreichung produktionswirtschaftlicher Ziele, in: Zeitschrift für Betriebswirtschaft 60 (1990), Nr. 4, pp. 423 - 442.

Knolmayer, G., Pfeiffer, H., EDI als Instrument einer JIT-Logistik, in: Beschaffung aktuell (1990), Nr. 5, pp. 30 - 35.

Kotler, P., Dubois, B., Marketing Management, 4[e] edition, Paris: Publi-Union 1981.

Krafcik, J.F., Triumph of the Lean Production System, in: Sloan Management Review 30 (1988), No. 1, pp. 41 - 42.

Kreckel, M., Communicative Acts and Shared Knowledge in Natural Discourse, London et al.: Academic Press 1981.

Kroeber-Riel, W., Vorteile der Business Graphik: Zu den Wirkungen von Bild und Graphik auf das Entscheidungsverhalten, in: Information Management 1 (1986), Nr. 3, pp. 17 - 23.

Kuhn, T.S., The Structure of Scientific Revolutions, 2nd ed., Chicago-London: University of Chicago 1970.

Kunerth, W., Praxis der Sachnummerung, Düsseldorf: VDI 1974.

Laidet, A., Les EDI en Plein Chantier, in: Télécoms 1 (October 1990), pp. 66 - 72.

La Londe, B.J., Emmelhainz, M.A., Electronic Purchase Order Interchange, in: Journal of Purchasing and Materials Management 21 (1985), No. 3, pp. 2 - 9.

Lallande, A., Electronic Networks Raze the Paper Mountain, may even Save the Firm, in: International Management (March 1986), No. 3, pp. 51 - 57.

Lancaster, K., Consumer Demand: A New Approach, New York-London: Columbia University 1971.

Langen, C., Tegelhoff, M., Btx-Rechnerverbund im Lebensmittelhandel, in: SAVE aktuell (1989), Nr. 3, pp. 9 - 11.

Lee, E., Selecting Communications Services for EDI, in: M.Gifkins/D.Hitchcock (eds.), The EDI Handbook - Trading in the 1990s, London: Blenheim 1988, pp. 156 - 164.

Lee, R.M., Finding International Contracting Opportunities: AI Extensions to EDI, in: J.DeGross/M.Alavi/H. Oppelland (eds.), Proceedings of the Eleventh International Conference on Information Systems (Copenhagen), Baltimore: ACM 1990, pp. 1 - 13.

Lefkon, R.G., How Connectivity Standards Help, in: Datamation 35 (1989), No. 18, pp. 44 - 45.

Lehmann, H., Integration, in: E.Grochla (Hrsg.), Handwörterbuch der Organisation, 2. Aufl., Stuttgart: Poeschel 1980, cols. 976 - 984.

Leibenstein, H., Bandwagon, Snob and Veblen Effects in the Theory of Consumers' Demand, in: Quarterly Journal of Economics 64 (1950), No. 2, pp. 183 - 207.

Leinfuss, E., Digital's EDI Remedy, in: Datamation 36 (1990), No. 19, pp. 63 - 73.

Leong-Hong, B.W., Plagman, B.K., Data Dictionary/Directory Systems: Administration, Implementation and Usage, New York et al.: Wiley 1982.

Lewis, B.A., Pucelik, F., Magic Demystified: A Pragmatic Guide to Communications and Change, Lake Osevego: Melamosphous 1982.

Lindner, H., Streifzug durch die moderne Physik, Köln: Aulis 1973.

Lindsay, P.H., Norman, D.A., Human Information Processing - An Introduction to Psychology, 2nd ed., San Diego et al.: Harcourt Brace Jovanovich 1977.

Litecky, C.R., Intangibles in Cost/Benefit Analysis, in: Journal of Systems Management 32 (1981), No. 2, pp. 15 - 17.

Litwin, W., Abdellatif, A., Multidatabase Interoperability, in: IEEE Computer 19 (1986), No. 12, pp. 10 - 18.

Loomis, M.E.S., Data Communications, Englewood Cliffs: Prentice Hall 1983.

Lyngbaek, P., McLeod, D., An Approach to Object Sharing in Distributed Database Systems, in: M.Schkolnick/C.Thanos (eds.), Proceedings of the Conference on Very Large Databases (Florence), s.l.: VLDB Endowment 1983, pp. 364 - 375.

Lyngbaek, P., McLeod, D., Object Management in Distributed Information Systems, in: ACM Transactions on Office Information Systems 2 (1984), No. 2, pp. 96 - 122.

Maciejewski, P.G., Internationale Standardisierung elektronischer Kommunikation, in: Computer Magazin 18 (1989), Nr. 3, pp. 49 - 52.

Mackintosh, E., Lewin, D., EDI (Electronic Data Interchange) in Europe - The Business Opportunity, Summary Report, London: Ovum 1990, pp. 10 - 12.

Mag, W., Kommunikation, in: E.Grochla (Hrsg.), Handwörterbuch der Organisation, 2. Aufl., Stuttgart: Poeschel 1980, cols. 1031 - 1040.

Malone, T.W., Modeling Coordination in Organizations and Markets, in: Management Science 33 (1987), No. 10, pp. 1317 - 1332.

Malone, T.W., What is Coordination Theory?, National Science Foundation Coordination Theory Workshop, Cambridge: MIT 1988.

Malone, T.W., Yates, H., Benjamin, R.I., Electronic Markets and Electronic Hierarchies, in: Communications of the ACM 30 (1987), No. 6, pp. 484 - 497.

Malone, T.W., Yates, H., Benjamin, R.I., The Logic of Electronic Markets, in: Harvard Business Review 67 (1989), No. 3, pp. 166 - 169.

Mansfield, E., Technical Change and the Rate of Imitation, in: Econometrica 29 (1961), No. 4, pp. 741 - 766.

Maraschiello, B., EDI: An End to the "Paper Chase", in: Handling & Shipping Management 26 (1985), No. 11, pp. 48 - 52.

March, J.G., Simon, H.A., Organizations, New York-London-Sydney: Wiley 1958.

Mark, L., Roussopoulos, N., Information Interchange between Self-Describing Databases, in: W. Kim et al. (eds.), Database Engineering, Washington: IEEE Computer Society 1987, pp. 170 - 176.

Markus, M.L., Toward a "Critical Mass" Theory of Interactive Media, in: Communication Research 14 (1987), No. 5, pp. 491 - 511.

Marsh, D., Legal Considerations - 2, in: J.Sanders/P.Coathup (eds.), EDI'88, Conference Proceedings (London), London: Blenheim 1988, pp. 85 - 88.

Marshall, P., The Case for Catalogs, in: Apparel Industry Magazine (June 1989), pp. 48 - 52.

Martin, A., Die empirische Forschung in der Betriebswirtschaftslehre, Stuttgart: Poeschel 1987.

Martin, J., Strategic Data-Planning Methodologies, Englewood Cliffs: Prentice-Hall 1982.

Martin, J., Information Engineering, Book I: Introduction, Englewood Cliffs: Prentice Hall 1989.

Martin, J., Information Engineering, Book II: Planning & Analysis, Englewood Cliffs: Prentice Hall 1990a.

Martin, J., Information Engineering, Book III: Design & Construction, Englewood Cliffs: Prentice Hall 1990b.

Mason, J., EDI is Starting to Take off, in: Computerworld 23 (1989), No. 5, p. 110.

McEvoy, N., EDIFACT versus 'Special' Message Syntaxes, in: EDI Analysis (March 1990), pp. 10 - 11.

McFadden, F.R., Hoffer, J.A., Data Base Management, 2nd ed., Menlo Park et al.: Benjamin Cummings 1988.

McFarlan, F.W., Information Technology Changes the Way You Compete, in: Harvard Business Review 62 (1984), No. 3, pp. 98 - 103.

McGuffog, T.B.C., Message Standards for EDI, in: M.Gifkins/D.Hitchcock (eds.), The EDI Handbook - Trading in the 1990s, London: Blenheim 1988, pp. 40 - 55.

McGuffog, T.B.C., The Pivotal Role of Standards in Successful EDI, in: J.Sanders/P.Coathup (eds.), EDI'88, Conference Proceedings (London), London: Blenheim 1988, pp. 69 - 74.

Meffert, H., Benkenstein, M., Wertkette, in: DBW 49 (1989), Nr. 6, pp. 785 - 787.

Mehnen, H., EDIFACT - Syntax, Messages, Design, in: dc: deutsche congress gesellschaft starnberg mbH (Hrsg.), EDI 89 Report, Starnberg: dc.starnberg 1989, pp. 245 - 265.

Meier, A.R., EDI Tunes Up for Major Growth Phase, in: Business Communications Review (1989), No. 5, pp. 58 - 62.

Meijer, A.H., Electronic Data Interchange for Product Structure Data, in: International Journal of Computer Integrated Manufacturing 2 (1989), No. 4, pp. 220 - 228.

Mertens, P., Die zwischenbetriebliche Kooperation und Integration bei der automatisierten Datenverarbeitung, Meisenheim am Glan: Anton Hain 1966.

Mertens, P., Zwischenbetriebliche Integration der EDV, in: Informatik-Spektrum 8 (1985), Nr. 8, pp. 81 - 90.

Mertens, P., Industrielle Datenverarbeitung 1 - Administrations- und Dispositionssysteme, 7. Aufl., Wiesbaden: Gabler 1988.

Mertens, P., Plattfaut, E., Informationstechnik als strategische Waffe, in: Information Management 1 (1986), Nr. 2, pp. 6 - 17.

Mertens, P., Schumann, M., Hohe, U., Informationstechnik als Mittel zur Verbesserung der Wettbewerbsposition - Erkenntnisse aus einer Beispielsammlung, in: K.Spremann/E.Zur (Hrsg.), Informationstechnologie und strategische Führung, Wiesbaden: Gabler 1989, pp. 109 - 135.

Metcalf, T., How and Where to Start and How to Keep Going, in: J.Sanders/P.Coathup (eds.), EDI'88, Conference Proceedings (London), London: Blenheim 1988, pp. 39 - 49.

Metzger, M.B. et al., Business Law and the Regulatory Environment, 6th ed., Homewood: Irwin 1986.

Meyer, B.E., Überbetriebliche Logistik im Rahmen von CIM, in: H.Wildemann (Hrsg.), Planen und Steuern der Produktion, München: gfmt 1987, pp. 409 - 436.

Meyer, J., Eine leise Revolution, in: Sysdata (1988a), Nr. 6, pp. 34 - 37.

Meyer, J., EDI - Datenströme statt Papierfluten, in: Computerworld Schweiz (1988), Nr. 25, pp. 13 - 19.

Milbrandt, B., EDI: Making Business More Efficient, White Plains: Automated Graphic Systems 1987.

Monczka, R.M., Carter, J.R., Implementing Electronic Data Interchange, in: Journal of Purchasing and Materials Management 24 (1988), No. 2, pp. 2 - 9.

Moore, G., An End to the Paper Chase?, in: Electronics & Power 33 (1987), No. 9, pp. 554 - 556.

Morris, J., Communications Options for EDI, in: Blenheim Queensdale (ed.), EDI '89, Conference Proceedings (London), London: Blenheim 1989, pp. 61 - 63.

Moshos, G.J., Data Communications - Principles & Problems, St. Paul et al.: West 1989.

Müller-Berg, M., Hohe Wachstumraten vorausgesagt, in: Handelsblatt (1991), Nr. 110, p. 25.

Mulder, K., Value Added Network Services - Future Developments: An Outlook, in: C.Chang/D.Hitchcock (eds.), The VANS Handbook, 2nd ed., London: Blenheim 1989, pp. 221 - 234.

Mulder, K., The EDI Market in Europe, in: S.Schaff (ed.), Legal and Economic Aspects of Telecommunications, Amsterdam et al.: North-Holland 1990, pp. 653 - 660.

Myrach, T., Jordan, A., Implementierung und Vergleich mehrerer Methoden zur Identifizierung von Datenelementen im Data Dictionary ROCHADE, Arbeitsbericht Nr. 22, Institut für Wirtschaftsinformatik, Bern: Universität Bern 1990.

N.N., An Overview of Value Added Networks (VANs), in: Datapro Research (ed.), Datapro Report CS15-725, Delran: McGraw Hill 1988a, pp. 101 - 112.

N.N., Protocol Conversion Systems, in: Datapro Research (ed.), Datapro Report CS15-500, Delran: McGraw Hill 1988b, pp. 101 - 106.

N.N., The Strategic Value of EDI, in: I/S Analyzer 27 (1989), No. 8, pp. 1 - 13.

N.N., Multiple Standards that Bar the Way, in: Euromoney (July 1990), Supplement, pp. 8 - 10.

Navathe, S., Elmasri, R., Larson, J., Integrating User Views in Database Design, in: IEEE Computer 19 (1986), No. 1, pp. 50 - 62.

Nevins, J.L., Whitney, D.E (eds.), Concurrent Design of Products & Processes, New York et al.: McGraw-Hill 1989.

Newman, C., EDI in Search of a Critical Mass, in: Communications 3 (1986), No. 11, pp. 43 - 44.

Newman, J., Harvey, S., Contracts made by Electronic Mail: Legal Issues, Technology and Services, in: H.Smith (ed.), Computer-Based Message Services, Proceedings of the IFIP WG 6.5 Working Conference on Computer-based Message Services (Nottingham), Amsterdam et al.: North Holland 1984, pp. 237 - 246.

Niederman, F., Brancheau, J.C., Wetherbe, J.C., Information Systems Management Issues in the 1990s, MISRC-WP-91-08, Management Information Systems Research Center, Minneapolis: University of Minnesota 1990.

Nijssen, G.M., Data Structuring in the DDL and Relational Model, in: J.W.Klimbie/K.L.Kofferman (eds.), Data Base Management, Amsterdam: North-Holland 1974, pp. 363 - 379.

Nogossek, G., Zivilrechtliche Probleme elektronischer Kommunikationssysteme im anglo-amerikanischen Recht, in: Computer und Recht 2 (1986), Nr. 6, pp. 353 - 359.

Nolan, R.L., Managing the Crises in Data Processing, in: Harvard Business Review 57 (1979), No. 2, pp. 115 - 126.

Norris, D.M., Waples, E., Control of Electronic Data Interchange Systems, in: Journal of Systems Management 40 (1989), No. 3, pp. 21 - 25.

Norris, R.C., Business Data Interchange, s.l.: Auerback 1984.

Norris, R.C., Electronic Data Interchange, in: R.E.Umbaugh (ed.), Handbook of MIS Management, 2nd ed., Boston-New York: Auerbach 1988, pp. 717 - 730.

Norris, R.C., The Industrial Politics of EDI Communications Standards, in: Information Strategy 7 (1990), No. 1, pp 18 - 22.

Notto, R.W., EDI Standards - A Historical Perspective, in: N.C.Hill/J.V.Hansen (eds.), EDI Forum, Founding Issue, Oak Park: EDI Publications 1989, pp. 120 - 127.

Nowacki, H., Austausch von CAD-Daten über Rechnernetze, in: CIM Management 6 (1990), Nr. 2, pp. 4 - 9.

OECD (ed.), Quarterly National Accounts, (1991), No. 1, OECD: Paris 1991.

Oliver, P., Marwell, G., Teixeira, R., A Theory of the Critical Mass. I. Interdependence, Group Heterogeneity, and the Production of Collective Action, in: American Journal of Sociology 91 (1985), No. 3, pp. 522 - 556.

Olson Jr., M., The Logic of Collective Action, Cambridge: Harvard University 1965.

Oren, S.S., Smith, S.A., Criticial Mass and Tariff Structure in Electronic Communications Markets, in: The Bell Journal of Economics 12 (Autumn 1981), pp. 467 - 487.

Oren, S.S., Smith, S.A., Nonlinear Pricing and Network Externalities in Telecommunications, in: Proceedings of the Sixth International Conference on Computer Communication (London), Amsterdam: North Holland 1982, pp. 685 - 690.

Orr, J.N., Electronic Data Interchange, in: Computer Graphics World 12 (1989), No. 10, pp. 109 - 112.

Owen, G., Game Theory, Philadelphia-London-Toronto: W.B. Saunders 1968.

Özsu, M.T., Valduriez, P., Principles of Distributed Database Systems, Englewood Cliffs: Prentice-Hall 1991.

Palmer, D., The Enabling Factors for EDI, in: M.Gifkins/D.Hitchcock (eds.), The EDI Handbook - Trading in the 1990s, London: Blenheim 1988, pp. 165 - 174.

Parsons, G.L., Information Technology: A New Competitive Weapon, in: Sloan Management Review 25 (1983), No. 1, pp. 3 - 14.

Payne, R.A., EDI Implementation: A Case Study, in: Journal of Systems Management 40 (1989), No. 3, pp. 14 - 20.

Peckhâm, J., Marynski, F., Semantic Data Models, in: ACM Computing Surveys 20 (1988), No. 3, pp. 153 - 189.

Petri, C., Externe Integration der Datenverarbeitung, Berlin et al.: Springer 1990.

Pfeiffer, H., Activity-based Cost Accounting, Arbeitsbericht Nr. 10, Institut für Unternehmensrechnung und Controlling, Bern: Universität Bern 1990a.

Pfeiffer, H., The Diffusion of Electronic Data Interchange - Selected Results of an International Empirical Investigation, Working Report No. 23, Institute of Business Informatics, Berne: University of Berne 1990b.

Pfeiffer, H., Case Study "Philips Fissiau", Unpublished Study Report, Bern 1990c [Publication by EC-Commission in Process].

Picot, A., Betriebswirtschaftlicher Nutzen von Electronic Mail, in: Information Management 2 (1987), Nr. 2, pp. 61 - 67.

Picot, A., Zur Bedeutung allgemeiner Theorieansätze für die betriebswirtschaftliche Information und Kommunikation: Der Beitrag der Transaktionskosten- und Principal-Agent-Theorie, in: W.Kirsch/A.Picot (eds.), Die Betriebswirtschaftslehre im Spannungsfeld zwischen Generalisierung und Spezialisierung, Wiesbaden: Gabler 1989, pp. 361 - 379.

Picot, A., Kosten und Nutzen schwer kalkulierbar, in: Die Computer-Zeitung (18. April 1990), Nr. 9, p. 28.

Picot, A., Neuburger, R., Niggl, J., Ökonomische Perspektiven eines "Electronic Data Interchange", in: Information Management 6 (1991), Nr. 2, pp. 22 - 29.

Plattner, B. et al., Datenkommunikation und elektronische Post - X.400: Die Normen und Ihre Anwendung, 2 Aufl., Bonn et al.: Addison-Wesley 1990.

Pope, N., Meeting EDI User Requiremements with X.400 Now and in the Future, in: N.C.Hill/J.V.Hansen (eds.), EDI Forum, Founding Issue, Oak Park: EDI Publications 1989, pp. 153 - 159. Also in: M. Gifkins/D.Hitchcock (eds.), The EDI Handbook - Trading in the 1990s, London: Blenheim 1988, pp. 217 - 228.

Pope, N., Vanguard EDI and X.400 Study, London: HMSO 1988.

Porter, M.E., Competitive Strategy, New York-London: Free Press 1980.

Porter, M.E., Competitive Advantage, New York-London: Free Press 1985.

Porter, M.E., Millar, V.E., How Information Gives You Competitive Advantage, in: Harvard Business Review 63 (1985), No. 4, pp. 149 - 160.

Quarterman, J.S., Hoskins, J.C., Notable Computer Networks, in: Communications of the ACM 29 (1986), No. 10, pp. 932 - 971.

Ram, S., Chastain, C.L., Architecture of Distributed Data Base Systems, in: Journal of Systems and Software 10 (1989), No. 2, pp. 77 - 95.

Ramberg, J., Electronic Transfer of Rights to Goods in Transit, in: H.B.Thomsen/B.S.Wheble (eds.), Trading with EDI - The Legal Issues, London: IBC Financial Books 1989, pp. 185 - 195.

Raver, N., Hubbard, G.U., Automated Logical Database Design, in: IBM Systems Journal 16 (1977), No. 3, pp. 287 - 312.

Reichwald, R., Straßburger, F.X., Innovationspotentiale von ISDN für die geschäftliche Kommunikation, in: Die Betriebswirtschaft 49 (1989), Nr. 3, pp. 337 - 352.

Rihaczek, K., Sicherheitsfragen bei der EDI-Kommunikation mit Geschäftspartnern, in: dc: deutsche congress gesellschaft starnberg mbH (Hrsg.), EDI 89 Report, Starnberg: dc.starnberg 1989, pp. 145 - 155.

Rivest, R.L., Shamir, A., Adleman, L., A Method for Obtaining Digital Signatures and Public-Key Cryptosystems, in: Communications of the ACM 21 (1978), No. 2, pp. 120 - 126.

Robertson, T.S., Gatignon, H., Competitive Effects on Technology Diffusion, in: Journal of Marketing 50 (July 1986), pp. 1 - 12.

Robinson, D.G., Stanton, S.A., Electronic Data Interchange, in: R.E.Umbaugh (ed.), Handbook of MIS Management, 2nd ed., Boston-New York: Auerbach 1988.

Robinson, P.J., Open Document Architecture (ODA), in: Eledis (1990), No. 5, pp. 4 - 7.

Rockart, J.F., The Changing Role of the Information Systems Executive: A Critical Success Factors Perspective, in: Sloan Management Review 24 (1982), No. 1, pp. 3 - 13.

Roden, H., EDIFACT im Spiegel der grundlegenden Entwicklungen im Europa nach 1992 in: E.Rösch (Hrsg.), EDIFACT as a Strategic Instrument in European Competition, Colloquy Proceedings, Kolloquium D, Thirteenth European Congress Fair for Technical Communications, Velbert: Online 1990, pp. D-2-01 - D-2-18.

Rogers, E.M., Diffusion of Innovations, 3rd ed., New York-London: Free Press 1983.

Rogers, E.M., Communication Technology - The New Media in Society, New York-London: Free Press 1986.

Rogers, E.M., Kincaid, D.W., Communication Networks: Toward a New Paradigm for Research, New York: Free Press 1981.

Rohlfs, J., A Theory of Interdependent Demand for a Communications Service, in: Bell Journal of Economics and Management Science 5 (1974), No. 1, pp. 16 - 37.

Rösch, E., EDIFACT im Spannungsfeld moderner I+K Entwicklungen, in: dc: deutsche congress gesellschaft starnberg mbH (Hrsg.), EDI 89 Report, Starnberg: dc.starnberg 1989, pp. 213 - 229.

Ross, G., EDI over X.400 - The Implications, in: Electronic Message Systems 88, Conference Proceedings (London), London: Blenheim 1988, pp. 251 - 264.

Roos, G., The Modern Alternative, in: H.B.Thomsen/B.S.Wheble (eds.), Trading with EDI - The Legal Issues, London: IBC Financial Books 1989, pp. 41 - 60.

Sacher, D., Electronic Mail (X.400), ODA, EDIFACT - welche Zusammenhänge gibt es?, in: SAVE aktuell (1989), Nr. 3, pp. 19 - 21.

Sadhwani, A.T., Sarhan, M.H., Electronic Systems Enhance JIT Operations, in: Management Accounting 71 (December 1987), pp. 25 - 30.

Sadhwani, A.T., Kim, I.-W., Helmerci, J., The Impact of Electronic Data Interchange on Internal Controls, in: Journal of Accounting and EDP 5 (Fall 1989), pp. 23 - 31.

Sahal, D., Patterns of Technological Innovation, Reading et al.: Addison-Wesley 1981.

Sanders, J., EDI Development Groups, in: M.Gifkins/D.Hitchcock (eds.), The EDI Handbook - Trading in the 1990s, London: Blenheim 1988, pp. 117 - 125.

Sarich, A. (ed.), Electronic Data Interchange and Paperless Trade - The Implementation Guide, 2nd ed., Brussels: EUROMATICA 1988.

SAS Institute Inc., SAS© User's Guide: Basics, Version 5 Edition, Cary: SAS Insitute Inc., 1985a.

SAS Institute Inc., SAS© User's Guide: Statistics, Version 5 Edition, Cary: SAS Insitute Inc., 1985b.

Schatz, W., EDI: Putting the Muscle in Commerce & Industry, in: Datamation 34 (1988), No. 6, pp. 56 - 64.

Scheer, A.-W., Computer Integrated Manufacturing, Berlin et al.: Springer 1987a.

Scheer, A.-W., Betriebsübergreifende Vorgangsketten durch Vernetzung der Informationsverarbeitung, in: Information Management 2 (1987b), Nr. 3, pp. 56 - 63.

Schindler, P.E. et al., EDI is Coming at you, in: InformationWeek (October 5, 1987), pp. 20 - 27.

Schlageter, G., Stucky, W., Datenbanksysteme: Konzepte und Modell, 2. Aufl., Stuttgart: Teubner 1983.

Schmoll, T., Der Einsatz von EDI-Standard-Lösungen in: EWI (Hrsg.), Electronic Data Interchange EDI 90, Elektronischer Geschäftsverkehr mit EDIFACT: Perspektiven, Anwendungspraxis, Erfahrungen, Starnberg: EWI 1990, pp. 83 - 88.

Schneider, M., Message-Handling-Systeme (I), in: Computer und Recht 4 (1988), Nr. 9, pp. 767 - 774.

Schneider, M., Message-Handling-Systeme (II), in: Computer und Recht 4 (1988), Nr. 10, pp. 868 - 873.

Scholz, B., CIM-Seminar: Schnittstellen zum Austausch produktdefinierender Daten, in: CIM Management 5 (1989), Nr. 5, pp. 17 - 20.

Schubenel, R., EDIFACT ja - aber... - Die Kunst ist das Weglassen -, in: Coorganisation (1989), Nr. 2, pp. 19 - 23.

Schumann, M., Abschätzung von Nutzeffekten zwischenbetrieblicher Informationsverarbeitung in: Wirtschaftsinformatik 32 (1990), Nr. 4, pp. 307 - 319.

Schumann, M., Hohe, U., Nutzeffekte strategischer Informationsverarbeitung, in: Angewandte Informatik 30 (1988), Nr. 12, pp. 515 - 523.

Schwab, R., EDI - der Erfolgsfaktor, in: IBM Panorama 3 (1989), Nr. 11, pp. 25 - 27.

Schwarze, J., Daten- und Datenbankorientierung in der Betriebswirtschaftslehre, in: Angewandte Informatik 29 (1987), Nr. 2, pp. 51 - 58.

Scott Morton, M.S., The Impact of Information Technology on Organizations in the 1990s, in: Siemens Review (Mai 1989), Nr. 3, pp. 36 - 41.

Scott, P., Trends in Communications, in: J.Sanders/P.Coathup (eds.), EDI'88, Conference Proceedings (London), London: Blenheim 1988, pp. 89 - 93.

Seibt, D., Ausgewählte Probleme und Aufgaben der Wirtschaftsinformatik, in: Wirtschaftsinformatik 32 (1990), Nr. 1, pp. 7 - 19.

Seither, M., EDI Reaches Critical Mass, Creates Opportunities for Integrators, in: Mini-Micro Systems 21 (1988), No. 7, pp. 17 - 19.

Selig, J., EDV-Management: Eine empirische Untersuchung der Entwicklung von Anwendungssystemen in deutschen Unternehmen, Berlin et al.: Springer 1986.

Sen, A., Ching, C., Schema Translation: A Three-Level Semantic Abstraction Approach, in: Information Systems 11 (1986), No. 3, pp. 255 - 270.

Shannon, C.E., Mathematical Theory of Communication, in: Bell System Technical Journal 27 (1948), pp. 379 - 423 and 623 - 656.

Shannon, C.E., Weaver, W., The Mathematical Theory of Communication, Urbana: University of Illinois 1949.

Shaw, L., Electronic Data Interchange, in: Engineering 230 (1990), No. 3, pp. 33 - 34.

Sherick, D., Legal, Auditing and Security Aspects, in: Tradelink (ed.), EDI Asia 89, Conference Proceedings (Honkong), Hongkong: Tradelink 1989, pp. 65 - 73.

Sheth, A.M., Larson, J.A., Federated Database Systems for Managing Distributed, Heterogeneous, and Autonomous Databases, in: ACM Computing Surveys 22 (1990), No. 3, pp. 183 - 236.

Sibler, A., Wettbewerb spielt sich zur Zeit bei kundennahen Angeboten ab, in: Computerwoche 17 (1990), Nr. 48, pp. 41 - 44.

Silber, S., A Case for Electronic Document Interchange, in: Infosystems (1987), No. 1, p. 58.

Simon, H., Die Zeit als strategischer Erfolgsfaktor, in: Zeitschrift für Betriebswirtschaft 59 (1989), Nr. 1, pp. 68 - 93.

Sloman, M., Kramer, J., Distributed Systems: What? Why? and Where?, in: Datapro Research (ed.), Datapro Report CS20-500, Delran: McGraw-Hill, pp. 101 - 110.

Smith, J.M. et al. Multibase - Integrating Heterogeneous Distributed Database Systems, in: A.Orden/M.Evens (eds.), Proceedings of the National Computer Conference (Chicago), Reston: AFIPS 1981, pp. 487 - 499.

Smithers, R., Bailey, D., The IBM EDI Service, in: M.Gifkins/D.Hitchcock (eds.), The EDI Handbook - Trading in the 1990s, London: Blenheim 1988, pp. 187 - 194.

Sokol, P.K., EDI: The Competitive Edge, New York: McGraw-Hill 1989.

Spaccapietra, S., Parent, C., View Integration: A Step Forward in Solving Structural Conflicts, rapport de recherche, Lausanne: Ecole Polytechnique Federale de Lausanne 1990.

Staehle, W.H., Management, 4. Aufl., München: Vahlen 1989.

Stahlknecht, P., Einführung in die Wirtschaftsinformatik, 4. Aufl., New York et al.: Springer 1989.

Stalk Jr., G., Time - The Next Source of Competitive Advantage, in: Harvard Business Review 66 (1988), No. 4, pp. 41 - 51.

Stalk Jr., G., Hout, T.M., Competing Against Time, New York-London: Free Press 1990.

Stallings, W., Data and Computer Communications, 2nd ed., New York-London: Macmillan 1988.

Stamper, D.A., Business Data Communications, Menlo Park et al.: Benjamin/Cummings 1986.

Stanton, C., EDI: UK Leads the Way, in: Automation (UK) 26 (1989), No. 3, pp. 35 - 38.

Stark, H., DFÜ - Kommunikation mit Lieferanten, in: Beschaffung aktuell (1990), Nr. 9, pp. 66 - 71.

Stern, L.W., Kaufmann, P.J., Electronic Data Interchange in Selected Consumer Goods Industries: An Interorganizational Perspective, in: R.D.Buzzell (ed.), Marketing in an Electronic Age, Boston: HBS 1985, pp. 52 - 73.

Sternberg, H., SINFOS schließt die Lücke in der Datenkommunikation, in: Coorganisation (1988), Nr. 4, pp. 16 - 18.

Stevens, L., Users Say EDI Cuts Inventory Costs, Speeds Product Delivery, in: Computerworld 22 (1988), No. 18, pp. 53 - 57.

Stolz, H., Sicherheitsaspekte beim VANS-Einsatz, in: EWI (Hrsg.), Value Added Networks & Services VANS 91, Starnberg: EWI 1991, pp. 363 - 378.

Stone, E.F., Research Methods in Organizational Behavior, Glenview-London: Scott, Foresman 1978.

Stranger, J., The Importance of X.400 and Related Standards, in: Electronic Message Systems 88, Conference Proceedings (London), London: Blenheim 1988, pp. 1 - 9.

Straub, D.W., Wetherbe, J.C., Information Technologies for the 1990s: An Organizational Impact Perspective, in: Communications of the ACM 32 (1989), No. 11, pp. 1328 - 1339.

Strunz, H., CASE, in: Information Management 3 (1988), Nr. 2, pp. 64 - 65.

Stucky, W., Krieger, R., Datenbanksysteme, in: K.Kurbel/H.Strunz (Hrsg.), Handbuch Wirtschaftsinformatik, Stuttgart: Poeschel 1990, pp. 837 - 856.

Sundblad, G., Communication - Aspects - Networks, in: H.B.Thomsen/B.S.Wheble (eds.), Trading with EDI - The Legal Issues, London: IBC Financial Books 1989, pp. 63 - 69.

Sutton, C.J., Economics and Corporate Strategy, Cambridge et al.: Cambridge University 1980.

Suzuki, A., "SINFOS" in Japan - Item Code File Service, in: Coorganisation (1988), Nr. 4, pp. 25 - 28.

Szyperski, N., Strategisches Informationsmanagement im technologischen Wandel. Fragen zur Planung und Implementation von Informations- und Kommunikationssystemen, in: Angewandte Informatik 22 (1980), Nr. 4, pp. 141 - 148.

Talaysum, A.T., Hassan, M.Z., Goldhar, J.D., Scale vs. Scope Considerations in the CIM/FMS Factory, in: A.Kusiak (ed.), Flexible Manufacturing Systems: Methods and Studies, Amsterdam-New York-Oxford: North Holland 1986, pp. 45 - 59.

Tate, L., EDI in the UK: Suppliers' Response to Business Requirements, in: C.Chang/D.Hitchcock (eds.), The VANS Handbook, 2nd ed., London: Blenheim 1989, pp. 131 - 140.

Taylor, G.J., Howard A.E., A Study to Draw a Correlation between EDIFACT and ASN.1, Final Draft, London: Department of Trade and Industry, Information Technology Standards Unit s.a.

Teece, D.J., The Diffusion of an Administrative Innovation, in: Management Science 26 (1980), No. 4, pp. 464 - 470.

Teng, J.T.C., Galletta, D.F., MIS Research Directions: A Survey of Researchers' Views, in: Data Base 21 (1990), No. 2 and 3, pp. 1 - 10.

Thomas, G.P., Steen, M., Profits through Technology, in: Petroleum Management (February 1987), pp. 40 - 45.

Thomas, H.E., EDIFACT: Firmenübergreifender elektronischer Geschäftsverkehr nach Normen, in: Office Management 35 (1987), Nr. 10, pp. 50 - 54.

Thomas, H.E., Strategische und organisatorische Aspekte von EDI, in: dc: deutsche congress gesellschaft starnberg mbH (Hrsg.), EDI 89 Report, Starnberg: dc.starnberg 1989, pp. 25 - 59.

Thomas, H.E., Elektronischer Geschäftsverkehr in einem Europa ohne Handelsschranken, in: EWI (Hrsg.), Electronic Data Interchange EDI 90, Elektronischer Geschäftsverkehr mit EDIFACT: Perspektiven, Anwendungspraxis, Erfahrungen, Starnberg: EWI 1990, pp. 161 - 171.

Thompson, J.D., Organizations in Action, New York: McGraw-Hill 1967.

Thomsen, H.B., Background, in: H.B.Thomsen/B.S.Wheble (eds.), Trading with EDI - The Legal Issues, London: IBC Financial Books 1989a, pp. 11 - 37.

Thomsen, H.B., UNCID and Communication Agreements, in: H.B.Thomsen/B.S.Wheble (eds.), Trading with EDI - The Legal Issues, London: IBC Financial Books 1989b, pp. 153 - 173.

Thomsen, H.B., Wheble, B.S. (eds.), Trading with EDI - The Legal Issues, London: IBC Financial Books 1989.

Thunis, X., Questions of Liability in Value Added Network Services: The Case of Electronic Funds Transfers, in: S.Schaff (ed.), Legal and Economic Aspects of Telecommunications, Amsterdam et al.: North-Holland 1990, pp. 681 - 699.

Tornatzky, L.G., Klein, K.J., Innovation Characteristics and Innovation Adoption-Implementation: A Meta-Analysis of Findings, in: IEEE Transactions on Engineering Management EM-29 (1982), No. 1, pp. 28 - 45.

Trajtenberg, M., Yitzhaki, S., The Diffusion of Innovations: A Methodological Reappraisal, in: Journal of Business & Economic Statistics 7 (1989), No. 1, pp. 35 - 46.

Tsichritzis, D.C., Klug, A. (eds.), The ANSI/X3/SPARC Framework Report of the Study Group on Database Management Systems, in: Information Systems 3 (1978), No. 3, pp. 173 - 191.

Tsichritzis, D.C., Lochovsky, F.H., Hierarchical Data Base Management, in: ACM Computing Survey 8 (1976), No. 1, pp. 105 - 123.

Tsichritzis, D.C., Lochovsky, F.H., Data Models, Englewood Cliffs: Prentice-Hall 1982.

Tufte, E.R., The Visual Display of Quantitative Information, Cheshire: Graphics Press 1983.

Turnbull, P., The Impact of EDI upon Business Organisation, in: M.Gifkins/D.Hitchcock (eds.), The EDI Handbook - Trading in the 1990s, London: Blenheim 1988, pp. 11 - 23.

Tweddle, D., EDI in International Trade: A Customs View, in: M.Gifkins/D.Hitchcock (eds.), The EDI Handbook - Trading in the 1990s, London: Blenheim 1988, pp. 139 - 146.

Ullman, J.D., Principles of Database Systems, 2nd ed., Rockville: Computer Science 1982.

Venitz, U., CIM-Rahmenplanung, Berlin et al.: Springer 1990.

Venkatraman, N., Zaheer, A., Electronic Integration and Strategic Advantage: A Quasi-Experimental Study in the Insurance Industry, Management in the 1990s Working Paper No. 89-072, Cambridge: MIT, 1989.

Venkatraman, N., Kambil, A., Strategies for Electronic Integration: Lessons from Electronic Filing of Tax-Returns, Management in the 1990s Working Paper No. 90-080, Cambridge: MIT 1990.

Vervest, P.H.M., Innovation in Electronic Mail, Amsterdam et al.: North-Holland 1987.

Vetter, M., Strategie der Anwendungssoftware-Entwicklung, Stuttgart: Teubner 1988.

Vogel, D.R., Wetherbe, J.C., MIS Research: A Profile of Leading Journals and Universities, in: Data Base 16 (1984), No. 1, pp. 3 - 14.

von Weizsäcker, C.C., Die wirtschaftliche Bedeutung von Mehrwertdiensten, mimeo: Köln 1987.

Walden, I., EDI and the Law, in: C.Edwards/N.Savage/I.Walden (eds.), Information Technology & The Law, 2nd ed., London: Macmillan 1990, pp. 239 - 252.

Walker, R., The Pivotal Role of Standards in Successful EDI - 2, in: J.Sanders/P.Coathup (eds.), EDI'88 Conference Proceedings, London: Blenheim 1988, pp. 75 - 81.

Warnecke, H.-J., Die Zielgröße "Zeit" wird wichtiger als die Kosten, in: Blick durch die Wirtschaft (1988), Nr. 171, p. 7.

Warner, T., Why in the World - EDIFACT, in: N.C.Hill/J.V.Hansen (eds.), EDI Forum, Founding Issue, Oak Park: EDI Publications 1989, pp. 129 - 131.

Webb, K., Using EDI to Maximise Stock Availability with Minimum Stock Levels, in: J.Sanders/P.Coathup (eds.), EDI'88 Conference Proceedings, London: Blenheim 1988, pp. 51 - 54.

Weede, E., Jagodzinski, W., Einführung in die konfirmatorische Faktorenanalyse, in: Zeitschrift für Soziologie 6 (1977), Nr. 3, pp. 315 - 333.

Weid, H., Wettbewerbsvorteile durch Informationstechnik, in: Wirtschaftswissenschaftliches Studium 18 (1989), Nr. 9, pp. 414 - 416.

Wertz, C.J., The Data Dictionary: Concepts and Uses, Amsterdam: North Holland 1986.

Wetzel, W., Statistische Grundausbildung für Wirtschaftswissenschaftler, Band II: Schließende Statistik, Berlin-New York: de Gruyter 1973.

Wheble, B., Creating Legal Relationships with Trading Partners, in: M.Gifkins/D.Hitchcock (eds.), The EDI Handbook - Trading in the 1990s, London: Blenheim 1988, pp. 126 - 138.

Wheble, B.S., EDI and the Documentary Credit, in: H.B.Thomsen/B.S.Wheble (eds.), Trading with EDI - The Legal Issues, London: IBC Financial Books 1989, pp. 196 - 204.

White, R., Quick Response: What is it?, in: Apparel Industry Magazine (December 1985) pp. 40 - 42.

Wienand, H.J., Nummernsysteme - Verwirrspiel oder Herausforderung der Organisation, in: Elektronische Rechenanlagen 22 (1980), Nr. 3, pp. 130 - 134.

Wiener, N., Cybernetics or Control and Communication in the Animal and the Machine, Paris-Cambridge-New York: Herman-Technology-Wiley 1948.

Wiener, N., The Human Use of Human Beings - Cybernetics and Society, London: Eyre and Spottiswoode 1950.

Wierzewski, J., Kommunikation mit EDI-Partnern: Nutzung von Value Added Networks & Services (VANS), in: EWI (Hrsg.), Electronic Data Interchange EDI 90, Elektronischer Geschäftsverkehr mit EDIFACT: Perspektiven, Anwendungspraxis, Erfahrungen, Starnberg: EWI 1990, pp. 105 - 114.

Wiese, H., Netzeffekte und Kompatibilität, Stuttgart: Poeschel 1990.

Wigglesworth, P., A Review of the Business Implications of EDI in the U.K., in: N.C.Hill/J.V.Hansen (eds.), EDI Forum, Founding Issue, Oak Park: EDI Publications 1989, pp. 165 - 168.

Wightman, D.W.L., Competitive Advantage through Information Technology, in: Journal of General Management 12 (1987), No. 4, pp. 36 - 45.

Wildemann, H., Just-In-Time-Informationsflußgestaltung, in: CIM Management 4 (1988), Nr. 5, pp. 4 - 12.

Wildemann, H., Kundennahe Produktion und Zulieferung: Eine empirische Bestandsaufnahme, in: DBW 50 (1990a), Nr. 3, pp. 309 - 331.

Wildemann, H., Neben Kosten und Qualität kann der Faktor Zeit im Wettbewerb zum entscheidenden Element werden, in: Handelsblatt (9. Oktober 1990b), Nr. 195, p. 26.

Wildemann, H. (ed.), Just-In-Time-Produktion, München-Düsseldorf: gfmt/Handelsblatt s.a.

Willenz, N., Walker, R., Danikiewicz, E., Introduction to UN/EDIFACT, s.l.: UN/ECE 1989.

Williams, R., Rice, R.E., Rogers, E.M., Research Methods and the New Media, New York-London: Free Press 1988.

Williamson, O.E., Markets and Hierarchies, New York-London: Free Press 1975.

Williamson, O.E., Transaction-Cost Economics: The Governance of Contractual Relations, in: The Journal of Law and Economics 22 (1979), pp. 233 - 261.

Wilmot, R.W., International Trends and Developments in EDI, in: J.Sanders/P.Coathup (eds.), EDI'88, Conference Proceedings (London), London: Blenheim 1988, pp. 15 - 21.

Wittmann, W., Produktionstheorie, Berlin-Heidelberg-New York: Springer 1968.

Womack, J.P., Jones, D.T., Roos, D., The Machine That Changed The World, New York et al.: Rawson, Collier, Maxwell Macmillan 1990.

Yannakoudakis, E.J., The Architectural Logic of Database Systems, Berlin et al.: Springer 1988.

Yin, R.K., Case Study Research, Beverly Hills: Sage 1984.

Zentes, J., Nutzeffekte von Warenwirtschaftssystemen im Handel, in: Information Management 3 (1988), Nr. 4, pp. 58 - 67.

List of Acronyms and Abbreviations

ADL	Arthur D. Little, Inc.
AFIPS	American Federation of Information Processing Societies
AIAG	Automotive Industry Action Group
ANOVA	Analysis of Variance
ANSI	American National Standards Institute
AS	Application System
ASC	Accredited Standards Committee
ASCII	American Standard Code for Information Interchange
ASN.1	Abstract Syntax Notation No. 1
AU	Access Unit
AWV	Arbeitsgemeinschaft für wirtschaftliche Verwaltung e.V.
BCS	British Computer Society
BSP	Business Systems Planning
ACM	Association for Computing Machinery
CAD	Computer Aided Design
CASE	Computer Aided Software Engineering
CBIS	Computer Based Information Systems
CCITT	Comité Consultatif International Telégraphique et Telephonique
CEFIC	Conseil Europćen des Fédérations de l'Industrie Chimique
CEO	Chief Executive Officer
cf.	confer
CIM	Computer Integrated Manufacturing
CIO	Chief Information Officer
CSDN	Circuit Switched Data Network
CV	Converter
DBA	Database Administrator
DBMS	Database Management System
DD	Data Dictionary
DD/DS	Data Dictionary/Directory System
DDL	Data Description Language
DEC	Digital Equipment Corporation
DIN	Deutsches Institut für Normung e.V.
DML	Data Manipulation Language
DNSCE	Direction Nationale des Statistiques du Commerce Extérieur
DoF	Degrees of Freedom
DP	Data Processing
DSS	Decision Support Systems
E-Mail	Electronic Mail
e.g.	*exempli gratia*
EAN	European Article Number
EBCDIC	Extended Binary Coded Decimal Interchange Code
EBDI	Electronic Business Data Interchange
ECE	Economic Commission for Europe
ECMA	European Computer Manufacturers' Association
EDI	Electronic Data Interchange (Electronic Document Interchange)
EDIFACT	Electronic Data Interchange For Administration Commerce and Trade

EDIFICE	EDI For Companies with Interest in Computing and Electronics
EDIFICE	Electronic Data Interchange Forum for Companies with Interests in Computers and Electronics
EDMD	Electronic Document Message Directory
EDP	Electronic Data Processing
EDSD	Electronic Document Segment Directory
EFT	Electronic Funds Transfer
EFTA	European Free Trade Association
EII	Electronic Information Interchange
EIS	Executive Information Systems
EOQ	Economic Order Quantity
ERM	Entity-Relationship Model
ES	Expert Systems
FMS	Flexible Manufacturing System
FTAM	File Transfer, Access, and Management
FTP	File Transfer Protocol
GEISCO	General Electric Information Services COmpany
GTDI	Guidelines for Trade Data Interchange
HBS	Harvard Business School
HDLC	High-Level Data Link Control
i.e.	*id est*
IA	Interchange Agreement
IA5	International Alphabet No. 5
IBM	International Business Machines
IGES	Initial Graphics Exchange Specification
IOS	Inter-organizational Systems
IPMS	Inter-Personal Messaging System
IRR	Internal Rate of Return
IS	Information System
ISDN	Integrated Services Digital Network.
ISO	International Standards Organization
ISO/OSI	International Standards Organization/Open System Interconnection
IT	Information Technology
ITA2	International Telegraph Alphabet No. 2
JEDI	Joint EDI group
JIT	Just-In-Time
LAN	Local Area Network
LISREL	Linear Structural Relation
MDN	Managed Data Network
MHS	Message Handling System
MIS	Management Information Systems
MIT	Massachusetts Institute of Technology
MODEM	Modulator/Demodulator
MRP	Material Requirements Planning
MS	Message Store
MTA	Message Transfer Agent
MTS	Message Transfer System
N.N.	*nomen nescio*
ODA	Office Document Architecture

ODETTE	Organization for Data Exchange Through Teletransmission in Europe
ODIF	ODA Interchange Format
OECD	Organization for Economic Cooperation and Development
OFTP	ODETTE File Transfer Protocol
OSI	Open Systems Interconnection
p.	page
PAD	Packet Assembler/Disassembler
PC	Personal Computer
PCP	Pragmatic Communication Problem
PDAU	Physical Delivery Access Unit
pp.	pages
PSDN	Packet-Switched Data Network
PSTN	Public Switched Telephone Network
PTO	Public Telephone Operator
QL	Query Language
QR	Quick Response
RCS	Remote Computer Service vendor
RFQ	Request for Quote
RJE	Remote Job Entry
s.a.	*sine anno*
s.l.	*sine loco*
s.l.e.a.	*sine loco et anno*
SAD	Single Administrative Document
SAS	Statistical Analysis System
SCP	Semantic Communication Problem
SDLC	Synchronous Data Link Control
seq.	*sequens*
seqq.	*sequentes*
SET	Standard d'Echange et de Transfer
SME	Small and Medium-Sized Enterprise
SNA	Systems Network Architecture (IBM)
STEP	Standard for the Exchange of Product Model Data
SWIFT	Society for Worldwide Interbank Financial Telecommunication
TCP	Technical Communication Problem
TDCC	Trade Data Coordinating Committee
TDED	Trade Data Elements Directory
TEDIS	Trade Electronic Data Interchange Systems
TRADACOMS	Trade Data Communication Standards
TTDB	Trade Transaction DataBase
U.S.	United States (of America)
UA	User Agent
U.K.	United Kingdom
UN	United Nations
UN-GTDI	United Nations Guidelines for Trade Data Interchange
UNCID	UNiform rules of Conduct for Interchange of trade Data by teletransmission
UNECE	United Nations Economic Commission for Europe
UPC	Uniform Product Code
VADS	Value Added and Data Service
VAN	Value Added Network

VANS	Value Added Network and Services
VAS	Value Added Service
VDA	Verband der Automobilindustrie
V.P.	Vice President
vs.	versus
WAN	Wide Area Network
ZI	Zero Inventory